V. D. Segre

ISRAEL

A SOCIETY
IN TRANSITION

LONDON
OXFORD UNIVERSITY PRESS
NEW YORK   TORONTO
1971

Oxford University Press, Ely House, London W.1

GLASGOW NEW YORK TORONTO MELBOURNE WELLINGTON
CAPE TOWN SALISBURY IBADAN NAIROBI DAR ES SALAAM LUSAKA ADDIS ABABA
BOMBAY CALCUTTA MADRAS KARACHI LAHORE DACCA
KUALA LUMPUR SINGAPORE HONG KONG TOKYO

SBN 19 215172 X

Printed in Great Britain by
Western Printing Services Ltd, Bristol

ISRAEL: A Society in Transition

The Library of
Sir Ben Helfgott MBE

To Rosetta
Twenty Years After

Preface

On a winter's day in 1938, a few months after the promulgation of the antisemitic legislation in Italy, I happened to attend, at the age of sixteen, a meeting of Italian Fascist Jews in Turin to discuss the idea of a 'patriotic' raid on the premises of the pro-Zionist Jewish publication *Israel*. Less than a year later, in September 1939, I landed in Palestine knowing very little about the movement which I had decided to join and in which I have been involved ever since.

As an Italian Jew I tended to look on Zionism as a Jewish version of the Italian Risorgimento. It has been my good fortune to come into contact—through personal experience—with new forms of Jewish self-expression: kibbutz life, underground work, Israeli army service and diplomacy. Without having become a specialist in any of these fields, I feel that I have acquired sufficient familiarity with the subject of Israel to dare to write about it.

This book was made possible by the generous help of institutions and the guidance of friends and scholars in the field. I am grateful to the Wolfson Foundation which, by establishing a Fellowship in Israeli Studies at St. Antony's College, Oxford, permitted me to spend two years in that atmosphere of detached involvement which only an Oxford College can provide, to Sir Isaiah Berlin and to Mr. F. W. D. Deakin, the former Warden of St. Antony's, as well as to the Governing Body of St. Antony's College, to the Massachusetts Institute of Technology, and more particularly to the Director of the Department of Humanities, Professor Richard Douglas, and to Professor Bruce Mazlish.

I am deeply indebted to the many friends who have suggested ways in which the book might be improved: Mr. Chimen Abramsky, Mr. Hanoch Bartov, Sir Isaiah Berlin, Mr. Arieh Eliav, Dr. Walter Eytan, Mr. Jon Kimche, Mr. R. A. May, Mr. Amos Oz, Dr. David Patterson, and Dr. Michael Bar-Zohar, who have read some or all of my manuscript.

There are, however, two people to whom my debt goes beyond their contribution to this book: Professor Josef Agassi of Boston University, for his invaluable guidance and for sharing with me the fruits of a distinguished mind; and Mr. Albert Hourani of St. Antony's College, Oxford, for supervising my work with sympathetic insight, placing his knowledge of the Middle East at my disposal, and providing an inspiring example of academic impartiality.

Last but not least, I am deeply grateful to Miss Carole Burden of the Oxford University Press, for her care in editing my original text, to Miss Susan Lermon, and to Mrs. Helen Baz for preparing the index.

V.D.S.

Jerusalem
April 1970

ACKNOWLEDGEMENT is due to the Central Bureau of Statistics, Jerusalem, for permission to reprint three tables from the *Statistical Abstract of Israel* (1961).

Contents

Maps

Chapter 1

Introduction

The verb structure of classical Hebrew reflects the idea that traditional Judaism has of history:[1] there is no 'before' and no 'after' in divine revelation: sequences are of no importance, only events, and only those events which have a symbolic significance. In so far as Judaism can be said to have a general conception of history, it is an ethnocentric one, the Jew being God's testimony in human recorded time.[2]

This may explain to some extent why it is so difficult for responsible opinion in the State of Israel to make a clearer distinction between past, present, and future in any issue closely connected with collective Jewish feelings. More recent events, which have turned a people known to suffer from 'an excess of history and a lack of geography'[3] into a State suffering from an excess of geography and a lack of political history, have not simplified the issue.

This book takes into consideration, but is not predominantly concerned with, the Jewish approach to time and history. It does not dismiss as irrelevant the emotional link between the image of Moses ascending Mount Sinai some 3,500 years ago to receive the divine Commandments and the picture of the Chief Chaplain of the Israeli Army retracing the steps of Moses in a helicopter to commemorate biblical revelation. This book contends, however, that paradoxes—even one as fascinating as that of a non-Zionist French aristocratic Jewish banker, Baron Edmond de Rothschild, rescuing the Marxist-Zionist

---

[1] Classical Hebrew has no verb form equivalent to the present tense in English. There is a past tense, the so-called 'perfect', and a future tense, the so-called 'imperfect'. In continuous narrative, however, two further tense forms are also used of which that for the past tense may be described as being formed by pre-fixing 'vav' to the 'imperfect' tense, and the 'future' by pre-fixing 'vav' to the 'perfect'.

[2] Martin Buber, *Israel and Palestine: The History of an Idea* (London, 1952), pp. 77–8, considers Rabbi Liva Ben Bezalel (1520–1609), the alleged creator of the robot-like Golem, to be the founder of this specifically Jewish philosophy of history.

[3] Isaiah Berlin paraphrasing Herzen in a lecture at the Hebrew University, Jerusalem, in 1966.

agrarian society, originating from Russia, of Turkish Palestine—remain fundamentally *l'écume de l'histoire*: the froth of history.

In this book I am concerned mainly with the evolution of the Jewish community in the Holy Land—the 'Yishuv'—from a colonial, agrarian, and traditional Messianic society into that of an independent, industrial, and productivist State.

My aim is not to belittle or seek to prove the uniqueness of Jewish history, past or present, since I believe that every nation worth the name is unique in its own way—even if some appear to be 'more unique' than others. My aim is to look at the history of the Jewish national movement—and more especially at its concrete manifestations in Israel in the last twenty years—from that particular and ambiguously elastic angle which contemporary social and political scientists call 'modernization'. Unique as the Jewish people and its history may appear, however, the process of economic, social, political, and ideological change which has taken place among the Jews of Palestine, and then of Israel, is not fundamentally different from the process of change which has taken place in other colonial and traditional societies in our time. This process is not contradictory to the more specific and universal trends of Jewish history and character, but the conditions in which the Jewish people lived and continue to live throughout the world—conditions of geographical dispersion (Diaspora) and national regrouping, of ethnic minority and of religious universalism, of social and racial discrimination, and of an osmosis into the intellectual *élites* of our times—appear extraordinary and sometimes contradictory and absurd, at least by current standards of political and social logic.

This apparent lack of logic may be the result of the difficulty of grasping the essence of the historical development of the Jews. Whether we agree with Toynbee that the Jews are 'fossils' who do not behave like fossils, or with Sartre that the Jews and the Jewish problem are a mere reflection of modern society,[1] we are perplexed at the apparently insoluble riddle of the Jew. We feel that the solution of this riddle is located somewhere in the encounter of a 'Promised Land' and a 'Chosen People', but we are at a loss when we try to define these two elusive—perhaps mythical—terms. The gauges by which such terms could be measured—those of religion, nationhood, etc.—are themselves confused and imprecise, and particularly so when applied to Jews and Judaism.

The temptation to overcome the difficulty of the definition by using

---

[1] Arnold J. Toynbee, *A Study of History*, vol. VIII (London, 1954), pp. 272–313; J.-P. Sartre, *Réflexions sur la question iuive* (Paris, 1946).

instead the imprecision of paradox is thus very great. I know I have not been immune to it in this book. But I feel I can be somehow excused because I am a Jew and Jews are intrinsically paradoxical: they claim both a small country and the whole world for their homeland; they have the most parochial and the most universal religious traditions for their sources of inspiration; they are an integral part of and a constant witness to the course of humane and, more specifically, Western civilization; they represent linguistically, religiously, culturally, and politically the only uninterrupted link of physical and cultural continuity between the ancient past and our chaotic present; they have participated, antagonized, and fertilized with their ideas and their actions throughout the centuries, as if time and geography could not change their nature.[1]

When one speaks of Israel, either of its past or its present, one speaks of two things: of a certain land in the Middle East and of a certain people whose origins are also in the Middle East.

The concept of the Promised Land is easier to grasp than that of the Jewish people, in spite of the many changes in boundaries which it underwent throughout the centuries. It remains fundamentally the Land of Canaan promised to Abraham when he was, according to archaeological evidence, still a member of the polytheistic society of the Euphrates some 4,000 years ago. The divine promise to Abraham was, significantly, conditional, the Bible tells us, on the willingness of the forefathers of the Jews to exchange the land of their birth for an unknown land of promise. Thus, the Land of Canaan, which later became the cradle of the Jewish nation, was also the first stop in a Jewish migratory movement which, it seems, has continued ever since.

Patriotism is shrouded in myth wherever it occurs: among ancient Jews and ancient Greeks, modern Ghanaians and modern Americans. But myths may differ. The ancient Greek myth, accepted by the descendants of the Dorian Horde which conquered the land, was the myth of the *autochthon*—literally, 'the son of his fatherland who was born from the earth'. The myth is preserved in the contemporary word 'fatherland' (which incidentally exists also in modern Hebrew—*moledet* and *mechorah*—the first being a Hebrew neologism, the second ancient Greek). There is no ancient Hebrew word for 'fatherland'. It is not the country which made Abraham; it was Abraham and his descendants who made Canaan into the Promised Land. The Bible makes this very

---

[1] Nathan Rotenstreich, in *The Recurring Pattern—Studies in Anti-Judaism in Modern Thought* (London, 1963), p. 123, refutes Toynbee's thesis of Jewish 'fossilization', arguing that while 'the renaissance of a fossil may constitute a paradox . . . the allegedly paradoxical nature of this renaissance is no proof against its reality'.

clear: the land is not promised until Abraham shows interest and even undergoes tests of his loyalty.

When the land was no longer inhabited by the Jews, it was still the 'Holy Land', but, strangely enough, it also ceased to play an autonomous role on the stage of human history. Canaan then became Palestine—a land which owes its name to passing conquerors from beyond the sea; it became the Latin Kingdom of Jerusalem, under the Crusaders, who saw their mission linked not with the land, but with the Holy Sepulchre; it became part of the *vilayets* (provinces) of Beirut, Damascus, and Syria under the Turks. I shall not attempt to summarize the geopolitical evolution of the Holy Land, which has filled volumes of religious and historical interpretations throughout the centuries. The country with which we shall be mainly dealing is British Palestine, officially established by a League of Nations decision on 24 July 1922, then sliced in 1948 into a Jewish State, an Egyptian Gaza, and a Jordanian (West Bank) zone of occupation, and finally encompassing its original Mandatory boundaries through the 1967 Jewish-Arab War and the Israeli occupation of the West Bank, which extended also to Sinai and the Syrian Golan Heights.

British Palestine covered an area of 30,000 square kilometres—of which 20,000 are now Israel—a country a little bigger than the island of Sicily. British Palestine stretched for more than 500 kilometres between the mountains of Lebanon in the north and the Red Sea, along the Gulf of Aqaba in the south. It is, in spite of its eastern and southern deserts, a country which is easily accessible from all sides, a kind of 'lowlands' of the Middle East bridging Africa and Asia, the Mediterranean Sea and the Indian Ocean. Archaeologists keep reminding us that Palestine is an historical crossroads of imperial lines of communications linking the Euphrates Valley with the Mediterranean and Syria with Egypt and Africa.

In present times, as in the past, Palestine has remained, mainly because of its geographical position, a land of mixed population, of many religions, cultures, and ethnic minorities. There is really no great difference between the crowds of Arabs, Druzes, Jews, Christians, and Moslems who mix today in the narrow streets of Old Jerusalem and those who mixed in the streets of Roman Caesarea some eighteen centuries ago. Perhaps the most significant change from the past is that the Jews now occupy the coastal region of Palestine which once was the stronghold of the Philistines. Modern Israelis have broken with their ancestors' almost exclusively rural traditions and have mastered the maritime skills of their former enemies. In spite of all the changes which occurred through centuries of crowded and tragic events in Jewish history, in spite of the fluctuating numbers of the population of the Holy Land, Palestine has today a population similar in number to that of second-century Judea.[1] In Israel on the West Bank and in Gaza there are some 2,500,000 Jews and 1,500,000 Arabs today, less than the population of Sicily, which is not, after all, one of the most developed parts of the Mediterranean. It is important to remember these figures. One does not fully appreciate the history of the Jews in their land if one does not constantly recall the fact that the Jewish population of Palestine has never been greater than that of a modern medium-sized European city such as, for instance, Milan.

For a small population to play a great historical role is by no means a prerogative of the Jews. Athens had a population of about 30,000 free citizens and no more than 100,000 inhabitants at the time of its greatest splendour and of its vital struggle with Persia. But Athens has disappeared from the scene of active history while the Jews of Palestine continue, as in the past, to puzzle the conscience of the world and challenge the political balance of the great empires of today.

This is only one of the many attributes of the Jews which make it so difficult to place them. What are they, in fact? A race, a nation, a State with a worldwide Diaspora? A Diaspora with a recurrently reconstructed political centre? I shall not attempt to discuss a problem for which I think no one has any solution to offer. When the Israeli Government, in 1958, attempted to give a simple administratively workable answer to the question 'Who is a Jew?', it fell from power. Paradoxical though it be, the only country in the world in which the Jews have been defined as a national group independently of their religious belief is Soviet Russia.[2]

---

[1] The population of Palestine at the time of King Solomon, tenth century B.C., has been estimated at three-quarters of a million. At the time of the destruction of the Jerusalem Temple by Titus in A.D. 70, 4 to 5 million Jews were supposed to be living in Palestine, of whom 1,100,000 (according to Josephus Flavius) or 600,000 (according to Tacitus) were killed during the war. In the second century, prior to the great Jewish revolts under Trajan and Hadrian, the Jewish population in the Roman Empire is believed to have reached 6 to 7 million (out of a total of 35 million), of whom 5 million probably still lived in Palestine. See W. F. Albright, 'The Biblical Period', in *The Jews, Their History, Culture and Religion* (ed.), Louis Finkelstein (Philadelphia, 1949), vol. I, pp. 42–50; J. Juster, *Les Juifs dans l'empire romain, leur condition juridique, économique et sociale* (Paris, 1914), p. 210, 2–3. For the geopolitical boundaries of ancient Palestine before and after the Roman conquests, see *The Jewish Encyclopedia*, vol. IX, pp. 498–500.

[2] Birobidjan, a Soviet autonomous region in East Siberia on the Chinese border, was allotted for Jewish settlement in 1928 on the initiative of President Kalinin. Its Jewish population was estimated at 25,000 to 50,000 in 1959. *The Standard Jewish Encyclopedia* (London, 1962), col. 320.

Whatever the Jews may finally be, it cannot be refuted that, for some twenty centuries before the Christian era, they fought a revolutionary battle against the whole social, religious, and political conception of the polytheistic world of their time. They fought, suffered, and revolted time after time in order to be able to hold to their belief that God is One. However, in giving Judaism the characteristic of militant monotheism, we must not overlook those events of the last two thousand years or so. Through the battle for monotheism in a polytheistic world, the ancient Jews developed a particular inclination for struggles against the stream, usually fought against political, military, and ideological odds, and in the course of these, the battles lost heavily outnumbered those that seemed won. It was only when Judaism looked back at the ruins of the civilizations and empires which it encountered in its long peregrinations through time and over continents, that it could realize the measure and the feeling of its extraordinary vitality. Conversely, it was the combination of vitality and despair which developed the Messianic ideal—the belief in a better world to come on this earth—and linked the idea of the return to the Land of Israel—to Erez Israel—with the desire to speed the advent of the Messiah.[1] Thus for many centuries, in fact from the time of the return from the Babylonian exile (sixth century B.C.) to the great upheaval created in the seventeenth century by the most famous of the false Messiahs, Sabbatai Zevi,[2] 'Zionism'— namely, the desire and the attempt to return to Zion—had always been associated with the idea of final Messianic redemption.

During these centuries the Jewish presence in Palestine continued unbroken, in spite of radical attempts—such as those of Emperor Hadrian in the second century—to obliterate even the traces of Judaism in Judea and especially in Jerusalem.[3] The constant efforts of the Jews to return to Palestine from the 'Exile', for which we have documentary evidence from the ninth century onwards, were both a proof of the attachment

---

[1] The physical link of the Jew with the land, the Divine Promise to the Patriarchs, and the idea of the final redemption are, according to Martin Buber, op. cit., pp. 3–34, the three rings of the same moral, religious, historical and national consciousness on which Jewish identity has been based throughout the centuries.

[2] Sabbatai Zevi Ben Mordecai, b. 1626 in Smyrna, d. 1676. He proclaimed himself the Messianic redeemer in 1648 and finally embraced Islam. On the social and psychological impact of the Sabbatean movement on the Jews of the seventeenth century, see Gershom G. Scholem, *Major Trends in Jewish Mysticism* (2nd ed., London, 1946), p. 287, and the interesting article by Robert Alter, 'Sabbatai Zevi and the Jewish Imagination', in *Commentary*, June 1967. He was to be followed by the last of the false Jewish Messiahs, Jacob Frank, from Podolia, who was converted to Catholicism in 1759 and died after an adventurous life in 1791.

[3] Where the Romans built a new city called Aelia Capitolina after the Jewish revolt led by Bar Kochba (A.D. 132), and where the Jews were forbidden to resettle.

of the Jewish people to the Holy Land and a manifestation of their belief in practical Messianism. It is significant that the first break with 'Messianic Zionism' did not occur—as has sometimes been claimed[1]— in modern times and through secular Zionism and Jewish nationalism, but under the impact of early European enlightenment. It is true, as Arthur Hertzberg claims, that it was the 'Copernican revolution', announced by Zionism and marking a fresh beginning in Jewish history, that claimed Zionism's ultimate values derived from the general *milieu* and not from the Divine Will; but it was Baruch Spinoza, that extraordinary rationalist Jewish rebel, who, in a famous passage in his *Tractatus*,[2] contended that new conditions of world society, not a divine miracle, might bring about the fulfilment of the hopes of Messianic return.

Such an approach was naturally consistent with the new intellectual climate of Europe brought about by the advancement of the Age of Reason—a revolutionary time in which Jews, not as such, but in the split personalities of Spanish *conversos*,[3] still played a considerable role. Modern historical researches on the contribution of Spanish *conversos* to the social change in Western Europe and to the development of the Spanish American colonial empire have shown the impact of the religious and social marginalism of the Jewish *conversos* and crypto-Jews on sixteenth- and seventeenth-century Europe. Thus, for instance, Américo Castro has been able to collect ample evidence of the role played by Jewish *conversos* as instigators of innovation and change in Renaissance Europe. He is probably right to link the phenomenon with the peculiar situation of social and psychological instability in which the Jewish *conversos* found themselves as marginal and influential elements in Christian society.[4] Professor Baer has for his part described the reactions of religious Jews towards the *conversos* in the fifteenth and sixteenth centuries—and vice versa—which, strangely enough, recall the heated arguments between Jewish assimilationists and Zionists before the First World War.[5]

---

[1] For instance, in Arthur Hertzberg, *The Zionist Idea : a Historical Analysis and Reader* (New York, 1959), p. 18.

[2] Baruch Spinoza, *The Political and Religious Tractate* (Eng. trans., New York, 1951), vol. I, p. 56. I am grateful to Mr. C. Abramsky for having brought this passage to my attention.

[3] *Conversos* or *marranos* (Spanish for 'swine') were the Jews who became converted to Catholicism in Spain and Portugal at the end of the fifteenth and beginning of the sixteenth century but secretly retained their faith.

[4] Américo Castro, *The Structure of Spanish History* (Princeton, 1954), ch. 13, 'The Spanish Jews'; 14, 'The Presence of the Jew in Literature and Thought'.

[5] Y. Baer, *A History of the Jews in Christian Spain* (Philadelphia, 1961–6), vol. II, pp. 270–483.

Perhaps the most remarkable example of innovation made in Spanish political thought by a *converso* haunted by the psychological instability of his own situation was the colonial reform preached by Bishop de las Casas, a converted Jew, on behalf of the American Indians. His *Brevissima relación de la destruyción de las Indias* not only paved the way for the substitution of African slave-labour for Indian but also contained a new approach to the whole concept of colonization. It seems to me safe to argue that it is the tension created by the increasing involvement of the Jews—converted at first, later secularized—in non-Jewish modern society and not Jewish religious particularism which is becoming the core of the Jewish problem in Western society.

After the French Revolution Jewish assimilation was accompanied by the increasing popularity of Tacitus' old belief in Jewish inadaptability to 'normal' society and Hegel's conception of the Jewish national 'soul' in terms of *odium generis humani*. Tacitus proclaimed some eighteen centuries ago that 'everything which is sacred to the Romans is profane to the Jews, while what the Romans regard as impure is possible among the Jews'.[1] To Hegel, Judaism was a religion for slaves. 'The fate of the Jewish people', he said, 'is the fate of Macbeth who stepped out of nature itself, clung to alien Beings, and so in their service had to trample and slay everything holy in human nature, had at last to be forsaken by his gods (since these were objects and he their slave) and be dashed to pieces on his faith itself.'[2] Thinkers as different as Sombart, Lenin, and Kaufman share, although obviously with different intentions and conclusions, the view of the abnormality of the fate of the Jew.[3] No wonder the idea of abnormality, coupled with the catastrophically negative view of the role of the Jew in society, should have been adopted by Arab nationalism, which is far more of a by-product of European post-Hegelian thought than Zionism. Whatever its truth, as far as the position of the Jew in Western Christian society is concerned, such a view certainly seems inconsistent with the realities of Jewish life in the vast Jewish settlement of Eastern Europe—until the beginning of our century—and even more inconsistent with the realities of Jewish life in the non-Christian world, mainly in the Islamic countries.

[1] *Histories* 5, 2–5.

[2] Georg Wilhelm Friedrich Hegel, *Early Theological Writings*, trans. T. M. Knox, with an Introduction, and Fragments trans. by Richard Kroner (Chicago, 1948); quoted in N. Rotenstreich, op. cit., p. 49.

[3] W. Sombart, *The Jews and Modern Capitalism*, trans. M. Epstein (London, 1913); V. I. Lenin, 'National Culture', October–December 1913; *idem*, 'The National Spectre of "Assimilation" ', October–December 1913, in R. F. Andrews (ed.), *What Lenin Said about the Jews* (London, 1929); Yehezkel Kaufman, *Toledot Haemunah Hayisreelit* (A History of the Israelite Faith), 8 vols. (Tel Aviv, 1956).

The Jewish settlement of Eastern Europe, and certainly ghetto society until the time of Jewish emancipation, was a very traditional, conservative type of society, in which the impact of Jewish marginalism was very limited. It is difficult to disagree with Professor Scholem's view that heresy, being closely connected with mysticism and Messianism, appears as a consistent trend of 'conservative revolutionarism' in a tight, traditional Jewish society.[1] One may also be tempted to advance a more speculative opinion and ask if the irrational attachment of so many modern, totally secularized Jews to Palestine and their equally irrational rejection of any alternative territorial solution to the Jewish problem—such as Baron de Hirsch's Jewish colonization attempts in the Argentine,[2] the British proposal to the Zionist Organization to investigate the possibility of Jewish settlement in Uganda,[3] and the Soviet offer of an autonomous Jewish territory in Birobidjan initiated by the State—may not be explained in terms of secular Jewish mysticism. The irrational but real attachment of the Eastern European Jews—religious masses and secularized *élites*—to Palestine deeply impressed Theodor Herzl during his first trip to Russia in 1900, and considerably strengthened his belief that political Zionism could turn from a Jewish national philanthropic organization aiming at overcoming antisemitism into a powerful Jewish national movement. He died in 1904, fully realizing the unbridgeable gap existing between the fundamentally 'secular' Zionists, the Territorialists, who thought only in terms of expediency and *Realpolitik*, and those perhaps equally non-religious Zionists, the Zion-Zionists, for whom the return to the Land of Israel was an irrevocable, even if irrational, commitment. Herzl tried, at the Sixth Zionist Congress in 1903, to reach a compromise between the two sides with the idea of a *Nachtasyl*, a temporary refuge outside Palestine in which Jews could train for the last leg of the trip. He failed because the *Nachtasyl* was not so much a tactical compromise as a betrayal of Zionism in disguise.[4]

[1] Gershom G. Scholem, 'Religious Authority and Mysticism', *Commentary*, Nov. 1964.

[2] Baron Maurice de Hirsch, French philanthropist and industrialist, 1831–96; founder of the Jewish Colonization Association (I.C.A.) in 1891, which was set up mainly to transport persecuted Russian Jews to South America. For his relations with Herzl and Zionism see Alex Bein, *Theodor Herzl: A Biography* (London, 1957), pp. 124 ff.

[3] Before the Uganda offer (which in fact consisted of a proposition made by the Foreign Office to Herzl's representative in London, Leopold Greenberg, to investigate the possibility of Jewish settlement on the Guas Ngishu Plateau) Cyprus, El Arish, and Sinai had been under consideration as sites for possible Jewish settlements. See documents and correspondence, Foreign Office, 2 (785), East Africa; Oskar K. Rabinowicz, *A Jewish Cyprus Project: Davis Trietsch's Colonization Scheme* (New York, 1962); Alex Bein, op. cit., pp. 412 ff.

[4] Alex Bein, op. cit., pp. 455 ff.

If we turn from Jewish traditional society in Eastern Europe to the position of the Jews in Islam, we can see even more easily how inconsistent is the theory of the inherently subversive nature of the Jew. In the Moslem countries the Jews were, like the Christians, a separate group with unequal political rights in the theocratic Moslem world. But they were completely integrated from the social and cultural point of view and never represented an element of ferment or change. Quite the contrary, they were to be found consistently in basic agreement with conservative groups such as government administration, merchants, legal authorities, and moderately progressive, although never revolutionary, scientific and literary trends.[1] It was through religious differentiation, perpetuated and preserved by the Moslem system of personal law and by a theocratic society, that the Jewish national identity and the idea of the return to Zion were kept alive. The efforts of the Duke of Naxos,[2] the powerful Jewish prince of the sixteenth-century Ottoman Empire, to reconstruct Tiberias as an autonomous Jewish settlement and to protect the persecuted Jews of the papal territories in Italy are a typical example of such an attitude, as well as of the political power which Jews could muster in the Ottoman Empire.

The theory of the Jewish disposition to change and ferment change seems thus quite false when applied to the Jewish people as a whole. Jews were integrated as well as marginal, conservative as well as carriers of ferment and change into the non-Jewish society in which they lived, according to the time and place. If a Jewish destiny and mission exist—and I find no difficulty in accepting this idea—their meaning seems to me to be a divine prerogative. I am as suspicious of Jewish determinism and Jewish historicism as I am of any other form of determinism, historical or otherwise. Thus it seems safe to me to argue that while the Jews, both in their own traditional society and in non-Christian societies, embodied conservatism and social stability, they turned into increasingly important instigators of change in modern Europe, where they remained marginal to Western society, in spite of the growing secularization of Christian society and the growing secularization of the westernized Jew. The reason for this paradoxical situation is to be found in the rise since the end of the eighteenth century of certain new secular Western religions, such as nationalism, Marxism,

[1] S. D. Goitein, *A Mediterranean Society: The Jewish Communities of the Arab World as Portrayed in the Documents of the Cairo Geniza*, vol. I (University of California Press, 1967), pp. 70–3.

[2] Joseph Nasi, Duke of Naxos, Turkish financier and diplomat of Jewish–Portuguese origin, was born at the beginning of the sixteenth century and died in Constantinople in 1579. *The Jewish Encyclopedia*, vol. IX, pp. 172–4.

racism, and so on, which were far more intolerant than the old theocratic faiths.[1] But it was also during this period, the century and a
half from Jewish emancipation through the French Revolution to the
massacre of the Jews by Nazi Germany, that many Jews and non-Jews
were convinced that the centuries-old struggle between Church and
Synagogue was at last on the point of weakening under the shock of
Enlightenment and liberalism.

A Jewish thinker who had much influence on the development of
contemporary Zionist thought, Nachman Krochmal (1785–1840),[2] believed not only in Enlightenment but in the fact that the whole purpose
of Jewish history was to make the Jews a vehicle of Enlightenment.
Now it was felt that the responsibility for carrying the torch of human-
ism and monotheism had finally passed into non-Jewish hands (especially after the French Revolution, some of his followers said); a new era
and new tasks were opening before the Jews. It was expressed in the
Hebrew slogan 'Ish le-ohalo, Israel'—'Each to his tent, O Israel';
meaning that, from now on, each Jew could choose his own way,
including the one leading to the Land of Canaan, which growing
national consciousness now made a more appealing 'tent' to disengaged
Jews and to the modernizing Jews in search of a cause. The Zionist
movement was born in a passionate and confused search for change
and escapism, which best found its expression in the Russian-
Jewish provincial literature of the fermenting Tsarist empire of the
mid-nineteenth century.[3] And with it arose a new task, a new internal
and external up-stream battle for the Jewish return to their homeland.

The odds facing the Zionists, and later even more the Israelis, once
more looked formidable. About a century after Krochmal's death, in
1955 to be precise, in a distant corner of the world, Bandung in Indonesia, the developing nations declared that one of the most serious dangers
to the freedom and development of the some 1·5 billion Afro-Asians
was tiny Israel, with its two million inhabitants. Today the Zionist
State is at odds with the Arabs, and with the Communist world, France,

---

[1] See J. L. Talmon, *The Origins of Totalitarian Democracy* (London, 1952).

[2] Known in Hebrew by the acronym *Ranak*, an historian and philosopher from Galicia
in Eastern Europe. Author of 'The Guide of the Perplexed of the Time' (*Moreh Nevukhe
HaZeman*). For a collection of his works see S. Rawidowicz, ed., *Kitvei Rabbi Naḥman
Krochmal* (Berlin, 1924; in Hebrew). For a concise essay, stating the principles and activities
of pre-Herzl Palestinophiles, see Naḥum Sokolow, *Ḥibbath Zion* ('The Love of Zion') (Jerusalem, 1934), ch. 7: 'Nachman Krochmal, The Revival Theory', and ch. 8: 'The Conclusions of Krochmal's Theory', pp. 43–50.

[3] See David Patterson, *The Hebrew Novel in Czarist Russia* (Edinburgh, 1964).

and large sections of 'progressive' Western intellectual circles, which are so often influenced by Jews.

I mention these interesting but quite trivial manifestations of irritation of the 'great' and the 'small' of the world with Israel not because I think they are important or relevant to the subject under discussion—which is the evolution of Israel from a colonial to an industrialized society—but to stress the strange fact that this modern evolution, marking the disengagement of the nationalist Jews from their Diaspora status, is carried out once more according to the pattern of an uphill battle against impossible odds.

Why should this be so? Is it because the return of at least some of the Jews to the Land of Canaan is resulting in the insoluble tribal confrontation of two peoples—the Arabs and the Jews—in times of almost exasperating nationalism? Or is it because Israel, alone among contemporary countries engaged in nation-building experiments, possesses a special brand of 'cosmopolitan' nationalism in this era of political atomization and scientific unity? Why are Arabs, Communists, Negro activists, and so many 'progressive' Jews so vehemently opposed to the new Jewish State? Is it because Zionism represents the revolt of the traditional victim? It may sound a foolish suggestion, however, at a time when violence is so exalted. Yet the fact is that no execution in modern times has aroused so much opposition over the world as that of an acknowledged criminal and convicted murderer, Adolf Eichmann. Evidently, where Israel is concerned, anything can be questioned, even if the question is prima facie an irrelevant one. And so it is dangerous to attempt to compile a list of questions: a few may be relevant, but the majority are not. Also, the questions often get confused and entangled and may be the confused expression of all sorts of ambiguities: modernization of traditional societies; Western technical superiority not yet mastered by the East; effective mobilization of the masses for a national goal, attempted and failed at by the majority of newly independent countries; the inability of nationalism to produce statehood and political control or sufficient economic and industrial power. So is the widespread hostility to Israel due to the fact that, in a time of racial strife, the most oppressed 'race' in the West is attempting to establish in the Middle East a pluralistic State in which the Jewish concept of universalism is put to the test again? Or is it because, in a period of declining Communist ideological power, socialist Israel proves that Marxism can coexist with capitalism and that democracy and colonial development are not necessarily political antitheses?

I hope to be able to show how much the success of the Zionist revolution is to be attributed to the uncoordinated actions of men deeply convinced of their human role and dignity, rather than to numerical majorities and minorities or to the acceptance of the rules of historical determinism.

Thus this book is intended to cover mainly the period from 1917 to 1957 and it deals with the question of how a small number of Jews in Palestine built institutions and won a war for the independence of a Zionist State without being able to solve the 'Jewish Problem'.

In a second book, which will deal in detail with the period from 1958 to 1968, I hope to be able to describe what seems to me the beginning of a new revolution of the Israeli Jews in the post-industrial, atomic era, namely the creation of a Jewish pluralistic metropolis in the Middle East. I do not know if the conclusions that have been reached are valid and I do not intend to argue in favour of any of them. But it seems to me that Israel, in its present striving to survive as a new, modern, pluralistic, industrialized State in a still traditional but fast-changing, agrarian, homogeneous Arab Middle East, is once more moving along the Jewish road of a minority struggle against immense hostile majorities.

I feel it fair to request the reader at this stage to accept tentatively the meaning I give to some recurrent words so charged with emotion that they can wreck an argument even before it has been fully expounded.

One of these words is the adjective 'colonial' which I often attach to Zionism, to the Yishuv of Palestine, and to the State of Israel. It is somehow ironic that the word 'Yishuv' has a favourable connotation, although *yishuv* means 'colony', both literally and historically, while the word 'colony' has a derogatory meaning in literature about Israel. This word is used here, unless otherwise stated, to describe the early result and ideas of a more or less organized transfer of Jews from countries of long residence (it is difficult to speak of 'fatherland' for the majority of Jews) to one of more recent residence in the Middle East. I therefore use the words 'colonial' and 'colony' in the strict sense of ancient Greek or early American settlements, not necessarily in the sense of more recent colonial conquest or of the politically and militarily protected establishments of expatriate *colons* in a foreign land—such as the European expatriates in Africa.

When speaking of Jews and Judaism, I use the words 'tradition' and 'traditional' in the sense of accepted rabbinical tradition, which was the only tradition the Jewish masses knew and grew up in in Eastern Europe, Asia, and Africa till the first decade of the twentieth century.

Finally, I use the term 'agrarian' in connection with groups which, whatever their declared ideology might be, have a predominant and vested interest in the direct or indirect control of agricultural land and production, whether as owners or producers.

Chapter 2

From Enlightenment to Socialism

In the beginning there was Enlightenment. And I mean not only the beginning of Zionism, but the beginning of the belief that the Jewish question, which had been a religious riddle for centuries, understandable only in terms of the Divine Will, could be handled intelligently by men. This, of course, was one of the tenets of eighteenth-century philosophy; a belief in man's ability to remould the world through reason and knowledge and to free himself from the bondage of ignorance and superstition.

How Enlightenment (the Hebrew word meaning both Enlightenment and the cultural, religious, psychological movement of modernization connected with it is *haskalah*) came to the Jews is well known.[1] It coincided both in Western and in Eastern Europe (where the majority of European Jews lived at the time) with the French Revolution and the Napoleonic conquests, although it had earlier roots of its own. For some rabbis it was, in fact, a portentous ultimate confrontation between Gog and Magog, and the popular mystic religious movement of Hasidism[2] in eighteenth-century Eastern Europe had certainly prepared the masses for coming changes.

But, as I have said, it was not only the French Revolution and Napoleon which were shaking the walls of the Jewish ghettos. In Jewish traditional society itself, more and more voices were raised in favour of change, of cultural and scientific progress, of the adaptation of the medieval Jewish community life to contemporary conditions. Rabbi Elijah of Wilna (the Sage of Wilna), a violent opponent of Hasidism as a potentially heretical movement, welcomed the Enlightenment and even published a geometry text in Hebrew.

[1] Jacob S. Raisin, *The Haskalah Movement in Russia* (Philadelphia, 1913); J. Meisl, *Haskalah* (Berlin, 1919).

[2] Founded by Rabbi Israel Ben Eliezer (*c.* 1700–60), better known in Hebrew as Baal Shem Tov (The Master of the Good Name), it was fully developed by Dov Ber of Meseritz and Jacob Joseph of Polonoye. See Martin Buber, *Tales of the Hasidim* (New York, 1947–8), and *Hasidism* (New York, 1948), and Patterson, op. cit., ch. 6, 'The Cultural Dilemma', pp. 157–88.

After a delay, which was caused by their peculiar situation, the Jews of Europe were experiencing the effects of the revolutionary ideas which had been at work in the Christian world from the time of the Reformation. Naturally in Western Europe the movement was more advanced than in Eastern Europe. Here the masses of the Jews lived as an oppressed minority in the most backward and culturally deprived part of the Continent, as a consequence of the anarchy which followed in the wake of the Cossack invasions in the seventeenth century, when the privileged life enjoyed by the Jews in Poland and Lithuania over the previous 400 years came to an end.[1] But even here Enlightenment had come to stay; it meant, basically, two things: that the traditional values of Judaism began to be questioned by the Jews and that they saw for the first time in their long history the possibility of joining the Gentile world as equals on the condition that they give up some of their less important traditions and beliefs, namely their superstitions and taboos, and this strengthened the moral and intellectual values of the religion. Abbé Grégoire, the ardent advocate of Jewish emancipation in revolutionary France, saw clearly how emancipation could lead Jews to conversion by breaking the link between Church and Nation, thus solving the Jewish dilemma.[2] The rabbis of the Napoleonic Empire were summoned in 1806 by Napoleon to a general assembly—they called it by the ancient name of 'Sanhedrin'—to define once and for all the nature of Judaism, but skipped the dilemma by declaring, under the watchful eye of the Paris police, that they forfeited all the 'political laws' of Judaism 'which were intended to rule the people of Israel in Palestine when it possessed its own kings, priests, and judges', but not the religious laws, which are 'by their nature absolute and independent of circumstances and time'. It was an implicit acceptance of the Jewish reform movement, aimed at transforming the Jews simply into 'Israelites', but it did not solve the Jewish dilemma either in theory or in practice; in theory because it did not free the Jews from observance of the religious laws, the essence of which was the maintenance of a separate identity in the hope of Messianic redemption and return to the Promised Land; in practice, because the Jews at the Napoleonic Sanhedrin were mainly Western European Jews and represented only a small minority compared with the masses of Jews living in Eastern Europe. Here the Jews continued in their traditions, spoke their own language, and considered themselves, and were considered

[1] Raisin, op. cit., pp. 20–52.
[2] H. Grégoire, *Essai sur la régénération physique, morale et politique des Juifs* (1789), p. 123.

by their Gentile neighbours, to belong to a different, foreign nation.[1]

The confrontation between Judaism and assimilation brought about by the Enlightenment had similarities with the great confrontation of Judaism and Hellenism in the Roman Empire. A fundamental difference, however, was that in ancient times the distinction between religion and nationality could not be made (as it cannot in principle be made—and we shall see with what important consequences for the Jews of Israel—to this very day in Islam, where Church and State are not separate). Now, that is, since the French Revolution, it became possible for a European to divide his loyalties without losing his faith and head. This was the gist—and justification—of the teaching of the great prophets of Jewish Enlightenment, Moses Mendelssohn and Solomon Maimon.[2] They believed that science and religion could be reconciled and that knowledge would allow the Jew to participate as an equal in the life of the world outside the ghetto, without losing the prerogative and the dignity of being a Jew. These ideas were not exclusive to the modernizing group: the Orthodox spokesman of Jewish Enlightenment, Nachman Krochmal, declared that the Almighty's purpose in creating the Diaspora was to spread Enlightenment among the Gentiles.

It was a logical idea which did not work. Enlightenment never overcame antisemitism and never allowed the European Jew who continued to identify himself with Judaism to become completely assimilated into Gentile society, where he had been considered for so long as an object, and not a subject, of history. Whether it was the Jew who carried antisemitism with him, by the fact that he was (rather like the Negro in America) different in the matter of language, religion, customs, social structure, trades, etc., from the Gentile majority, or whether it was the endemic antisemitism of the Gentile—namely the failure of Enlightenment itself—which forced the Jew to remain different, in spite of his wishes, is a much debated question, to which J.-P. Sartre has added, since the Second World War, a modern, existentialist, and (like all the others) insufficient interpretation[3]—insufficient at least if one is to judge from the passionate attachment of the assimilated Jews to the State of

---

[1] See the interesting article by Max J. Kohler and Simon Wolf, 'Jewish Disabilities in the Balkan States', *American Jewish Historical Society*, XXIV, pp. 2–39.

[2] Rabbi Moses Ben Menahem Mendelssohn (1729–86), leading German representative of the Haskalah movement, translator of the Pentateuch into German; Solomon Maimon (1754–1800), one of the greatest Jewish philosophers, author of an autobiography (1783) which has been compared with Rousseau's *Confessions* and which is one of the most penetrating analyses of Jewish psychology of the Enlightenment. Raisin, op. cit., pp. 86–97.

[3] J.-P. Sartre, op. cit.

Israel which can only partially be explained as a reaction to bourgeois antisemitism. Perhaps it was the rise of Romanticism which was the main reason for the failure of Jewish Enlightenment. I shall not enter into this here, since the aim of this chapter is to deal with the ideological origins of Zionism.

My purpose is to show that through the Enlightenment crisis the European Jews were caught in a dilemma: they wanted to become part of the new, egalitarian, rationalist, Utopian, European society brought about by eighteenth-century ideals, and they were ready to give up part of their Jewishness, namely their separate national identity, in order to become citizens of the enlightened world. But the process was a long one, since the ideas of the Enlightenment did not permeate the Jewish masses of Eastern Europe until after the revolution they had brought about—the French Revolution—had failed to construct its Utopian world and after the Napoleonic Wars had stirred up nationalism all over the Continent. So, enlightened Jews who had broken with their national and in many cases also with their religious past found themselves nationally defenceless, in a world which, with Hegel and Marx, was now unprepared to offer the individual *droit de cité* in the new State and/or class society.

The doctrine of the emancipation of the Jews involved the view that their earlier status of subjection was no longer permissible; consequently, a 'Jewish problem' existed. Given the existence of this problem, it was logically possible to seek a solution for it in two different ways: by granting the Jews a new status of equality either individually, as citizens of the countries where they lived, or collectively, as a modern nationality.[1]

Both the Jews and the Gentile world were unprepared for either solution. By the time the Jews started to take full advantage of emancipation, rising nationalism in Gentile society had blocked their progress towards assimilation with antisemitism, while strengthening, through reaction, the new Jewish separatist, nationalist trend—Zionism. In both cases they became increasingly marginal to the society in which they lived, but also to their own, because of the dwindling influence of Jewish tradition on the Jewish *élite*.

Thus, Zionism was not simply the natural outcome of a spontaneous Jewish social upheaval; it was also one of the many reactions to the 'situational logic' of the time, in Karl Popper's sense,[2] by the Jews estranged from Jewish traditionalism by Enlightenment. By being so,

---

[1] Ben Halpern, *The Idea of the Jewish State* (Cambridge, Mass., 1961), pp. 58 f.
[2] Karl Popper, *The Open Society and its Enemies* (London, 1945).

it was naturally desynchronized, that is to say, over-extended; it was a reaction of Jews ideologically and intellectually involved in the social roles of eighteenth-century Enlightenment to the challenge—and rejection—of the nineteenth-century nationalist world.

From the moment Zionism was formulated to the time of its practical realization, namely the creation of the State of Israel in 1948, a lot more ideological and political water flowed under the bridge. So, in our own time, Zionism has found itself once more desynchronized, theoretically and practically, awkwardly transformed from oppressed nationalism, fighting antisemitism in Europe, into a European Jewish settlement fighting Arab nationalism in the Middle East.

The problem of Jewish national desynchronization, the stretching of its ideological content to cover its actions, is one of the themes of this book. I shall endeavour to elaborate it by describing the transformation of Israeli society from an agrarian into an industrial society which, I hope to show, is both cause and consequence of the multiple over-extension of Jewish nationalism.

In this chapter, however, I only intend to deal briefly with some aspects of Zionist ideology and with its prophets. First I shall discuss the early nineteenth-century Zionist thinkers, both Jewish and Christian, and the reasons for their failure to impress their ideas on the Jewish masses and the Jewish intellectuals of their time.

Then, I shall deal very briefly with the conditions of European Jewry in the second half of the nineteenth century. In this period three contradictory ideological reactions to antisemitism occurred—Zionism, assimilation, emigration to the West—and the first two, paradoxically, had their philosophical roots in the eighteenth-century Enlightenment. I shall conclude by describing the ideas and the personality of some of the Zionist leaders who played a major role in the translation of Jewish national Utopias into political realities.

The first practical formulations of the Jewish national Risorgimento were left to Christian politicians or authors sensitive to Jewish suffering but emotionally detached from Jewish traditionalism.

One of the first and most colourful of them was certainly Bonaparte, who in 1799 issued a call to the Jews of Africa and Asia to re-establish the glory of ancient Jerusalem by enlisting under his flag.[1] A detailed plan for Jewish political resurrection was also presented to the Directory in the wake of Bonaparte's conquest of Egypt. It was aimed at

---

[1] *Gazette nationale ou le moniteur universel*, No. 243, tridi, 3 prairial, an 7 de la République française une et indivisible (1799).

using the Jews as a pro-French 'colony' in the Near East. Later one of Garibaldi's comrades-in-arms, Benedetto Musolino, wrote a book to prove, from a strictly Christian point of view, the necessity of creating a Jewish State across the Sinai Peninsula.[1]

The idea of a Jewish State controlling the strategic route from the Mediterranean to the Red Sea seems to have occurred to Englishmen, such as Lord Shaftesbury, 1801–85,[2] and Laurence Oliphant, 1829–88,[3] who combined romanticism and philosemitism with political awareness of British strategic interests in the Middle East. Oliphant, who has had many streets named after him in Israel, was accompanied on one of his trips to the Holy Land by a Jewish 'bard' strongly influenced by German Romanticism, Naphtali Herz Imber (1856–1909), who composed a nostalgic song called 'The Hope', which later, and significantly, became Israel's national anthem.[4]

Laurence Oliphant enjoyed the political and emotional support of Disraeli who, in his novels *Tancred*, *Alroy*, and *Coningsby*, wrote of the return of the Jews to the Promised Land with romantic passion. A Swiss, Henri Dunant, the founder of the Red Cross, fought with little success for Jewish colonization of Palestine and founded a 'Society for the Colonization of Syria and Palestine' in 1878.[5]

Britain was interested in the protection of the Jewish religious minority in areas where France was already staking political and religious claims to the Catholic minorities, and Russia to the Orthodox ones. The London Government was thus favourable to the initiatives of some members of Britain's Jewish aristocracy on behalf of the 'overseas Jews'. Sir Moses Montefiore,[6] the great Jewish philanthropist, thus became a kind of Jewish British ambassador-at-large for his persecuted brethren. He pleaded their cause before the Sultan, the King of Morocco, the Russian Tsar, usually dressed in the uniform of a Captain of the London Municipal Guard. At this time, too, George Eliot made romantic Zionism a fashionable subject through her novel, *Daniel*

---

[1] Benedetto Musolino, *Gerusalemme ed il popolo ebreo* (reprinted, Rome, 1951).

[2] For Lord Ashley, 7th Earl of Shaftesbury's text of: 'Scheme for the Colonisation of Palestine, 25th September 1840', see Naḥum Sokolow, *History of Zionism 1600–1918* (London, 1919), vol. I, ch. XXIII, pp. 121 ff.

[3] Laurence Oliphant, *The Land of Gilead; With Excursions in the Lebanon* (Edinburgh, 1880), and *Haifa; or, Life in Modern Palestine* (Edinburgh, 1887), which contains one of the earliest descriptions of Zionist–Arab agricultural co-operation and conflict in Palestine, pp. 10–16. See also Margaret Oliphant, *Memoir of the Life of Laurence Oliphant* (Edinburgh, 1891).

[4] His other famous song 'Guard on the Jordan' was copied from the nationalistic German song 'Guard on the Rhine'.

[5] See the account in Richard J. H. Gottheil, *Zionism* (Philadelphia, 1914), pp. 40–6.

[6] See Louis Loewe, *Diaries of Sir Moses and Lady Montefiore* (London, 1890).

Deronda (1876), while Alexandre Dumas *fils* brought the idea of the Jewish return to the Holy Land to the Paris theatre with *The Wife of Claude*.

More than romantic sympathy and philanthropy was, however, needed to transform the growing, incoherent Jewish national aspiration into a political movement. It demanded programmes and direct social, economic, and moral incentives. As might be expected, the first translators of the centuries-old Jewish hope of return to Zion into a modern national concept were religious leaders. Rabbi Judah Alkalai (1798–1878) was a Sephardi[1] traditionalist, born in Sarajevo—in what is today Jugoslavia—and the leader of several Jewish communities of the Christian part of the then Ottoman Empire. He was undoubtedly influenced, like so many people in his time, by the Greek national revolt. His belief that the 'Redemption of the Jews' and the physical return of the Jewish People to Palestine could be brought about by national revival is already present in a booklet called 'Hear, O Israel', published in 1855. But it was the charge of ritual murder brought against the Jews of Damascus in 1840 at the instigation of the Franciscan friars—and its tragic consequences[2]—that convinced Rabbi Alkalai of the need for the Jews to save themselves and their ancestral values by buying back their former country from the Turks and returning to it *en masse*.

Although Alkalai couched his nationalistic ideas in the most traditional language and type of argument, he failed to elicit any response from either Jewish Orthodoxy or Reform Judaism. One of his few partisans was, however, Herzl's grandfather, Simon Loeb.

Another early Zionist, Rabbi Zvi Hirsh Kalisher (1795–1874),[3] born in Posen in the part of Poland recently acquired by Prussia, was not more successful. Like Alkalai he was stirred by the example of local nationalism, this time of the Poles against Russia. But, unlike Alkalai, he lived in an area which, lying astride the border of the old pietist ghetto society of the Pale of Settlement and the new, modernizing,

---

[1] *Sepharad*, in Hebrew, means Spain, *Ashkenaz* means Germany. The great division between the Jews of Spanish origin (*Sephardim*) and of German and European, other than Spanish, origin is geographical, linguistic (Sephardim speak Ladino, Ashkenazim speak Yiddish), and liturgical. After the expulsion of the Jews from Spain many Sephardim moved to Islamic countries and the Balkans. See Rabbi Judah Alkalai, *Kitvei* (Writings), vol. 1 (Jerusalem, 1944).

[2] Father Thomas, Superior of the Franciscan Convent in Damascus, disappeared on 5 February 1840. Jews were accused and tortured by the local Turkish officials until a Note from nine Consuls persuaded the then ruler of Syria, Mehemet Ali, to release them.

[3] Author of *'Emunah Yesharah* (The Correct Belief), 1843–70, and the pamphlet *Derishat Zion* (The Claim of Zion), 1862; and see Naḥum Sokolow, *Ḥibbath Zion*, ch. 4, 'The Message of Rabbi Hirsh Kalisher', pp. 17–28.

westernized Judaism assimilating itself in Germany, was also an area of strong Jewish social tension.

Kalisher, of course, belonged to the traditionalists. All his ideas were therefore expressed in the most orthodox language. He never believed that Redemption could be an exclusively human realization, and he was convinced that it could not be a sudden miracle and that it would require a long, painful effort involving the national goodwill of the Jews themselves. But he was no more successful than Rabbi Alkalai.

The assimilationist Jews, who believed in the possibility of Jewish integration into Gentile society through the 'equality', 'liberty', and 'fraternity' proclaimed by the Enlightenment, also believed, as the fathers of the French Revolution did, that religion was superstition and that the Jewish national religion was a particularly backward superstition.[1] The appeal of Kalisher and Alkalai to the Jews to return to their homeland as part of the involvement in the 'national' scheme of Messianic Redemption made no sense to rational minds. It also made little sense to Jewish Orthodoxy, but for entirely different reasons.

Jewish traditionalism represented a heroic and effective way elaborated by the rabbis through the centuries of dispersion and persecution of keeping their people morally and physically alive. Since Roman times they had developed, practised, taught, and suffered for the preservation of a religious particularism, which was in fact the best guarantee for the preservation of the national identity of a dispersed nation. With this code of ethics and religious behaviour the Jews enclosed themselves well before the Christians threw the walls of the material ghetto around them. In the ghetto of Jewish traditionalism, Jewish values, Jewish nationalism, Jewish pride and dignity had been salvaged to an incredible extent. Jewish Orthodoxy could not give up such a secure system to take the political and national risk of an organized mass return of the Jews to Palestine, even one backed by the nationalist Orthodoxy of pious men and Kalisher and Alkalai.

We shall have to return to this aspect of rabbinical opposition to Zionism in the Jewish Diaspora when we discuss the problem of the *Kulturkampf* in the State of Israel. Here I only wish to stress the fact that the early Zionist religious appeals for the return of the people to the Holy Land did not move the Jewish traditionalists of the time. The

---

[1] On the impact of assimilation on Russian Jewry see Y. Kaufman, 'Ḥevlei Temiah' (The Pains of Assimilation), in *Hashiloach*, vol. XLVI, iii–vi; *Jerusalem* (in Hebrew), p. 278; and Dr. S. Bernfeld, *Dor Tahpuchot* (The Subversive Generation), vol. II (Warsaw, 1898); S. M. Dubnow, *History of the Jews in Russia and Poland*, trans. I. Friedlaender (Philadelphia, 1916–20).

rabbis of the ghetto were convinced—like many responsible leaders of today's colonial societies—that their first duty was to avoid innovation liable to create illusions, to bring about, as so many false Messiahs had done throughout Jewish history, additional tragedy and disgrace on the Jewish people. If the Jews wanted to return to their homeland before the divine call, they were welcome to do so individually or in groups, but not as a nation.

The ideas of another—the greatest—early Zionist thinker, Moses Hess (1812–75),[1] failed for the same reason. He was, unlike Kalisher and Alkalai, an assimilated Jew, although born of a religious family.

Moses Hess was an unusual man, whose life story has been told by many scholars, past and present.[2] He was born in Bonn and soon turned from Jewish traditionalism to the teachings of Hegel. He mixed freely in the intellectual circle round Karl Marx and Friedrich Engels, went to Paris as a journalist, contributed to the *Rheinische Zeitung* edited by Marx, and even managed to be sentenced to death in the 1848 German revolution.

The Communist Manifesto, which at one time Hess was asked to draft, put an end to his political collaboration with the founders of 'scientific socialism'. After that, he lived in France for many years, immersing himself in scientific—mainly anthropological—studies, and completely cut off from his family in Germany. In 1862 he wrote his prophetic book *Rome and Jerusalem* which contains some of the best-reasoned arguments in favour of the Jewish national return to Zion. The book passed almost unnoticed and was soon forgotten by his contemporaries. In fact Hess's family found it so offensive that they ordered the last edition to be burnt in order to remove the 'offence',[3] but not before it had caught the imagination of the great Jewish historian, Heinrich Graetz, who recognized its importance as early as 1864.[4] It was its fate to be rediscovered by the Zionist politicians at the end of the century, long after the death of its author, of whom Herzl said, 'Everything we have attempted can be found in his work.'

Hess was, in spite of his connection with socialism, a romantic nationalist and a believer in the humanistic message of the French Revolution. 'Until the French Revolution', he argued, 'the Jewish people was the only people in the world whose religion was at once national and universalist. . . . Since the French Revolution, the French

[1] See Moses Hess, *Rome and Jerusalem* (1862), trans. Maurice J. Bloom (New York, 1958).
[2] For example, Theodor Zlocisti, *Moses Hess* (Berlin, 1921); Isaiah Berlin, 'The Life and Opinions of Moses Hess', The Lucien Wolf Memorial Lecture, 1957 (Cambridge, 1959).
[3] *Die Welt*, 11, No. 9, p. 16.   [4] Gottheil, op. cit., p. 38.

as well as the other peoples who followed them, have become our noble rivals and faithful allies.'[1] With ideas of this kind he could certainly not be regarded with favour by Jewish Orthodoxy, aware as it was of the anti-religious content of French rationalism. Hess himself, incidentally, had no illusions about the 'insurmountable obstacle to the realization of our patriotic aspirations' which 'rigid Christian dogma' and 'unbending Jewish Orthodoxy' would put in his way unless they both agreed to be 'revived' by his national call for Jewish redemption. He wrote: 'Just as Orthodox Jews would consent to a return to Palestine only on the condition that the ancient sacrificial cult be reintroduced in the new Jerusalem, so the Christians would give assistance to such a project only on the condition that we Jews bring our national religion as a sacrifice to Christianity at the holy sepulchre.'[2] He would certainly have been surprised at the precision of his forecast if he could have listened to the conversation between Herzl and Pius X and to the reasons adduced by the Pope against the Zionist movement.[3]

As for the assimilationist, progressive Jews, they had even more reason to ignore Hess's appeals. He claimed, quite correctly, that Jewish rationalists had as little reason for remaining within the world of Judaism as the Christian rationalists for clinging to Christianity, and that their duality no longer had a *raison d'être*. The German assimilationist Jews, who made frantic efforts to identify themselves with their Gentile environment, were doomed to failure since, he said, with deep foresight, the Germans hate the religion of the Jews 'less than they hate their race'. Neither reform, nor conversion, nor education, nor emancipation would thus open the gates of German society to them. Curiously enough, Hess is still more often attacked in our day by assimilated, progressive Jews[4] than by Orthodox ones.

So, as things stood with European Jewry in the nineteenth century, no one was ready to listen to the early Zionist appeals. Alkalai, Kalisher, and Hess were forgotten and Jewry continued its march into the twentieth century, more and more estranged from the old, traditional religious way of life, more and more committed to the road of assimilation to a hostile Gentile world, which was thronged up to Hitler's time by thousands of Jews who firmly believed that they could become completely assimilated into Gentile society.

---

[1] Hess, op. cit., pp. 61–2.
[2] Hess quoted in Hertzberg, op. cit., p. 135.
[3] Theodor Herzl, *The Complete Diaries*, trans. H. Zohn (New York, 1960), vol. IV, pp. 1, 602–4.
[4] Berlin, op. cit., p. 35, and, for example, in Hal Draper, 'The Origins of the Middle East Crisis', *New Politics*, vol. VI, no. 1, Winter 1967.

We must digress a moment to look into the conditions of the Jews in 1880. Although many European countries had emancipated their Jewish citizens—following the revolutionary events of 1848—the total number of Jews who benefited from these liberal measures was still very limited.

No statistics exist for the total number of Jews living in the various countries of the world by the end of the century. Those living in the Islamic countries aroused the interest of their western co-religionists only in time of misfortune, such as that I have already mentioned which befell the Jews of Damascus in 1840, following the charge of ritual murder brought against them by the Franciscan friars. But on the whole their existence was considerably more secure and comfortable than that of most of their European brethren.

In Western Europe a fraction of the Jewish people was engaged in the intense battle for modernization. There were those who fought for complete assimilation; those who felt with Moses Mendelssohn that a new *Jüdische Wissenschaft* (Jewish learning) should replace the old rabbinical learning of the ghetto, thus giving a new cohesive identity to modern Judaism. And finally there were the Orthodox who fought a losing battle to maintain the old Jewish way of life and traditional code of ethics in a changing world, which was becoming more and more alienated from the 'godly Society'.

The situation in Eastern Europe was totally different. In this part of the Continent, particularly in the fifteen provinces of western and southern Russia called the Pale Settlement, lived the majority of Jews. By their very number—not less than two million by the end of the century—they constituted a compact, homogenous, culturally self-sufficient society, practically untouched by modernism.

It was, paradoxically, an oppressed minority society which socially stood well above the Gentile population among which it lived.

Catherine II, in establishing the Pale of Settlement, had not only reversed her previously favourable policy towards the Jews, but sought by this to restrict the movements of the hated Jewish minority, which the partition of Poland had suddenly increased by at least one million souls in the largest ghetto there has ever been. But she intended also to make sure that the Russian Jews should not enjoy the relative autonomy which the Polish Jews used to have under their communal organization, the 'Kahal', and a kind of national ruling body, called the 'Council of the Four Lands'.[1] Her successor, Alexander I, transformed the Kahal into an organization for collecting Jewish taxes and at the

[1] Raisin, op. cit., pp. 43–5.

same time issued, in 1804, a set of comprehensive regulations for the Jews, known by the name of 'The Constitution of the Jews' and under which the Jews were to live in fear for the next fifty years. It was a paradoxical piece of legislation which on the one hand created a 'New Judea' and on the other hand tried to destroy it. In the Pale of Settlement the Jews seldom came into contact with outside civilization. They wrote and prayed in Hebrew, spoke Yiddish among themselves and local Slavonic dialects with their neighbours. They could not intellectually 'russify' themselves because the Russian culture of the time consisted of ideas imported from the West. They were asked to become farmers, but only in the most inhospitable parts of the Empire; they were allowed to go to universities, but on the condition that they should take compulsory courses in Christian religion.

The life of the Russian Jews became an inferno under Alexander's brother and successor, Nicholas I, who decided that the Jewish question would be best solved by forcibly enrolling them into the Army, after a 'preparatory' educational period starting at the age of 12. To obtain the necessary 'quotas' of boys the Tsarist officials used the community leaders who were thus forced to become instruments of their own people's oppression.[1] Nicholas's reign was a period of expulsions and pogroms for the Jewish population of Russia, who became dejected and miserable beyond imagination. No wonder that the liberalizing measures of Nicholas I's son, Alexander II, appeared to the Jews to be a miracle and a sign that Russian society was finally choosing the path of liberalism. After 1855 the Jews were no longer obliged to part with their young sons by compulsory conscription into the Army; they began to enjoy a measure of autonomy in the Pale of Settlement while the richest among them were even allowed to live outside the restricted areas.

A new Jewish 'intelligentsia' was thus created. Its members spoke Russian, it was full of hope in future collaboration with the Russians, and it took a great interest in Russian thought, culture, and political ideology. It was, however, a very limited even if important group, and the Jewish masses remained faithful to their traditional religious culture.

In the Pale of Settlement where 95 per cent of Russian Jews resided, they represented 12 per cent of the total population but controlled 30 per cent of the textile industry and 70 per cent of the commerce. Fifty-one per cent of the Jewish population was concentrated in the towns, as against 12 per cent of the non-Jewish population. At the age of 10, Jewish children were one and a half times more literate than the

[1] Dubnow, op. cit., vol. II, pp. 22 ff.

non-Jewish children. In monetary terms, the Jewish population disposed of a liquidity superior to that both of the landed aristocracy and of the farmers. Thus, they were the natural financiers of both.[1] The situation was not fundamentally different in Romania and the Austro-Hungarian Empire, and it was similar in some respects to that of the Asian minority in contemporary East Africa. The situation of the Jews in Russia was a perfect example of social superiority linked with ethnic inferiority, thus inviting inter-professional, inter-class, inter-communal strife. When the Government allowed this strife to break out in 1881, it produced a catastrophe and a shock of unexpected magnitude and consequence.

The pretext for the 1881 pogroms, which shattered more than 150 Jewish communities (as a diversionary measure of Russian internal policy), was the assassination of Alexander II.[2]

His successor, Alexander III, was less responsible for the tragic events which befell the Jews than his reactionary courtiers, especially Constantine Petrovich Pobyedonostzev, the main instigator of the new antisemitic policy, who aimed at driving 'one-third of the Jews out of Russia, one-third to apostasy, and one-third to death', and at making them the scapegoats of the Government's anti-liberal policy.

In 1882 the 'Temporary Rules' issued by the commission investigating the causes of the pogroms, under the direction of Count Ignatiev, became the rules according to which the Jews of Russia were afterwards forced to live. Jews were forced out of the agricultural areas of the Pale of Settlement; they were submitted to a strict *numerus clausus* in the schools and universities; their trade was hindered, so that many Jewish artisans found themselves financially ruined. With the approach of the Russo-Japanese war more violence, culminating in the Kishinev pogrom in 1903, was openly instigated by the authorities as a way of distracting the Russian population from the hardships imposed by the Government's policy.

Three Jewish movements were—in time—born out of these dramatic events: Jewish Socialism, Americanism, and Zionism. I shall not discuss the first movement, the 'Bund', that anti-Zionist and yet national Jewish workers' organization of Eastern Europe, which Johnpoll has

---

[1] I. M. Rubinow, 'Economic Condition of the Jews in Russia', *Bulletin of the Bureau of Labor*, no. 72, Department of Commerce and Labor (Washington, 1907); and Arthur Ruppin, *The Jews in the Modern World* (London, 1934), ch. III.

[2] The reason officially advanced by the Russian press was that a Jewess, Hesia Helfman, had participated in the plot against the Tsar. The first anti-Jewish violence broke out on the eve of the Jewish Passover, on 27 April 1881 in Elizabethgrad, spread to Kiev on 8 May, to Odessa on 15 May, and then to the surrounding countryside.

so well described in his book *The Politics of Futility*.[1] I shall recall only that the Bund was born in the same year as the Zionist Organization—1897—and that it played a role in shaping, through bitter opposition, the conscience of the Zionist workers' groups.

The second, far more important Jewish movement created by Russian antisemitism is what I call Americanism, namely mass emigration to the United States, and in more limited numbers to South America.

The fact that two million Eastern European Jews, mainly from the Russian Empire, crossed the Atlantic between 1881 and 1914 to America is a phenomenon of particular importance for Zionism. It raises the question why so few Jews from Eastern Europe went to Palestine in the same period and what the Jewish American community means to the rest of the Jewish Diaspora in political and philosophical terms.

The problem is a fascinating one to which I shall return when speaking of the relations between the State of Israel and the United States. Here I shall limit myself to underlining two facts. The first, that the same shock of anti-Jewish events—the pogroms of 1881—was what sent the Jews to Palestine and the United States. The second, that the same eighteenth-century Enlightenment ideals which served as a catalyst in the Zionist Utopia also served as philosophical justification for the East European Jews establishing a new Diaspora in the New World.

This does not mean that the Jewish immigrants to America were motivated by any ideal other than the one of finding a haven from persecution. But in the United States the new immigrants also found themselves politically and ideologically conditioned by the small but influential Jewish community which had preceded them across the Atlantic. This community enjoyed a level of equality and freedom unsurpassed by any other Jewish community of the world; it had taken an active part in the American Revolution and now saw its status fully recognized by the new republic's constitution.

To give an idea of the difference in status between the Jews in the U.S.A. and the Jews in Europe, it is sufficient to recall that in 1789, three years before the Jews were considered citizens in France and eighty-five years before they were emancipated in Switzerland, kosher food was provided for them at the garden party given by the City of Philadelphia in honour of the new American Constitution.[2] At the time

---

[1] Bernard K. Johnpoll, *The Politics of Futility: The General Jewish Workers Bund of Poland, 1917–43* (Ithaca, New York, 1967).

[2] Joseph L. Blau and Salo W. Baron (eds.), *The Jews of the United States 1790–1840: A Documentary History*, 3 vols. (New York, 1963), p. xxiii.

there were only 3,000 Jews in the Union. They not only played an active role in American politics, but were conscious of that fundamental distinction between an American and a non-American Jew, namely that to be a Jew in America was one accepted way of being American, whereas to be a Jew in Egypt or in France was—and still is—to be considered somehow a foreigner by the respective nation.

The new immigrants in America found themselves confronted with a society which, for the first time since the destruction of the Temple of Jerusalem, considered the Jews not only equal but co-founders of the American Commonwealth. They were willing to believe that at last they were not exiles in a foreign land, but partners in a 'New Jerusalem' totally different from the 'Old World'. It was purest Enlightenment Utopia, a start *ex nihilo*. It is thus not difficult to understand why Zionism made so little impact on American Jewry, in spite of the passionate interest shown by the East European American Jews for the national home which their Eastern European Zionist brethren were building in Palestine.

Zionism was the third movement set in motion by the dramatic events of 1881. I have already shown how deeply these events shattered the faith of the Russian Jewish intelligentsia in the liberal evolution of Russian society. 'Close your eyes and hide your heads, ostrich fashion, as much as you like; if we do not take advantage of the fleeting moments of repose [of the pogrom] and devise remedies more fundamental than those palliatives with which the incompetents have for centuries vainly tried to relieve our unhappy nation, lasting peace is impossible for you,' wrote L. S. Pinsker, a distinguished doctor in Odessa, addressing himself to his fellow Jews.[1] At the time, he did not dare, or at least did not think it advisable, to sign his pamphlets with his own name, and just described himself as 'A Russian Jew'. But his pamphlet *Auto-Emancipation*, published in Odessa in 1882, was to become the inspiration for the first organized movement for the Jewish return to the homeland.

The movement, which had originally started in Romania, was the 'Ḥibbath Zion' (Love of Zion) and its members called themselves the 'Ḥovevei Zion' (Lovers of Zion).[2] They were a mixed group: some religious, others not; some very simple people, and others young, idealistic university students, too educated to accept a return to ghetto culture, too clear-sighted to trust the forces of Russian liberalism,

[1] Leo Pinsker, *Auto-Emancipation: An Appeal to His People by a Russian Jew* (Berlin, 1882), quoted in Hertzberg, op. cit., p. 182.

[2] See Naḥum Sokolow, *Ḥibbath Zion* (Jerusalem, 1935).

especially after the significant silence of men like Tolstoy over the 1881 massacres (although later, in 1903, he strongly protested against the Kishinev pogrom, in a famous pamphlet called 'I Cannot Keep Silent'). They were also too proud to embark on the road of a new West European or American exile. So they decided to go to Turkish Palestine where they were to be supported by committees organized on their behalf all over Russia and, later, by the French Baron Edmond de Rothschild.

In the year in which Pinsker's *Auto-Emancipation* was published, 1882, the first Jewish colony in Palestine, Rishon-le-Zion (First to Zion), was founded south of Jaffa. The young Jewish students from Russia who set it up had been moved by the writings of thinkers as different as Smolenskin,[1] A. D. Gordon,[2] and Lilienblum,[3] who had little in common apart from the intellectual *malaise* brought on by the frustrations of assimilation and antisemitism.[4] Significantly, they called themselves by the name 'Bilu', an acrostic of the biblical verse: *Beith Yaakov lehu veneelcha* (House of Jacob, let us rise and go). With this motto they established, in a romantic and unplanned agricultural crusade, the villages of Zichron-Yaakov in Samaria, Rosh Pinah in Lower Galilee, and Wadi Hanin, south of Jaffa; they reinforced the colony of Petach Tikwah, founded in 1878 by Jews from Jerusalem, and in 1883 they founded Yesud Ha Maalah in Galilee. Strangely enough, these were the boundaries the Jews were prepared to accept in 1937, when the partition of Palestine was first envisaged by the British Government.

The 'Hovevei Zion' were idealists who set the ball of the return to Zion rolling but who still lacked a clear-cut programme.[5] It took thirteen more years for the programme to mature in the mind of an assimilated Austro-Hungarian Jew, Theodor Herzl, and one more shock, the

[1] Peretz Smolenskin (1842–85), founder of the magazine *Hashahar* (The Dawn), a most important literary contribution to the revival of Hebrew and Jewish nationalism. Author of *'Am Olam* (Eternal People), 1872, and *'Et Lataat* (Time for Planting), 1875, on the theory of Jewish nationalism.

[2] See p. 43, n. 2 below.

[3] Moshe Leib Lilienblum (1843–1910), author of a pamphlet calling for the creation of a Jewish Colonization Society in Palestine.

[4] A climate of intellectual questioning and rebellion permeated most of the Jewish Hebrew newspapers from the sixties onwards; for example, *Hamagid* (The Teller), founded at Lyck in Eastern Prussia by Leo Silbermann; *Hakarmel* (The Carmel), founded in Wilna by S. J. Finn in 1860; *Ha-Zefirah* (The Dawn), founded by H. S. Slonimsky in Warsaw in 1862; *Hameliz* (The Advocate), founded at Odessa by A. Zederbaum in 1860.

[5] For a short account of the activities of the 'Hovevei Zion' see S. Ravikovitch, 'The Palestine Committee of Odessa: Its Origin, Development, and Activity', *The Maccabeans*, XIII, 16 et seq.

Dreyfus trial in Paris, to determine its final elaboration and almost immediate success.

Theodor Herzl was born in Budapest on 2 May 1860, the son of a rich merchant. It would be interesting to have a detailed psychological study of his relationship with his mother, who remained until his death, on 3 July 1904, the dominant influence in his life. It was she who raised him in the Nietzschean dream of Promethean realization. He was a realist with a romantic streak, German-speaking, alienated by assimilation and *milieu* both from Judaism and Hungarian patriotism. But one should not underestimate the influence of his grandfather, Simon Loeb, who had been a personal friend of Rabbi Alkalai, the forgotten precursor of the Jewish Risorgimento, on his early spiritual formation. Herzl's first brush with antisemitism at the University of Vienna did not shake his faith in the ultimate success of liberalism and rationalism over the existing obscurantism. Later he went to Paris as a correspondent of the *Neue Freie Presse* of Vienna, convinced that France was still the main hope for human progress and civilization and Russia the last bastion of obscurantism. His covering of the noisy antisemitic activities of Édouard Drumont, author of the best-seller *La France juive*, led him to the conclusion that antisemitism was a 'lightning conductor' universally used for drawing the 'revolutionary ire of the masses away from the real woes of society'. As a result of this revelation he wrote a play, *The New Ghetto*, in which, for the first time, the Jewish problem became a major theme in his work. The underlying idea of the play was, in fact, that a Jew, even the most assimilated one, lives in an invisible ghetto in the Gentile world. This idea still remains fundamental to the ideology and mythology of the modern Zionist movement.

For Herzl the moment of truth came, however, only two years later, with Captain Dreyfus's arrest and trial in 1894.

'The Jewish State', that booklet which set political Zionism in motion, was historically the outcome of the emotional crisis suffered by Herzl when he witnessed the shattering of his hopes in democratic France. It was in fact the elaboration of a long letter sent to Baron Maurice de Hirsch on 3 June 1895 (after an interview in which Herzl discussed the possibility of a political solution to the Jewish question) and of a much longer memorandum prepared for the Rothschild family on the same subject.

The refusal of both leading oligarchic and philanthropic Jewish families to take the Viennese journalist seriously made him the founder and the first leader of Jewish political Risorgimento.

Subsequent events in the history of Zionism are well known, documented, and studied in the many analyses of Zionism.[1] We shall not, therefore, delve into them, but rather look briefly at the extraordinary figure of Theodor Herzl.

Hertzberg says that Herzl was a man of the West, a journalist of European reputation whose stature among his East European Jewish brethren was enhanced by his standing in the Western Gentile world.[2] I would accept this description and I would also agree with Hertzberg that, although Herzl wrote his book 'in the presence of the two gods of the *fin-de-siècle* (progressive) intellectual, Marx and Nietzsche', he did not follow either of them. He was too Marxist to allow himself to be labelled Utopian and too Nietzschean to renounce his eighteenth-century belief in the ability of men to change the world. Hertzberg is also right when he explains Herzl's political Zionism as the dialectical synthesis of the inevitable clash between the omnipresent antisemitism (thesis) and *malaise* of the Gentile world regarding the persisting Jewish problem (antithesis). Where I think his analysis falls short is on the evaluation of the role of antisemitism—a positive force 'which made sense—the visa to the Jews' passport into the world of modernity'.[3]

Herzl certainly had an optimistic view of antisemitism and his 'official' visits to the arch-Jew-baiters, the leaders of Tsarist Russia, were motivated by political realism and by his belief that the Russian Government was as fed up with the Jewish question as the Jews were with the Russian régime.

Such an analysis was probably correct and it holds good not only for Tsarist Russia but, in more recent times, for East European communist régimes. They seem, in fact, as relieved as Israel to see their Jews out of East European apartments and jobs, now coveted by the new Gentile communists.

The guiding principle behind Herzl's Zionist strategy seems to me to have been the idea of honour. Herzl, contrary to most of the assimilated, modernist Jews of his time, was a true aristocrat and, in this sense, he was more traditionally Jewish than many of the rabbis of his generation.

---

[1] Adolf Böhm, *Die zionistische Bewegung*, 2 vols. (Berlin, 1920–1), 2nd edition, vol. I (Berlin and Tel Aviv, 1935), vol. II (Jerusalem, 1937), remains the best work on Zionism; for the social climate of Eastern Europe in which Zionism germinated see also Ben Zion Dinaburg, *Sefer Hazionut* (The Book of Zionism), Tel Aviv, 1938. Naḥum Sokolow's *History of Zionism 1600–1918* (London, 1919) is a surprisingly pedestrian and unimaginative work for a Zionist leader who acted for many years as the 'Foreign Minister' of the movement; Theodor Herzl's *Diaries* are fascinating, indispensable, but often superficial reading; Richard Gottheil's *Zionism* is a concise and informative work. See also I. Cohen, *The Zionist Movement* (London, 1945).

[2] Hertzberg, op. cit., p. 49. [3] *Jewish Quarterly Review*, 1904–5, XVII, pp. 1–25.

The President of the World Jewish Congress, Naḥum Goldmann, in a speech in Basle on 18 October 1957, gave a very clear definition of what Jewish aristocracy meant up to the eighteenth century.

The notion of the 'Chosen People', which in the Old Testament possessed a considerable metaphysical and ethical value, became for the ghetto's Jew an ever renewed Messianic hope. The Jewish people reacted to attack, to persecution, to humiliation as a man reacts to a dog's barking. One takes cover from a dog; one runs away from a dog. But one is not offended by a dog. The ghetto's Jew considered his persecutors with the detachment due to a barbarian or to a heathen. He suffered physically, never morally. It sounds paradoxical but never a people felt so proud as the Jews of the ghetto: persecuted in this world they were conscious of being the chosen ones in the world to come; slaves of the barbarians, they felt they were the privileged of the Almighty.

It was this Jewish pride that Enlightenment and assimilation were destroying in the nineteenth century, as an inevitable price for Jewish equality within the Gentile society. For an assimilated Jew like Herzl, who apparently kept intact his inborn sense of dignity (he had significantly resigned from a fashionable students' association in Vienna because of their participation in a Wagnerian meeting which turned out to be antisemitic), honour became a bridge on which modern ideas could travel back into the Jewish soul and culture without destroying it.

Herzl did not build or invent a new road between modernism and traditionalism. He started by formulating a simplified slogan, expressing in a nutshell the complex and often contradictory Jewish national aspirations in his time: 'A nation without land must go to a land without nation.' When he saw his idea enthusiastically received, he refused to go into the details of the national goods which he promised to deliver: he loaded the whole Jewish question, complete with antisemitism, on to the fast-moving vehicle of honour and national dignity, and without being asked by anyone, sat at the driver's seat, with antisemitism and Jewish nationalism as his, often recalcitrant, horses.

He, indeed, possessed the necessary qualities for such a feat. He had a royal bearing and a charismatic personality. He impressed people with his mixture of greatness and humility. His early death, at the age of 44, after a short meteoric career as the uncontested leader of nationalist Jews, crowned him with immediate legend. He was not a man of learning and was almost totally ignorant of Judaism, but he was deeply civilized and honest. A religious agnostic, he was—paradoxically—an unshakeable believer.

Before him [said Naḥum Goldmann in the same speech], the Jewish people, as a political factor, as an active fighting group capable of taking decisions, did not exist. The Jews who had died heroically at the stake had never been able to present themselves as a unit in order to negotiate instead of begging. Herzl was the first Jewish statesman in 2,000 years. . . . He spoke in the name of the people as if this people already existed, as if it was already organised. All this was fiction but it is through this fiction that a people was created.

The President of the World Zionist Organization omitted to say that this was also pure Utopia and that Herzl made the greatest contribution towards the realization of Utopia in a century of hate of and of disbelief in Utopia.

This alone should be sufficient to explain Herzl's difficulties in putting his ideas across, within and without the Jewish community. But he possessed and used skilfully another powerful ingredient from his alchemistic laboratory of Jewish Risorgimento, an ingredient which was to remain a particular source of antagonism and dissent within the Zionist movement itself and inside the Jewish Diaspora: the ingredient of honour.

'Honour', said Montesquieu, 'is the foundation of monarchy, the binding force of aristocracy.' In his way, Herzl, who of course lacked any sort of institutional control over the Jewish people, proved this to be singularly true in modern times and of the Jewish people. His movement enjoyed much support among the masses of the European Jewish population but remained, for better or for worse, an *élite* movement. By the very fact of being a select society within a select society—the chosen people of the Bible—Zionism opened an aristocratic rift, a battle of legitimacy, the intensity of which reminds one, somehow, of the older Jewish-Christian rift for the control of *verus Israel*. This time it was of course no longer a question of being faithful to the Father or to the Father and Son together. Still, the rift was again closely connected with the legitimacy of God's presence and role in God's own people.

Who was in fact to be the new legitimate ruler of reunited and independent Judaism in Palestine? The Almighty, who established his Covenant with the Patriarchs and renewed it with the fugitives from Egypt? Or the new gods of the world, State, Nation, Historical Determinism, and so on? More than sixty years after Herzl's death the question is still unanswered and as far from solution as it was during his lifetime, especially in Israel where the new State created by Zionism has been unable to define its own nature to the point of being unable to give itself a constitution. We shall see in a later chapter how the stubborn

refusal of the minority religious parties to recognize any constitution except the Divine Law of Mount Sinai succeeded in crystallizing
an opposition which transcended the borders of affiliation to particular
political parties.

The question of the control of the source of legitimacy raised by
Herzlian Zionism remained closely connected with the monopolization
of power in Judaism, a problem derived from legitimacy itself. It
expressed itself throughout the years in a triangular fight of *élites* for
exclusive influence over the modern national version of *verus Israel*. On
one side there was the confrontation between Zionism and assimilation,
expressed especially in Reform Judaism. Moses Hess had predicted the
inevitable clash between those who were proud of being Jews and those
whose attempts to disguise themselves in the Gentile world was given
away by 'their Jewish noses'. This was only to be expected, since the
central argument of the Jewish assimilationists was the need to dissociate religion and nationality and insist on the universality of Judaism.
This is still the main argument of the 'progressive Left' against 'tribal
Zionism'. Lucien Wolf, the British Jewish leader who so strongly
opposed the idea of Britain offering a Jewish State to the Jews, defended,
more than half a century ago in an article significantly entitled 'The
Zionist Peril', the idea that the Jews were 'not the nation of a kept prin-
cipality but the holy nation of a kingdom of priests'.[1] Claude Montefiore,
another leading British Jew, wanted not Zionism but Jewish 'self-puri-
fication and brave endurance to await the better time that civilization
will shortly bring'.[2] But bound up with these lofty ideas was the fear of
successful Jews that Zionism might endanger the position they had
attained in Gentile society. 'The Zionists', wrote Laurie Magnus, 'are
part-authors of the anti-semitism they profess to slay.'[3] It is often
claimed that the appearance of the Jewish State has disturbed the harmony among Jews and Arabs in the Islamic world. And one cannot
suppress a twinge of irony on rereading the words of Ludwig Geiger,
who proclaimed some sixty years ago that 'Zionism is as dangerous to
the German spirit as are Social Democracy and Ultramontanism . . .
a chimera; for the German Jew is a German in his national peculiarities, and Zion is for him the land of the past, not of the future'.[4]

Of course, not all the rabbis were united in their opposition to Zionism. The 'Ḥovevei Zion' movement had been founded by one of them,

[1] *Jewish Quarterly Review*, 1904–5, XVII, pp. 1–25.
[2] *The Judaeans, 1897–9* (New York, 1899), pp. 86 et seq.
[3] *Aspects of the Jewish Question* (London, 1902), p. 18.
[4] In *Die Stimme der Wahrheit*, I, 1905, pp. 165 et seq., quoted in Gottheil, op. cit., p. 102.

Rabbi Mohilever.[1] The great Rabbi of Palestine, Rabbi Kook,[2] was to become one of Zionism's sturdiest and most enlightened supporters. In Italy Zionism was for years carried on the shoulders of the local religious leadership,[3] while in England leading Talmudic authorities joined with the Dutch rabbis in extending qualified support to Zionism.[4] But many other religious leaders, such as the Chief Rabbi of Vienna, Dr. Gudenmann, wavered between support and opposition.[5] 'The role of the Jews', he said, 'led them in the exactly opposite direction to the one preached by Zionism—as solvers of nationalism and preachers of internationalism.'[6] The Central Conference of American Rabbis proclaimed that Zionism 'infinitely harmed' the Jews by confirming the assertions of their enemies that the Jews were foreigners.[7] And the Association of Rabbis in Germany made an 'historic' declaration (16 July 1897) to the effect that the attempts of the Zionists to found a Jewish national State in Palestine were contrary to the Messianic promises of Judaism as laid down in Holy Writ, although there was no opposition to the 'noble plan to colonize Palestine'.[8] This idea of Jewish colonization unconnected with the establishment of a national State preceded by eighty years the ideological declaration against Israel made in 1968 by the Palestinian 'El Fatah' guerrilla organization.[9]

On the second side of the triangle was the confrontation between Herzl's political Zionist *élite* and Ahad Haam's 'spiritual Zionist' *élite*, both competing for the control of the masses of alienated, but barely assimilated Jews.

Ahad Haam's real name was Asher Ginzberg but he preferred to be known by the Hebrew equivalent of 'One of the People'.[10] He was a typical Jewish Eastern European intellectual with a passionate desire to rule and enough common sense to recognize his inability to lead.

---

[1] Rabbi Samuel Mohilever (1824–98) was not involved in Zionist activities till the end of the fifties. See Sokolow, op. cit., p. 221, and his speech at the First Zionist Congress (1897), quoted in Hertzberg, op. cit., pp. 401–5.

[2] Rabbi Abraham Isaac Kook (1865–1935); see Kurzweil, op. cit., ch. 10, 'Rabbi Kook', and pp. 294–8.

[3] Rabbi David Prato, Chief Rabbi of Italy, and particularly Rabbi M. D. Cassuto, later Professor of Bible at the Hebrew University of Jerusalem, and Rabbi Dante Lattes, author of one of the best concise works on the history of Zionism—*Il Sionismo* (Rome, 1928).

[4] Gottheil, op. cit., pp. 97–8.   [5] ibid.   [6] ibid., p. 100.

[7] *Yearbook of the Central Conference of American Rabbis*, 1897–1898, p. xli.

[8] *Allgemeine Zeitung des Judenthums*, no. 29, 16 July 1897.

[9] See *Jeune Afrique*, no. 427, 10–16 March 1969; *Le Nouvel Observateur*, 3–9 February 1969.

[10] Leon Simon, *Ahad Haam/Asher Ginzberg, A Biography* (London, 1960). For a short essay, see Norman Bentwich, *Ahad Haam and His Philosophy* (Jerusalem, 1927); and Harry Sacher, *Zionist Portraits and Other Essays* (London, 1959), pp. 46–51.

Physically and culturally he was the very opposite of Theodor Herzl. He possessed no charismatic power, no imposing personality. If Herzl looked the very example of assured late Victorian dignity, Ginzberg was the personification of that soul-and-mind searching Russian anti-romantic revolutionary intellectual, universally recognized since Lenin's appearance on communist propaganda posters.

He was dictatorial in his behaviour towards other authors, as editor of the periodical *Hashiloach*. One of Palestine's leading writers, Brenner, called him 'Effendi', and philosophically speaking he was far from original and never admitted how much he had derived from the writings of Hume.

Aḥad Haam was not a traditionalist; he believed in the new secular mission of the Jewish people. He rejected the rule of both rabbinical and politico-national *élites* but wanted the people to be ruled by a new aristocracy of learning, no longer based on 'the Book' but rather on 'books'. He went as far as planning the creation of a secret order of new Jewish secular scribes capable of offering their own 'rabbinical' guidance to the masses willing to accept the new Messianic version of Judaism, his 'spiritual Zionism'.

This type of Zionism was, in Ginzberg's view, the only possible legitimate form of Zionism, and totally opposed to Herzl's political brand, especially on the vital question of Jewish survival. What Zionism should care for, he claimed, were the 'needs of Judaism', not Herzl's 'needs of the Jews'. The Jewish hero could not be the Aryan 'blond beast' or any other conventional type of superman. It was the '*Tzadik*', the Jewish 'just man', freed from the straitjacket of rabbinical code but not from the moral duties derived from his aristocratic position as a Jew. 'A political idea which is not grounded in our culture', said Ginzberg after the First Zionist Congress in 1897, 'is apt to seduce us from loyalty to our own inner spirit and to beget in us a tendency to find the path of glory in the attainment of material power and political domination, thus breaking the thread that unites us with the past and undermining our historical foundation.'[1]

The obvious shortcoming in Aḥad Haam's aristocratic secular theory of the 'Chosen People' was his inability to define what the normative selector for 'spiritual Zionism' should be, once traditional rabbinism and political power were rejected. But this shortcoming was irrelevant to the fact that with Aḥad Haam the triangular battle of *élites* for the control of the Jewish masses and identity became complete: the rabbinical *élite* against the political and the spiritual Zionist

[1] Quoted in Hertzberg, op. cit., p. 56.

élites; the political Zionist *élite* against the rabbinical *élite* and spiritual Zionism; the spiritual Zionist *élite* against political Zionism and Orthodoxy.[1]

According to Aḥad Haam, the Jews were not yet ready for collective, practical national action. The nation had to be created in spirit first, in action afterwards; hence, a long period of preparation was necessary. This preparation could not and should not derive from a negative struggle. It could not, because 'negative action does not generate the positive social and moral qualities which political Zionism still lacks'.[3] It should not, because the most natural way of realizing Zionism is through a conquest of the national soul, not of the national markets; namely, the identification of Zionism with a 'national centre'. Palestine was the means for the national resurrection, not just the end. It could never solve the political and economic problems of all the Jews, but it could solve the problem of the Jewish nation by creating a 'national heart' capable of beating in unison for the Jews of Palestine and those of the Diaspora. Because Aḥad Haam valued the Jewish cultural and moral potential of the Diaspora and because he denied that a Jew living in Palestine and speaking Hebrew could be a truly 'national Jew' simply by virtue of this fact, his 'spiritual Zionism' became the major justification for Jewish hostility towards the State of Israel on the part of anti-Zionists. As to his claim to secular Jewish 'chosenness', he had to admit that it created insuperable problems.[3] So his programme, idealistic and logically perfect, in practice fell between these two stools.[4] And the outcome was tragic.

The outcome of this internal triangular fight among the Jewish leadership was to be tragic. Because of Orthodoxy's rejection of Zionism, large masses of religious Jews in Eastern Europe were not urged to emigrate to Turkish, later British, Palestine, whereby they could

---

[1] Aḥad Haam's chief works are: *Al Parashat Derachim* (At the Crossroads), 4 vols. (Berlin, 1921), which is a revised collection of the articles he published, mostly in *Hameliz*. They followed two famous articles, the first of which was called 'Lo Zeh Haderech' (This is Not the Way) published in *Hameliz* in spring 1889; it was a mature criticism of the Ḥibbath Zion movement. The second, written after a visit to Palestine in 1891, was published in several instalments in *Hameliz* after May 1891 and was called "Ehmet meEretz Israel' (Truths from Palestine). It was a bitter criticism of the Ḥovevei Zion colonization and it created a sensation in Jewish intellectual circles in Russia. These articles are among the large selection of Aḥad Haam's writings translated by Leon Simon in *Selected Essays* (Philadelphia, 1912); *Ten Essays on Zionism and Judaism* (London, 1922); *Essays, Letters, Memoirs* (Oxford, 1946).

[2] Aḥad Haam, 'Medinat Ha-Yehudim Ve "Zarat Ha-Yehudim" ' (The Jewish State and the Jewish Problem), 1897, quoted in Hertzberg, op. cit., pp. 262 ff.

[3] Hertzberg, op. cit., p. 65.

[4] See Dante Lattes, op. cit., pp. 73–80.

possibly, but by no means certainly, have reduced the chances of subsequent physical destruction in Nazi Europe; because of its dichotomy between the 'spiritual' and the 'political', Zionism never became a force with real attraction for the assimilated Jews; finally, because of political Zionism's insistence on the predominance of action over thought, because of its belief in the Nietzschean possibility for the determined man to change long-accepted realities of history and geography, Herzl's movement came to a perhaps not always inevitable head-on collision with the political resistance and obstacles it met on its way.

The fact that the direct heirs of Herzl's étatism turned out to be the most extremist political elements of the Zionist right—the Revisionist Party and later the 'Ḥerut' Party (with which I shall deal at length in the next chapter) is significant. They were also to be continually in opposition to the Government, until the 1967 June War.

No less significant is the fact that the direct heirs of Aḥad Haam's 'spiritual Zionism' became the representatives of that Jewish trend which considers the survival of the Diaspora, especially in the United States, at least as important as the establishment of a Jewish State. They also find themselves continually in opposition, as far as Zionism and Israel are concerned.

Micha Josef Berdichevsky (1865–1921), a collaborator on *Hashiloach*, expressed one aspect of Jewish impatience with Aḥad Haam's coldly logical arguments against religious Messianism and with the historicist trend which was strongly represented in all Zionist theory. He wanted to revolt against the past because it was past and against historicism because the Jew had, in his view, suffered too much from the 'slavery of the spirit'. 'We must cease to be Jews with an abstract Judaism and become simply autonomous Jews, a living people', he wrote in an essay significantly entitled 'The Inversion of Values'.[1] He went even further:

The redemption of Israel will not come about either through the efforts of prophets or of diplomats, but through the efforts of men acting for themselves and thus preparing the road for others. . . . A people is composed of individuals, each living for himself, in his own home. . . . We need egotistic men who will conquer the land to satisfy their private and collective aspirations, not to satisfy an abstract general good.[2]

Looked at in perspective, it was in the last resort Berdichevsky's

---

[1] M. J. Berdichevsky, *Baderech* (On the Road), 3 vols. (Leipzig, 1921–2); vol. II, *Shinui 'Arachim* (The Inversion of Values), p. 19.
[2] ibid., vol. III, *'Am Vaarez* (People and Land), p. 77.

impatience, accepted and translated by Jewish socialism into a collective movement, which could perhaps be defined as 'egotistic national Jewish labour', which carried the day.

But Socialist Zionism also had its own anarchist, existentialist trend: that expressed by Chaim Brenner, of whom it has been said that his 'personality, his capacity for friendship, for "love that verges on the angelic", his sufferings and tragic death in 1921 have stirred the deepest emotions of the Jewish people and caused him to be remembered not only as a pioneer of modern Hebrew but also as a martyr and a saint'.[1] In addition he was one of the greatest Zionist novelists, and perhaps the first of the Zionist Surrealists. Himself a man of profound doubts and contradictions, he wanted his writing to reflect the doubts and contradictions between Zionism and Judaism. He was passionately attached to the purity of the Hebrew language and wanted a completely free national consciousness, which to him meant a break with the 'hypnosis' of the Bible. He felt that Zionism had to be atheistic, not because he hated Judaism, but because he thought that religion had made the Jew bear the brunt of history and that the time had come for the Jew to renew himself by consigning himself for five hundred years to the silence of work. In fact, like so many Zionists and Israelis, he wished to escape through revolt from the constraint of having to live in a young, national present by the memories of an old, cosmopolitan past.[2]

Thus neither of the two main ideological trends, the 'étatist' and the 'spiritual', has been able to lead the battle for the material construction of the Jewish State. It was left to a third trend, Socialist Zionism, to succeed in the task, one of the reasons for its success probably being that it never shared the political lucidity—and the doubts—of the other two Zionist trends.

Socialist Zionism has always been conspicuous for its lack of originality and profundity. To survey the writing of its theoreticians, from Ber Borochov to Ben Gurion, is to take a boring trip over a sea of ideological incongruities, political banalities, cultural parochialism, and idealistic intellectualism. This was probably inevitable, since no clear-thinking mind could have put up with the contradictions of Zionism, Socialism, and Socialist Zionism. But, perhaps thanks to their lack of imagination, the Socialist Zionists had something which the others lacked, an ingredient far more vital for the building of a national home: faith and character, endless physical and moral courage and endurance, tactical ability and political pragmatism.

---

[1] Kurzweil, op. cit., p. 115.
[2] Joseph Chaim Brenner, *Ketavim* (Writings), vol. 1 (Tel Aviv, 1951).

The evolution of this trend and its realization will be discussed in the next chapter. Here I should like to describe briefly the concepts behind it and recall the names of the main theoreticians connected with it. We have already seen how, as far as political and spiritual Zionism were concerned, the intellectual task was a simple one: both movements developed their ideas from the premiss that the Jews were different from other people.

Herzl, a bourgeois Central European intellectual, imbued as all the modernizing Jews of his time were, with eighteenth-century rationalism and Utopism, justified the application of the *old* solution—the return to Zion—to the new version of the Jewish question, with an optimistic view of antisemitism. The hate for the Jews which the Jews carried with themselves around the world was, he claimed, the main moving force behind the Jewish Risorgimento, which was unique as it was indeed the outcome of antisemitism.

Aḥad Haam also played, in an entirely different way, with the idea of Jewish uniqueness. As I have mentioned, he accepted the traditional contention that the Jews were a chosen people, a light to lead the nations, and that this was the only reason and meaning for their survival and existence. His solution was to preserve the Jewish 'election' through the transfer of its interpretation and control from the hands of the rabbis to those of the secular scholars. He wanted to transform the People of the Book into the People of the books. Contrary to Herzl, whose main concern was for the physical security of the persecuted Jewish masses, Aḥad Haam cared chiefly for the survival of a Jewish spiritual *élite*, the essence of the people.

The Socialists, on the other hand, would have nothing to do with this 'bourgeois' élitism. If they were to be Zionist, then Jewish nationalism would have to be brought into alignment with the ideological premisses of the class struggle and in accordance with the rules which, Hegel and Marx had discovered, governed the course of history.

The Socialist Zionists were of course aware of the social and historical uniqueness of the Jewish people. But they wanted to fit this uniqueness into the new Marxist credo rather than the other way round.

Such a *tour de force* brought Socialist Zionists into open conflict with Jewish and non-Jewish Marxists from the time of Moses Hess onwards. From the very beginning to this day, Socialist Zionism and its leaders have been anathema to communists, to the Jewish Bund, to all types of contemporary radicalism, which have always appealed so strongly to Jewish intellectuals.

Things were made harder, in the beginning, by the internal contradictions in the Zionist movement itself. The first proletarian Zionist party was formed in Minsk in Tsarist Russia in 1900, three years after the birth of political Zionism; it called itself 'Poalei Zion' (Workers of Zion). It soon extended to Austria and the U.S.A. and involved itself early on in the Zionist quarrels over Uganda. The result was a split into three groups: the J.S.A.P.[1] or 'Sejmists' (from the Polish *sejm*, meaning 'parliament'), who stood for Jewish political autonomy in the Diaspora and were in favour of emigration to places other than Palestine; the Socialist Zionists, who were the extremists of non-Palestinian territorialism, but who, unlike the Sejmists, had no faith in the Diaspora and who wanted a Jewish State outside Palestine; and finally, the Poalei Zion, who stuck to Socialism, Zionism, and Palestine, in spite of the obvious contradictions that implied. They drew their inspiration from Dov Ber Borochov, the first thinker who tried to bridge the gap between Zionism and Marxism.[2] Born in the Ukraine in 1882, in the fateful year of the great pogrom, he grew up in Poltava, a place chosen by the Tsarist administration for deportation of political prisoners. It is possible that the highly political atmosphere of that town had something to do with his later Marxist tendencies. His association with Zionism was, however, natural, since his father was an active member of the 'Hovevei Zion' movement. When in 1906 the Poalei Zion emerged from the mosaic of Russian–Jewish Marxist factions, Ber Borochov wrote together with Izhak Ben Zvi, the future President of Israel, the first attempt at an ideological 'platform' for the new movement. It was the first serious attempt to accommodate Marxism and Zionism and it is interesting to see how near Borochov came with his solution to the thesis defended seventeen years later by Sultan Galiev, the Vice-Commissar for the Nationalities in Soviet Russia, at the famous Baku Conference for the Liberation of Oriental Peoples. Like Galiev, Borochov equated the situation of the oppressed nations with the status of the proletariat. It was a bold idea which contained the grain of the future Marxist 'colonial' revolution of conquered minorities against Russian imperialism, even of the Soviet brand. Galiev paid for it with his life.[3]

---

[1] The initials of the Jüdische Sozialistische Arbeiterpartei; see A. Tartakower, 'Zur Geschichte des jüdischen Sozialismus', in *Der Jude* (January 1924); and Böhm, op. cit., vol. II, p. 21 et seq.; Gottheil, op. cit., pp. 166–77.

[2] Amos Perlmutter, 'Dov Ber-Borochov: A Maxist-Zionist Ideologist', *Middle Eastern Studies*, vol. 5, January 1969, no. 1. Three volumes of Borochov's works, *Ketavim* (Writings), have been published in Hebrew by L. Levita and D. Ben Nahum (eds.) (Tel Aviv, 1955, 1958, 1965).

[3] A. Bennigsen and C. Quelquejay, *Les Mouvements nationaux chez les Musulmans de Russie: Le 'sultangalievisme' au Tatarstan* (Paris, 1960), pp. 167–8; also Hélène Carrère d'Encausse, *Réforme et Révolution chez les Musulmans de l'empire russe* (Paris, 1966), pp. 267–9).

Borochov's Socialist Zionism remains to this day a monstrous Jewish aberration of Marxism, equated by communists with Social Democratic heresy.

Ber Borochov in fact believed that the Jewish national struggle was waged, unlike the class struggle, not only for material advantages, but for values and possessions shared by all classes, namely political unity, political institutions, culture, and language, and for the achievement of nationhood. For the Jewish people, the struggle to achieve nationhood, through the return to its historical homeland, was thus a prerequisite of the class struggle. Once Jewish nationhood was assured, each of its component parts could go its own way and the class struggle begin, not vice versa.

But how could the Jewish occupation of Palestine be justified? Ber Borochov realized that this could not easily be explained and that 'this country will provide the line of greatest resistance'. But Palestine was also a derelict country. So derelict and poor, in fact, that 'big capital will hardly find use for itself there, while Jewish petty and middle capital will find a market for its products in both this country and in its environment'.[1] Thus the land forgotten by capitalism could be left to the most 'proletarian' people of the world, the Jewish nation.

It was a Jew, Karl Marx, who proclaimed, in *The Communist Manifesto* in 1848, that the worker had no fatherland. It was another Socialist Jew, Moses Hess, who proclaimed the right of the Jew, Socialist or not, to a fatherland. Jews were prominent at all stages of the development of Marxism. Singer and Bernstein, Rosa Luxemburg and Lassalle, Trotsky and Ana Pauker were Jews, but this did not make them or their fellow socialists and communists any more sympathetic to the Jewish cause. Many of the Jews killed in Russia were workers, but the British Socialists refused to join the Hyde Park demonstrations against the Kishinev pogroms of 1905, just as the Russian workers refused to make common cause with their Jewish compatriots.[2] Almost everywhere antisemitism was stronger than socialist brotherhood, and this remains true to this day in Russia, Poland, and Romania after decades of Marxist rule and the physical destruction of large sections of the Jewish communities there. No wonder, then, that classical Marxism never struck root in Palestine, although Marxist techniques were enthusiastically adopted. Franz Oppenheimer and his plan for co-operative settlements, rather than Lenin's Bolshevism, seemed to the Palestinian Jews

---

[1] Hertzberg, op. cit., p. 75.
[2] *Jewish Chronicle*, 26 June 1905, p. 10; and ibid., 22 December 1903, p. 29; and ibid., 29 December 1905, p. 14.

to offer a practical solution to the integration of socialist ideals and national needs in Palestine.[1]

Another important trend in Jewish socialism was represented by A. D. Gordon. Gordon was born in Russian Ukraine in 1856, became an early supporter of the 'Hovevei Zion' movement, emigrated to Palestine in 1904, and died there in 1922, the uncontested prophet of the 'back-to-the-land' Zionist religion.[2]

Gordon was not a socialist theoretician. In fact he can hardly be called a socialist. He represented 'pure soul', animated by a belief in total morality. His basic philosophy can be defined as the fight of man against alienation from nature. To him manual labour was the only way of returning to nature, and it could also be the ultimate expression of human fulfilment, a true religion of redemption.

By giving the labour movement in the Holy Land a spiritual significance, Gordon bridged, in his own Tolstoyan way, the gap between the mystical call of the religion of labour and the mystical call of the religion of Messianism. He gave a new universal meaning and dimension to the 'back-to-the-land' call of Zionism, especially when expressed through kibbutz collectivism.

Borochov, by the end of his short life (he died in 1917, returning from the United States to serve under Kerensky in Russia), had already become aware of the inconsistency of his own Marxist Zionist theories. Unlike Gordon, who remained to the end a prophet of international religious atheism, he made his appeal more and more to simple Jewish nationalism, deliberately forgetting to use in his speeches and articles the unbiblical noun of Palestine in favour of the more passionate one of 'Erez Israel' (Land of Israel).

Another socialist, Nachman Syrkin (1867–1924), tried to go further than this. He believed that through socialism the world could be freed of antisemitism as well as of any other social and political strife. But he saw that the process would take a long time, so he said that the Jews should fight for survival through a national State. Syrkin thus pleaded for the establishment of a Jewish State as the only way to solve the Jewish problem, but insisted that such a State should be conceived, from the beginning, in terms of socialism.[3] This is what indeed hap-

---

[1] Franz Oppenheimer, *Merchavia: A Jewish Co-Operative Settlement in Palestine* (New York, 1914). He put forward his plan to Herzl in 1902.

[2] Aaron David Gordon (1856–1922), *Michtavim Ureshimot*, ed. S. H. Bergmann and E. Shochat (Jerusalem, 1954); *Haadam Vehateva* (Man and Nature), ed. S. H. Bergmann and E. Shochat (Jerusalem, 1951); *Haumah Vehaavodah* (The People and Work), ed. S. H. Bergmann and E. Shochat (Jerusalem, 1952).

[3] See Hertzberg, op. cit., pp. 75–9, for an account of Syrkin's writings.

pened in Palestine, and from this point of view one can say that Syrkin was the most successful prophet of Socialist Zionism. But, to complete the picture, one should not forget another important, apparently self-contradictory, trend in the movement: socialist traditionalism.

Jewish nationalism being an integral part of Jewish religion, no nationalist Jewish group could avoid facing the challenge of tradition. Moses Hess had grasped the importance of the problem and hoped for a gradual evolution of Orthodoxy through a Jewish Risorgimento. The Socialist Zionists went a step further. They took upon themselves the task of preserving traditionalism, not as a religious way of life, but as a national culture.

For Berl Katzenelson (1887–1944), one of the central figures of Socialist Zionism in Palestine, the founder of the organ of the Jewish Workers' Federation, *Davar*, and of '*Am Oved* (the workers' publishing house), Jewish revolution could not be dissociated from Jewish tradition.

We like to call ourselves rebels, but may I ask, What are we rebelling against? Is it only against the tradition of our fathers? If so, we are carrying coals to Newcastle. Too many of our predecessors did just that. *Our rebellion is also a revolt against many rebellions that preceded ours* ... Primitive revolutionism which believes that ruthless destruction is the perfect cure for all social ills reminds one, in many of its manifestations, of the growing child who demonstrates his mastery of things and curiosity about their structure by breaking his toys. In opposition to this primitive revolutionism, our movement, by its very nature, must uphold the *principle of revolutionary constructivism*.[1]

For Katzenelson, true Socialist Zionism could thus realize its aims only by becoming the carrier not the destroyer of national tradition

From Jewish traditionalism to socialist traditionalism, via Enlightenment, assimilation, nationalism, and Marxism, the ideological circle of Zionism was completed. None of these trends could, however, have materialized without the emotional, anti-rational, anti-enlightenment, nationalist, and racial obscurantism of European antisemitism.

It was this negative force, not ideology, which pushed the Jews in their millions across the Atlantic and, when immigration to America was restricted after the First World War, to Palestine and later to Israel in their thousands. With them to Palestine came the new national institutions of Zionism, originally conceived in the context of the hopes and Utopias of the eighteenth century—those hopes and Utopias which first gave equality to the Jews through the American and French Revolutions—and later slowly matured in the tense atmosphere of uncompromising strife between Jewish and Arab nationalism.

[1] 'Revolution and Tradition' in Hertzberg, op. cit., pp. 390 and 392.

Chapter 3

From Utopia to National Home

In the previous chapter I dealt with trends in Zionist thought and I have tried to show some of the consequences of the desynchronizing of Zionism.

In this and in the following chapter, I shall deal with the institutions which were created in order to realize the Jewish national ideal in pre-Israeli Palestine, and with the climate of opinion in which these institutions evolved. The state of mind of the Jews, the Arabs, and the British in Palestine is important because the conflicting parties' understanding of their rights and duties, both historical and political, was probably as important as the structure of the institutions they built. These institutions were the outcome of tension between the participants in the 'Palestine Question'; the participants, both Jewish and Arab, were divided among themselves, on the ideological as well as the practical level.

Zionist ideologies have already been touched on. Arab anti-Zionist ideology did not really begin to develop until after the First World War—although it has been shown that the roots of Arab ideological opposition to Zionism go back to the pre-Balfour Declaration period.[1] However, both for the Zionists and for the Arabs, the tension became serious only after 1917. In Palestine the last days of the crumbling Turkish administration brought famine and terror to both Arabs and Jews, and reduced the Jewish community to some 50,000 persons;[2] a confusing situation was created militarily by the British victory, by the Arab revolt, by the Balfour Declaration, by the intense diplomatic activity which took place during the Allied military occupation of the Holy Land from 1917 to the establishment of the British Mandate in

---

[1] Neville Mandel, 'Turks, Arabs and Jewish Immigration into Palestine, 1882–1914', in *St. Antony's Papers*, no. 17, (Middle Eastern Affairs) Oxford, 1965, pp. 77–108.

[2] According to an internal census only 34,000 Jews were left in the cities of Palestine in 1916. There were 83,000 in the country as a whole in 1922 as against an estimated 589,000 Moslems and 71,000 Christians; see Norman Bentwich, *Palestine* (London, 1934), p. 16, and *Palestine Royal Commission Report* (London, July 1937), p. 32.

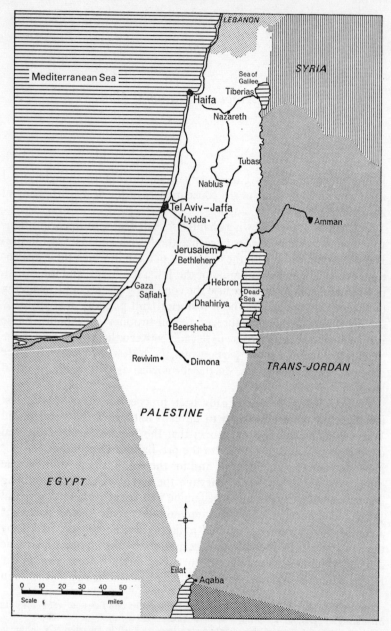

1 Palestine's Boundaries under the British Mandate

1922 and of that hybrid body known as the 'Jewish Agency for Palestine'.[1]

The story of the British, Jewish, and Arab struggle for Palestine makes fascinating reading. It has been told many times by partial and impartial historians, and of course by many of those who took part in the struggle.[2]

However, my main purpose in these two chapters dealing with the pre-Israeli Jewish national institutions, is to show: first, that the achievement of political independence was, for the Jews of Palestine, not the beginning but part of a process that was already well under way; this was not so in many other ex-colonies. Secondly, that the growth of Zionist institutions was affected not only by the natural tension between Zionist ideals and the actual situation in Palestine, but by the constant three-cornered conflict, both physical and ideological, between the British, the Arabs, and the Jews. Thirdly, that at the same time this battle was being fought on the larger stage of universal religious passions, world ideologies, and world-wide strategic and economic interests. A fact which gave even local problems (like the Jewish–Moslem conflict over the Wailing Wall) different dimensions and different angles from which to view the conflict at any given time. Thus the Jews spoke at the same time as colonials, as members of a world-wide Diaspora, and as representatives of a powerful international pressure group. The Arabs and their supporters, in Jerusalem, Damascus, Baghdad, and Beirut, spoke either from a situation of colonial subjection or as politically independent States. In London and Washington imperial interests and humanitarian involvement created powerful lobbies, and officials sympathetic to both parties could be found in Rome, and to the Arabs in Berlin. The British were busy justifying their presence in Palestine in terms of conflicting commitments to the Jews and the Arabs, imperial strategy, necessities of local colonial administration, Christian duties, and financial interests. No wonder that, in such

---

[1] The Jewish Agency for Palestine was recognized by Art. 4 of the League of Nations Mandate for Palestine. For details of its organization and work in the Mandate period see the *Palestine Royal Commission Report*, pp. 126–8.

[2] Christopher Sykes's *Crossroads to Israel, Palestine from Balfour to Bevin* (London, 1965) is the most recent and comprehensive study from a British source. J. C. Hurewitz, in *The Struggle for Palestine* (New York, 1950), offers a balanced view of the question and a detailed and valuable bibliography. George Antonius's *The Arab Awakening* (London, 1938) still remains the most lucid and intelligent defence of the Arab thesis. The Jewish case is forcefully stated in *The Jewish Plan for Palestine: memoranda and statements presented by the Jewish Agency for Palestine to the United Nations Special Committee on Palestine* (Jerusalem, 1947). The *Palestine Royal Commission Report* is an excellent concise document on the subject.

circumstances, ideas and institutions became increasingly flexible, creating and adapting themselves to standards of double-talk. These were originally diplomatic formulas meant to overcome the unexpected difficulties of conflicting circumstances. In the end, they became a kind of second nature, which made inter-community communications almost impossible. To understand the causes of the political confusion prior to 1948 one must go back to 1917.

The year 1917 was a crucial one for all the nations engaged in the First World War. Both sides were convinced that they had reached the very end of their resources and strength. It was a year of secret and frantic attempts to reach separate peace agreements, a year of German U-boat victories, of Russian and Italian military defeat, and of revolution in the East. It was the year of United States intervention and a time for both sides to use any diplomatic straws to keep the fire of war alive.

The Jews were commonly believed to be indispensable in this respect. Because the Allies valued their influence both in the United States and in Russia, without really caring much about the ultimate fate of the Middle East, the British Government issued, on 2 November 1917, the famous Balfour Declaration which was to become the first international recognition of Herzl's national dream.[1] Undoubtedly there were other considerations. The biblical vision and culture of men of great moral integrity, like Lord Balfour, had played a vital role in promoting the Zionist cause in Britain.[2] The extraordinary diplomatic ability of a man like Weizmann allowed the Zionists to make the best use of all favourable dispositions in Great Britain.[3] The British interest in using the Zionist cause against future French claims in the Middle East was also important.[4] It is possible that the officers and officials directly engaged in the operational planning of the war might have given some thoughts to the actual military contribution of the Jews in the Middle Eastern theatre of war. But it was the power of Jewry in the U.S.A. and in Russia which probably was the most influential factor on both sides of the front. In fact, at that time the Germans considered the Jews to be a most important revolutionary and anti-Tsarist element in Russia. They also hoped to gain their co-operation by proposing to create a Jewish State in the

---

[1] See Leonard Stein, *The Balfour Declaration* (London, 1961).

[2] Israel Cohen (ed.), *Speeches on Zionism by the Right Hon. the Earl of Balfour* (London, 1928).

[3] Isaiah Berlin, *Chaim Weizmann* (London, 1958). For a critical appraisal of Weizmann's diplomatic activities, see Oskar K. Rabinowicz, *Fifty Years of Zionism, A Historical Analysis of Dr. Weizmann's 'Trial and Error'* (2nd edition, London, 1952).

[4] Henry H. Cumming, *Franco-British Rivalry in the Post-War Near East: The Decline of French Influence* (London, 1938), pp. 30, 45–9.

'liberated' areas of Eastern Europe and promising the Jewish national movement every possible help, short of independence, in Palestine, which at the time still belonged to their Turkish allies.[1]

Intelligence officers of every type and nationality were active, with money and promises, all over the Middle East. Colonel Lawrence, who arrived in Djedda in October 1916, was one of the many British agents who tried to foment and support an anti-Turkish uprising in Arabia, not only as part of British strategy against the Turks in the Middle East but also as part of British strategy against the Germans in East Africa.[2] It was not an easy job, because of that lack of cohesion, discipline, and national aim among the Arabs which Lawrence himself describes so well in the *Seven Pillars of Wisdom*—where, however, no mention is made of the fact that Sherif Hussein of Mecca was still receiving money from the Germans while discussing the terms of his revolt with the British.[3] But it was a political and military feat crowned with outstanding success, even if this success had more effect on the fortunes of the Hashemite family than on those of Arab nations at large.

The feelings of the Arabs of Arabia and of the Middle East towards the political pre-eminence of the Mecca dynasty, which unfurled the banner of the Arab revolt in conjunction with the infidel but sympathetic Britain, did not coincide and soon diverged. But in 1917 the majority of Arab nationalists could not dissociate themselves from the historical, emotional, and political symbolism and the actual value of the Arab revolt. The fact that the Arabs fought more tenaciously and in far greater number under the Turkish flag than under the flag of Sherif Hussein,[4] that Feisal's conquest of Damascus[5] was as debatable as his effective military contribution to the war against Turkey;[6] all this paled before the fact that by the end of the war Sherif Hussein and his sons had become the living embodiment of Arab national revival.

---

[1] Leonard Stein, op. cit., ch. 13, 'Zionist Moves in Berlin', pp. 206–16. See also Max I. Bodenheimer, 'The Story of the Hindenburg Declaration', in the *Herzl Yearbook*, vol. II, ed. R. Patai (New York, 1959), pp. 56–77.   [2] Antonius, op. cit., p. 208.

[3] File Abt. la (*Weltkrieg*) IIG, 21.6.1915, Archives of the Foreign Ministry, Bonn, quoted in Kimche, op. cit., p. 5.

[4] Two divisions of Arab soldiers were employed almost continuously by the Turks throughout the War. The 25th Division fought bravely at Gallipoli. See Antonius, op. cit., p. 186.

[5] Zeine N. Zeine, *The Struggle for Arab Independence: Western Diplomacy and the Rise and Fall of Faisal's Kingdom in Syria* (Beirut, 1960), p. 28; Jean Pichon, *Sur la route des Indes un siècle après Bonaparte* (Paris, 1932), ch. v: 'L'Entrée dans Damas', pp. 115–33.

[6] This was in any case the opinion of the Turkish command which was able to keep the railway to Medina open and the town itself under Turkish control some 1,500 miles inside Arab-controlled territory; see Zeine, op. cit., p. 18, n. 1. For a French evaluation of Feisal's military efforts, see Pichon, op. cit., pp. 147–51.

To the Jews—who saw their return to Palestine in terms of their own ancient historical rights, who had just received international endorsement of their cause from the greatest powers of the world, who conceived their political presence in the Middle East in terms of the disruption of the Turkish empire, not of pan-Arabism, who were more sensitive to the Christian interests in Palestine and in Jerusalem than to the Moslem ones (who had their most important holy places in Arabia), and, finally, who were far more conscious of European influence than of Arab nationalism—the whole story of the Arab revolt sounded like a romantically inflated falsification of historical truth, of sound political judgement, of the potential forces present in Palestine.

They were convinced that the true interest of the British lay with them, rather than with the Arabs and resented the fact that the latter seemed to be benefiting from a myth which they had managed to create through the Arab rebellion and with British help. Besides, the Jews had been unable to transform their military contribution to the war into a recognized and publicized military feat, on which they could base their claim to Palestine.

The Zionists had also fought in the war, and particularly hard at Gallipoli, where they were not riding pure-bred horses, but driving supply mules. Later Palestinian Jewish refugees in Egypt and Russian Jews in England formed the Jewish Legion, the first Jewish military unit fighting for a Jewish national cause since the time of the Romans.[1] But the Legion, in which practically all the future political leadership of Israel and many members of the British Jewish aristocracy volunteered to serve (like Lionel de Rothschild), and the other pro-British activities of the Jews in Palestine, did not produce any hard political currency to bargain with after the war.[2] The Jewish Legion never became that Jewish army which its founder, Vladimir Jabotinsky, conceived as the army of the new Jewish State.[3] Its disbanding, following the Arab riots against the Jews in Palestine in 1919, had the opposite effect of the Arab capture of Aqaba or Feisal's triumphal entry in Damascus.[4] It did not help to establish the Jews as a military nation, but—Jewish apologists notwithstanding—underlined the different military, political, and power semantics of the Arab–Jewish confronta-

---

[1] V. Jabotinsky, *The Story of the Jewish Legion* (Eng. trans., New York, 1945). I have used an earlier Italian translation by M. Kingbail (Milan, 1935). See also J. H. Patterson, *With the Judaeans in the Palestine Campaign* (London, 1922).

[2] Anita Engle, in *The Nili Spies* (London, 1959), tells the story of the pro-British intelligence network established in Palestine by the Aaronson family. 'Nili' is an acronym of the Hebrew verse, 'The eternity of Israel is no lie'.

[3] Jabotinsky, op. cit., p. 253.   [4] Antonius, op. cit., pp. 223 and 238.

tion. No British military commander appreciated or sympathized much with the Jewish military effort. Quite the contrary, British officials in Palestine soon shared the view of the Arabs who felt themselves betrayed and 'sold out' to the Zionists in Palestine and to the French in the Levant. They resented being called on to carry out an impracticable policy, which seemed to them a cover for the Jews to reinforce their position in Palestine at the expense of the Arabs and of their friendship with Britain in the Middle East, by which they set great store.

The Zionists objected in London to these—at the beginning mainly local—reserves and hesitations on the part of the British to appreciate the unconditional friendship they were offering Britain, especially as they believed that they had made a more consistent military and political contribution, in men, brains, and money, to the allied victory than the Arabs.[1]

Weizmann's pathetic description of the first meeting of the Zionist delegation and the British authorities in Palestine is illuminating in this respect.[2] It was a bitter foretaste of the many disillusions, misunderstandings, compromises, ingenuities, and the double-talk which were to characterize the following thirty years of the British–Jewish relations in Palestine and influence, directly and indirectly, the growth and the purpose of Zionist institutions in Palestine.

One can distinguish three main groups of Jewish institutions in pre-Israeli Palestine: those of the Jewish community, those of the Zionist Organization, and those created by or linked with the Socialist Zionist movement.

The institutions of the Jewish community were the first to be recognized by the British, within the League of Nations' Mandate for Palestine.[3] They were important, not only for the role they played in shaping the political life of the Jewish community, but also as a training ground for Israeli democracy and self-government. In fact most of the political institutions and procedures of the Jewish State were later copied from those developed in the earlier Jewish community.

Already under the allied military Government, in the period from 1917 to 1920, the Yishuv started to prepare its community constitution which was finally approved in April 1920, after much political bickering, by general, direct, equal, and proportional vote, cast by all Jews

---

[1] Jabotinsky, op. cit., pp. 197–8. The Jewish Legion ended the war with 5,000 men.
[2] Weizmann, op. cit., pp. 271–3.
[3] For a concise description of Jewish and Arab communal institutions in Palestine, see the *Palestine Royal Commission Report*, pp. 126–35.

claiming six months' residence in Palestine. The first elected assembly which gathered in Jerusalem on 7 October 1920 had 314 members, representing 20 parties and 20,000 eligible voters, 70 per cent of whom had taken part in the elections.[1]

It was an interesting assembly from many points of view. Quite apart from the religious beliefs of its members, it was officially a religious assembly, since it officially represented the Jewish community. At the same time it was also a national one, because, according to Turkish law, which the British maintained in Palestine, no distinction could be made between nationality and religion. This distinction is still lacking in Israel today, with consequences which I shall discuss later.

Furthermore, it was an assembly made up of numerous parties, another feature which would remain prominent in Israeli political life, in spite of all attempts to change it through reform of the electoral system. Finally, the political trends reflected the three main political and ideological groupings of the Yishuv of the time: the religious, the socialist, and the oriental. The first two groupings have, as we shall see later, remained more or less unchanged in their respective strength. But the political status of the oriental group has changed considerably.

In the early days of the Palestine Mandate, the oriental group consisted of Sephardi Jews, the Jews of the Turkish Empire, who regarded themselves as much superior to the new immigrants from Central and Eastern Europe.[2] They were certainly not Zionists in the Herzlian sense, and neither were they capitalists or landed gentry. They were mostly merchants, conscious of being Jewish rather than Jewish nationalists.

In Turkish times the Zionist immigrants from Europe had tried to become assimilated to the Sephardi. One had only to look at the pictures of Ben Gurion or of the late President Ben Zvi, with Turkish fezes on their heads and badly cut clothes in the Constantinople fashion, to know who was practising social camouflage. And if one goes through the documents of the time, one cannot fail to perceive the snobbery with which the Sephardi notables treated the East European newcomers. Things were soon to change.

With the fall of the Ottoman Empire, the success of the London-based Zionist Organization in bringing about the Balfour Declaration, and with a Jew as first British High Commissioner in Palestine,[3]

---

[1] Marver H. Bernstein, *The Politics of Israel: The First Decade of Statehood* (Princeton, 1957), pp. 21 ff.

[2] Raphael Patai, *Israel Between East and West* (Philadelphia, 1953).

[3] Herbert Louis, Viscount Samuel; see John Bowle, *Viscount Samuel, A Biography* (London, 1957), especially chs. XII, XIII, XIV, pp. 167–237.

London and New York, not the capitals of the Middle East, became the centres of power as far as the Jewish community was concerned.

In the wake of political 'britannicization' of Palestine, anything connected with Turkey looked outmoded, 'colonial', corrupt, and useless. So were the Sephardi Jews, who lost their traditional political role as intermediaries with the ruling power. On the whole they kept themselves outside the new Zionist leadership of Palestine. They had little previous connection with the Zionist Organization of Western Europe, in particular, that of Great Britain, and little sympathy—being an urban group—with the agrarian, pioneering ideologies of the newcomers.

They certainly did not oppose the growth of Zionist authority. On the contrary, they found it of economic and national benefit. But they were cut off from it politically and socially. It was an important change, since the Sephardi were not only the traditional link with the Turkish authorities but also a link with the local Arab community. To this day the leaders of the Sephardi community in Israel claim that their relegation, by the European Zionists, to a secondary role in the political life and administration of the State, has diminished chances of a *rapprochement* with the Arabs.[1] This is probably true, although few Sephardi leaders have succeeded in explaining why they made so little effort to co-operate with the Zionist newcomers, especially under the Turkish administration.[2]

I shall not enter into a detailed examination of the Jewish community's internal political and organizational development under the British Mandate, but shall restrict the discussion to that of two well-known observations. The first is that during the mandatory period one of the major topics of internal political debate in the Jewish community was, as it remains today in the Jewish State, the measure of theocracy under which the Yishuv was supposed to live. In statistical terms, the religious Jews in Palestine under the Mandate were certainly less numerous than in the Israeli State. But, because of the religious structure of the Jewish community under the British administration, they made their weight felt.

The second observation touches on the internal organization of the Jewish community. The Jewish Assembly—Knesset Israel—elected a National Council (Vaad Haleumi) of thirty-six members, which ran the community affairs especially as regards the imposition of community taxes, and an Executive Committee. It is through these institutions that

---

[1] Eliyahu Sason, former Minister of Posts, in an interview with *Maariv*, 12 March 1963.
[2] Letter from S. Toledano, Prime Minister's Adviser for Arab Affairs, to *Le Monde*, May, 1966 (mimeographed), 14.

Israel formed its political personnel with the advantages and the disadvantages of a democratic training conducted in conditions of political and ideological parochialism.

As long as the Yishuv remained a small community and, on the whole, an *élite*, political, ideological, and economic differences could be fought out in a family atmosphere. At the same time the community bureaucracy, voluntary or paid, was split between the parties and the various communal laws. The parochialism of the Jewish community's bureaucracy soon became institutionalized and the splitting up of political personnel was to be carried on into the State of Israel.[1] It extended to the bureaucracy of the Zionist Organization, which perpetuated in Palestine some of the ideas and the habits of another type of Jewish parochialism; the parochialism of the Diaspora. Prior to the establishment of Zionist communal administration, the thousands of religious Jews who, throughout the centuries, had come to the Holy Land to pray and die, had lived mainly in the holy towns of Jerusalem, Safad (in Upper Galilee), Tiberias, and Hebron. Their material needs were met partly by limited local activities, but most by remittances which the Jews of the Diaspora willingly sent to their brethren who undertook the sacred duty of the return to the Holy Places.

Economically and administratively speaking, the most important institution of these religious Jewish communities was the 'Kollel', or central collector and solicitor of alms, who distributed them to his followers. Since each community could expect better and more generous understanding from the relatives and friends left behind in their towns of origin, the praying population of Palestine was divided according to the various home-town collectors: the Kollel of Bialystock, Vilna, etc.[2]

It was not a very reliable system but it worked under normal conditions. In times of trouble the Kollel system usually broke down, both at the source and at the receiving end. During the First World War the population of Jewish Palestine suffered tremendously from the disruption of communications with Russia and America, and 1916 and 1917 were years of misery, particularly for the Jewish urban population.

Things were soon to improve with the arrival of the British and the establishment in Palestine of a recognized Zionist communal administration. But the financial bureaucracy established by the Zionist Organization, although aiming at different, non-religious targets, adopted a system similar to that of the religious alms collectors. For a

[1] Bernstein, op. cit., p. 137.
[2] On the Kollel system, see Moshe Burstein, *Self-Government of the Jews in Palestine since 1900* (Tel Aviv, 1934), pp. 24–30.

long time it used the same methods, operated in the same territory, and remained imbued with the same petty, often arrogant, always defensive attitudes of the Kollel.

The Kollel was established and kept going by religious fervour and voluntary organization. The Zionist fund-collecting organizations were established by the various Zionist congress decisions. They became the economic ministries of the 'Jewish Agency', which raised £6,215,000 between 1921 and 1936.[1]

It took a long time for the Jewish Agency to become a reality.[2] It was formally constituted and recognized by the British Administration of Palestine in August 1929. Its structure was copied from the structure of the Zionist Organization. It had a council meeting of 224 people every two years; an administrative committee of forty members; an executive whose president was automatically the head of both the Jewish Agency in Palestine and of the world Zionist Organization, in which the Zionist Organization both inside and outside Palestine should have had an equal say, but the Zionists of the Diaspora never insisted on this. On the other hand the question of the participation of Jewish non-Zionist bodies in the Zionist Organization is still an open one.

In such a complicated organization grave internal tensions could not be avoided. The most serious crisis exploded in 1926 when Vladimir Jabotinsky, the founder of the Jewish Legion and a partisan, like Theodor Herzl, of political Zionism, came into open conflict with 'pragmatic' Zionism, namely Dr. Weizmann's policy of gradual development of the Jewish community in Palestine.

The story of Vladimir Zeev Jabotinsky (1880–1940) has not yet been fully dealt with by historians.[3] The personality of this Zionist leader, one of the greatest, without doubt, can be judged from the immense literary output he left on his death, most of it, however, consisting of journalism of little importance.[4] But behind the brilliance of the journalist and political pamphleteer were the genius of the linguist and the gifts of the orator and novelist.

Jabotinsky was accused of fascism and Ben Gurion, who went so far as to refuse permission for his public burial in Israel, called him

---

[1] *Palestine Royal Commission Report*, p. 127; S. N. Eisenstadt, *Israeli Society* (London, 1967), pp. 24–5.

[2] The Jewish Agency for Palestine was recognized by Art. 4 of the League of Nations Mandate for Palestine. For details of its organization and work in the Mandate period see the *Palestine Royal Commission Report*, pp. 126–8.

[3] But see Joseph B. Schechtman, *Rebel and Statesman: The Vladimir Jabotinski Story. The Early Years* (New York, 1956).

[4] e.g. E. Jabotinsky (ed.), *Baderech Lamedinah* (On the Road to Statehood) (Jerusalem, 1953); *Neumim* (Speeches), *1905–1926* (Jerusalem 1947); *Neumim, 1927–1940* (1948).

Vladimir 'Hitler' Jabotinsky. But he was nothing of the kind: he was a liberal imbued with nationalist romanticism, who saw in the Italian Risorgimento, and more particularly in Garibaldi, his ideal. He had a certain weakness for military show, liked uniforms and parades, and probably would have been delighted, as he once told an Italian friend, to have his memory perpetuated by an equestrian statue. But he was in no way a fascist, although some of his followers definitely were.

He was in many ways a tragic figure, impatient at the parochialism of the Zionist movement, ahead of his time in his political thinking: many of his ideas are being vindicated today by the Israeli State. But on the whole he brought more division than unity to the Jewish national movement and most of his superb intellectual qualities and energies were spent in sterile debate. His excellent translation of Dante into classical Hebrew and some of the pages of his best-known novel, written in Russian, *Prelude to Delilah*,[1] offer a hint of what he could have achieved if he had devoted more time to literary or historical work.

His name, however, remains linked, in the history of the Zionist movement, with the creation of the Jewish Legion in the First World War and with the organization of the 'Hagana', the Jewish defence movement in Palestine, in 1919. He was haunted by the idea that Jewish independence was conditional on the existence of a Jewish military force. After his efforts to use the Jewish Legion for the defence of the Yishuv during the Arab disturbances in 1919 had failed he himself had been imprisoned and sentenced to death by the British military authorities in Palestine for taking up arms while still in British uniform. On his release, he founded the 'Beitar' (after the Hebrew initials of Brit Trumpeldor) in 1923; a uniformed, paramilitary youth organization intended to provide the military backing for Jewish independence in Palestine. In Paris in 1925 he founded the International Union of Revisionist Zionists, which aimed at reviving Theodor Herzl's idea of achieving Jewish statehood through international recognition of Jewish sovereignty in Palestine. At the Seventeenth Zionist Congress, held in Basle in 1931, his group won 21 per cent of the seats and his idea of 'intensive colonization' was accepted while Weizmann, the leader of the opposing 'practical' Zionists, resigned in the wake of the British White Paper limiting, for the first time, Jewish immigration to Palestine. The strength of the Revisionist movement was much greater in Eastern Europe than in Palestine. In the fateful campaign for election to the Eighteenth Zionist Congress in 1933, Ben Gurion toured Eastern

[1] Vladimir Jabotinsky, *Prelude to Delilah* (Russian ed., 1926; English translation, New York, 1945).

Europe to fight against Jabotinsky's ideas. He won by making much use of the accusation—later proved unfounded—that the Revisionists had participated in the assassination of the brilliant socialist and political secretary of the Jewish Agency, Chaim Arlosoroff. In spite of everything, a political agreement was reached between the two men in 1935, but the refusal of the Histadrut (the federation of trade unions) to ratify it led Jabotinsky to break away from the Zionist Organization and found his own New Zionist Organization, which, until very recently, ran its own labour unions, health centres, youth clubs, in miniature opposition to and imitation of the Histadrut and other socialist institutions of the Palestinian Yishuv.

The Zionist Organization's contribution to Jewish Palestine was, on the contrary, impressive, especially in its non-political achievements. It created and contributed to the development of a formidable, autonomous educational organization starting from kindergarten and ending in academic institutions of international renown, like the Hebrew University of Jerusalem, and the Institute of Technology at Haifa. It provided most of the money for the acquisition and development of land. It helped with grants and loans, with the passages of immigrants from abroad, and with their installation in Palestine. It was to a large extent responsible for the development of an independent Jewish industrial and service infrastructure. It provided money and equipment for the defence organization, the Hagana, and, on the whole, successfully fulfilled the role of responsible Jewish government in British Palestine without having any authority to do so.

Most of the leadership of the Zionist Organization was closely connected on the one hand with the leadership of the Jewish Community (Vaad Haleumi) and on the other hand with the leadership of the socialist organizations, giving the Jewish Agency undisputed political control over Jewish national enterprise in the Holy Land.

How effective this political control was remains an open question, hotly debated during the whole period of the Mandate and for many years after the founding of the State of Israel. I shall not discuss it here. But even the most bitter critics of Jewish Agency policy admit that the Organization spent most of its diplomatic energy struggling against forces over which it had no control.

The first and most important negative force were the Jews themselves who did *not* come to Palestine at a time when their presence could have changed the political situation there. This had nothing to do with their ideological or religious tendencies; they simply preferred to remain in Europe, in spite of the growing antisemitism, or they chose to emigrate elsewhere. Those who came to Palestine did so over a long period of time and at a rate which had little to do with Zionist ideals and a great deal to do with Jewish persecution.

Historically, there was one long, uninterrupted flow of immigrants—combined with an equally uninterrupted flow of emigrants; in perspective, however, this trend appears as a succession of human waves, each one characterized by the country of origin of its members, their motives for coming, the rate of their arrival, and so on. In the history of Jewish Palestine, each wave of immigrants became a milestone in the development of the 'national home'. They were called *aliot*, plural of *aliah*—ascent—since a Jew 'goes up' to the Holy Land.

Two of the waves of immigration had taken place before the British conquest of Palestine.

The first *aliah* lasted from 1882 to 1903. It was an heroic, political, pre-Zionist *aliah*, which brought some 25,000 Jews, most of them Russian, who, fleeing from the pogroms of 1881, chose to go to one of the most unhospitable districts of the Turkish Middle East.

The newcomers' energies were quickly blunted by the harsh conditions in Palestine. Those who did not die of malaria quickly adapted to a colonial European way of life. In the twelve villages which they managed to establish with the help of Baron Edmond de Rothschild there were 473 Jewish workers in 1900.[1] It is interesting that the Jews were not the only immigrants in Turkish Palestine at the time. Members of German Protestant sects established at the same time wealthier agricultural colonies at various points in Palestine, such as Jaffa, Jerusalem, and Haifa. An agricultural German village north of Jaffa, Sarona, now in the heart of Tel Aviv, was later to become the main centre of Nazi anti-Jewish activities in Palestine between the two World Wars.[2]

It is also interesting to recall that the first *aliah* reached Palestine partly as a result of the capitulation rights held by the European powers —including Russia—in the Turkish Empire. The immediate reaction of the Ottoman authorities to the increasing numbers of Jews fleeing from Russia into Palestine was a negative one. It took the form of a publication of an Imperial Ordinance, displayed in April 1881 in the

[1] D. Ben Gurion, *Rebirth and Destiny of Israel*, 'Jewish Labor: The Origin of Settlement, an address before the Elected Assembly, March 2, 1932', p. 55.

[2] German Christian immigration into Palestine took place under the auspices of the 'Temple Society', a religious sect founded by Professor Christoph Hoffman of Württemberg, who tried to secure a 'firman' from the Porte in 1868 and, failing to obtain it, established the first colony at the foot of Mount Carmel at Haifa. See Oliphant, *Haifa*, pp. 17–27; also Habib Kenaan, *Moshavot HaGhermanim BeErez Israel* (German Colonies in Israel), Tel Aviv, 1967.

offices of Turkish consulates abroad, especially in Odessa, according to which all Jews were informed that they could settle in any part of the Ottoman Empire, but not in Palestine.[1] If Jews managed to do so, in spite of Turkish opposition, this was due to two factors: bribery, the usual way of overcoming administrative obstacles in the Ottoman Empire, and, as I have already mentioned, the fact that, as Russian citizens, they could claim capitulation rights. The first Arab and Turkish accusations of Jewish colonialism date back to this time.[2]

The second *aliah* extended from 1904 to 1913, ending on the eve of the First World War. It coincided with the beginning of organized political Zionism. Only 40,000 Jews out of the two and a half million which moved out of Eastern Europe in that period came to Palestine; and of those who came, more than half re-emigrated. But it was a wave which held the highest political potential for the future. Almost all the founding fathers of Israel: Ben Gurion, Levi Eshkol, Izhak Ben Zvi, the second President of Israel, were among these immigrants. More important, they gave Jewish Palestine three ingredients vital for its future independence: the kibbutz, the first Jewish defence organization, the 'Hashomer' (Watchman), and the first entirely Jewish town in the world, Tel Aviv, established in 1909 as a separate Jewish quarter of Arab Jaffa. Most important, this *aliah* brought with it to Palestine the idea of the *halutz*, the pioneer, that combination of the Jewish man of action and the nationalist, socialist ascetic. It emphasized the importance of manual work and it revived the Hebrew language. It was characterized by the ideological (Marxist) sectarianism of its members and by their will to create a new, larger framework of thought and action for the whole nation. It put new life into the political press with the appearance of *Hapoel Hazair* (1907) and *Aḥdut* (1910). It laid the foundations of the future labour exchanges, labour federation, and social services, and of the future political parties.[3]

Yet, the second *aliah* gave rise to persistent Islamic and Arab objections, and brought about the first tentative Jewish–Arab discussions on the possibility of collaboration. The little-known story of Arab–Jewish relations in this period has been studied in detail by a British scholar—Neville Mandel—in the light of the changing Turkish policy towards the two nationalities and of the internal problems of modernizing Turkey. Here I shall mention only one of his conclusions which seems

[1] *Hameliz* (1882), XVIII, 16, quoted in Mandel, op. cit., p. 80.

[2] Mandel, op. cit., p. 83.

[3] Eisenstadt, op. cit., pp. 19–24. For the revival of Hebrew, including a short appraisal of the role of the man who most contributed to it in Palestine, Eliezer Ben Yehudah, see Z. E. Kurzweil, *Modern Trends in Jewish Education* (New York, 1963), ch. 5, pp. 115–45.

to me to be of particular interest. Contrary to common belief, the two main trends of Jewish–Arab relations in Palestine—the trend in favour of collaboration and the trend in favour of open hostility—coexisted well before the British publication of the Balfour Declaration. For many years one of the mainstays of the political programmes of Arab politicians in the Ottoman Empire, used by them to win seats in local authorties or in the Turkish Parliament, was anti-Zionism.[1] Other Arab nationalists well before the First World War saw the confrontation between Jewish and Arab nationalism as crucial for Arab revival.[2] But at the same time contacts on both a personal and a communal basis existed. Unfortunately, when one community was ready to talk, the other no longer wanted to—and vice versa. The permanent stumbling block was, of course, the question of Jewish immigration—to which the Jews were passionately attached and the Arabs fiercely opposed. But one should not overlook the effects of the interference of the powers which then—as today—had a direct interest in the Palestine question. I shall discuss this problem later in the book.

The third *aliah*—35,000 strong—came to Palestine between 1919 and 1922. This relatively mass arrival of Jews from Europe and from the United States (many of whom were members of the Jewish Legion) was responsible for the first violent reaction of the Arab mob, directed especially against the old Jewish Orthodox community of Hebron. The disturbances were also used by the British Government as a justification for dividing the territory of the Mandate into two regions: Palestine, under direct British administrative control, and Transjordan, under Emir Abdullah, Feisal's brother.[3] More important perhaps, they allowed patterns of military activism to develop among both the Arabs and the Jews, with both of whom the British, after 1936, alternatively collaborated: an unusual sideline for the imperial administration.

One major event, however, was to have a permanent effect on the life and future of the Jewish community of Palestine in its early period. This was the creation in 1920 of the Histadrut—the Jewish federation of trade unions at Haifa. The Histadrut is discussed at length in another chapter. Here the most important point to remember is that during the meeting at which it was founded, and after a long ideological debate, the Histadrut agreed to share responsibility for the Jewish community's self-defence, and to help the underground military

[1] Mandel, op. cit., p. 95.
[2] Rashid Rida, *Al-Manar*, 1 June 1898, 108, quoted in Mandel op. cit., p. 89.
[3] The separation of Palestine from Transjordan was decided by Winston Churchill at the Jerusalem Conference in 1921, and the British Mandate over Transjordan explicitly announced on 26 May 1923.

organization, the Hagana, thus linking the socialist and military movements from the beginning.[1]

On the whole, the third *aliah* is remarkable for the great socialist 'push' it gave the Yishuv in the establishment of new, important socialist enterprises, such as the workers' bank, the workers' insurance company 'Hasneh', the engineering contracting firm 'Solel Boneh', the health insurance organization 'Kupat Ḥolim'.[2] The economic life of the Jewish community in Palestine at the time was hampered by the Polish Government's restrictions on the transfer of the immigrants' capital. This contributed indirectly to the creation of the Jewish 'Working Battalion', established to fight unemployment. It was also this *aliah* which saw the official international recognition of the 'national home', the first hesitation in the attitude of the British Administration towards the Jews, and the rising nationalistic opposition of the Arabs. If the second *aliah* was the *aliah* of the 'founding fathers', the third was the one which conceived the institutions, the style, and the strategy according to which the subsequent battles of Jewish nationalism were to be fought.

The fourth *aliah* was humanly, ideologically, and politically less significant than the previous ones. It took place between 1923 and 1926, and consisted of some 60,000 immigrants, who came to Palestine mostly as a result of the insecurity existing in the newly created Republic of Poland, which was still struggling for survival, and of the new restrictions on immigration imposed by the U.S.A. The immigrants of the fourth *aliah* established themselves mostly in the towns, and, significantly, their coming saw the organization of private industry with the fonnding of the 'Iḥud Baalei Hataasiah' (Manufacturers' Association) in 1925. So many of them left the country because of financial difficulties that in 1928 the number of emigrants was higher than the number of immigrants. Curiously enough, some of the Arabs and British began to worry about the possibility of Zionist 'bankruptcy'. The Arabs (who were naturally interested in selling land to the Jews) saw the prices of land go down. The British were worried about an economic recession which might reduce their main source of income from taxation, namely the Jewish community.

The trend was radically reversed after 1932, with the advent of Hitler to power. The fifth *aliah*, from 1934 to 1939, brought to Palestine some 225,000 immigrants, mostly from Germany. It brought a new

[1] Amos Perlmutter, *Military and Politics in Israel: Nation-Building and Role Expansion* (London, 1969), pp. 4–6. [2] Eisenstadt, op. cit., p. 29.

type of immigrant: middle-class, better educated than the previous East European immigrants, ideologically less involved but often possessing considerable financial means and technical knowledge. It was an immigration of technicians, who had decided to make the best of their banking, cultural, religious, and military experience in the new colonial environment of Palestine.[1]

The fifth *aliah* provided the skilled personnel for the creation of the new social, technical, and scientific infrastructures of the Yishuv. Whether in towns or in the countryside, in the socialist or private sectors, within the British Administration or outside it, the immigrants of the fifth *aliah* revolutionized existing Jewish society with their organizational capacity, their academic and operational experience, their initiative, and their resources. With them the balance of the internal population of the Yishuv changed irrevocably from the predominance of agriculture to that of the towns. And the whole of society became, for better or for worse, infinitely more European than it had ever been before.

This last wave of immigration before the Second World War coincided with what the British called the 'Palestine disturbances'. These took the form of open Arab guerrilla activity, which lasted from 1936 to the outbreak of the Second World War, and they gave the conflict in Palestine international significance.

Among the Europeans, the Italians and later the Germans were interested in using the Arab–Jewish conflict as a way of penetrating into the Middle East, shaking British rule, and counter-attacking the French and the British via the Arab nationalists after the Ethiopian war. In 1938 Mussolini held up 'the sword of Islam' in colonial Libya, and the Nazis were using the experience of the German non-Jewish settlers in Palestine to organize their intelligence nets in the Middle East.[2] If, in Egypt, the fascist-inspired nationalist 'green-shirts' movement had no greater success it is probably due to the fact that the equally nationalist 'Wafd' was pro-British out of fear of a possible replacement of British influence by Italian. However, quite apart from the activities of 'Misr-al-Fatah' (Young Egypt) there were plenty of people in Egypt ready to collaborate with the Italian agents, while the Germans were making important contacts with the Egyptian High Command.[3]

---

[1] *Haarez*, weekly supplement, 27 December 1968.

[2] *Akten zur deutschen auswärtigen Politik* (official documents of the Third Reich), E.V., 561, 564, 566, 576.

[3] Col. Anwar el-Sadat, in *Revolt on the Nile* (London, 1957), gives the details of the attempted anti-British plot organized by Egyptian army officers and German agents in 1942;

On the Arab side, it was mainly Iraq which supplied the Arab rebellion with men and arms to harass the Jewish community, although Arab activists could also find support among the bedouin tribes of Transjordan and the nationalists of Syria.

The British administration in Palestine was thus caught in the Arab–Jewish dilemma as never before. One official commission after another came to investigate the situation, but they only succeeded in infuriating both sides. The first Commission of Inquiry, headed by the Chief Justice of Palestine, Sir Thomas Hope, was set up to investigate the causes of the 1921 disturbances. The second commission came from England, headed by Sir Walter Shaw, to investigate the causes of the 1929 disturbances. The third, one-man investigation was conducted by Sir John Hope Simpson, who came at the suggestion of the Shaw Commission to investigate the economic problems of the country. He produced, in 1930, a White Paper, which for the first time linked Jewish immigration with the economic capacity of the country to absorb immigrants—a policy subsequently rejected in a letter from the Prime Minister, Ramsay MacDonald, to Weizmann which was immediately labelled the 'Black Letter' by the Arabs. In 1936 another commission, headed by Lord Peel, came to Palestine to investigate the causes of the renewed Arab disturbances. It proposed, in 1937, the partition of the country.[1] After the Second World War two more commissions were sent to Palestine, the Anglo-American Commission in 1946 and the United Nations Commission in 1947. But while the Arabs manoeuvred locally, trying to obtain concessions of principle against the 'Jewish Home' through the local administrators and the Colonial Office, the Zionists worked mainly in London, often reversing hostile decisions taken by the Government. It was over their policy towards Britain that the Jewish Agency and the Zionist Organization were most bitterly criticized by the Revisionists. The latter did not believe in Britain as most of the Zionist leaders did. They wanted to fight the London colonial Government as much as the Arabs did.

The first serious security crisis in Palestine had taken place in 1929, when hundreds of Jews were killed and wounded by Arab attackers,

---

see also Joseph B. Schechtman, *The Mufti and the Fuehrer : The Rise and Fall of Haj Amin El-Husseini* (New York, 1965). For an early summary of the unsuccessful Italian attempts to penetrate into the Arab world, see Elizabeth Monroe, *The Mediterranean in Politics* (Oxford, 1938), pp. 187–205. The most comprehensive study of German infiltration is to be found in Lukasz Hirszowicz, *The Third Reich and the Arab East* (London, 1966).

[1] *Palestine Royal Commission Report*, pp. 47 ff.

especially in places like Hebron where there were no Jewish defence groups. The disturbances gave impetus to a new policy of more active Jewish self-defence. In 1931 some members of the clandestine Jewish Army decided to establish in Jerusalem what they called the 'Hagana B', a more active branch of the Hagana controlled by a civilian committee composed of Revisionists, general Zionists, and members of the religious party. Jabotinsky was a member of this committee, the 'Irgun Zvai Leumi' (National Military Organization) or 'Ezel', according to its Hebrew initials. This organization still considered itself to be part of the Hagana, and in 1937, after a referendum, its commander, Abraham Theomi, formally reintegrated it into the Hagana. However, 65 per cent of the rank and file refused to take part in this merger and thus the Irgun became a completely separate military group.

In 1937 the Irgun had to take a vital decision: Arab troubles had started up again in 1936 and the Jewish community had to decide how to face the threat. The Hagana, the Yishuv leadership, and Jabotinsky supported the policy of *havlaga* (self-restraint), according to which clandestine Jewish military groups should only defend themselves, and not attack or counter-attack. On the other hand, the Irgun, now commanded by Moshe Rosenberg, wanted to take the initiative. The Irgun commander for the Jerusalem area, a brilliant young mathematician, David Raziel, and his second-in-command, a poet and student of classics, Abraham Stern, pushed hard for a decision. It was taken in the late summer of 1937, at a secret meeting of Jabotinsky and the Irgun leaders in Alexandria, and as a result the organization launched its first attack on 14 November 1937. It was the beginning of official Jewish terrorism, and of British repression of it. Raziel was arrested, and a young member of the Beitar, Shomo Ben Josef, was hanged, the first on the list of Jewish 'martyrs' of the resistance against the British. Meanwhile, in Europe, persecution of the Jews increased, war with Germany approached, and the British Government decided to appease the Arabs by issuing a White Paper which forbade the sale of land to the Jews over most of Palestine, limited immigration to 75,000 persons over five years, and announced its intention of creating an independent Jewish–Arab State in ten years where Jewish immigration would be allowed only with the Arabs' consent. It was the end of the 'national home' as the Jews intended it, but a violent reaction against Britain was staved off by the necessity of facing, with Britain, the greater threat presented by Hitler.

Jabotinsky fell in with Ben Gurion's formula: 'Fight Hitler as though the White Paper did not exist and the White Paper as though Hitler did not exist.' He tried in vain to persuade the British Government to create a Jewish Legion and died in New York in the middle of negotiations with Weizmann and Ben Gurion for a common military effort. Some of his followers, Raziel, and most of the Irgun, agreed to co-operate with the British. Raziel was released from prison and died in a British-organized commando operation in Iraq in 1941. Many of the members of the Beitar joined the British Army, but Abraham Stern refused to do so and founded a separate organization called the 'Lohamei Herut Israel' (or 'Lehi': Fighters for the Freedom of Israel), which intended to continue fighting the British, even if it meant soliciting the help of the Axis governments, with whom he tried unsuccessfully to make contact. He was tracked down and killed by British security forces in Tel Aviv in February 1942.[1]

The intricacies of Jewish internal and external policy in these crucial years have not yet been submitted to a critical historical analysis. When more is known of the relations between the leading and undoubtedly pro-British Zionist leadership, it will be easier to pass judgement. But whatever the weaknesses of Zionist diplomacy at that time, one should not forget that Zionists were not the only ones who had faith in the strength of British and French democracy in the face of fascist and Nazi provocation.

If the Zionist leaders could do little to increase Jewish immigration to Palestine when the safety of the European Jews was not yet in immediate danger, they were tragically helpless before the dangers of mounting antisemitism, which brought pressure to bear on the Jews and simultaneously whipped up anti-Zionist and anti-British Arab nationalists in Palestine.

The Zionist leaders, like so many European leaders, found themselves caught in the pincers of fascist and Nazi aggression and Franco–British appeasement.

It was in this confused atmosphere of hate, despair, and impending catastrophe that the Peel Commission was sent to Palestine to investigate the causes of unrest in the Mandate. The Commission compiled a

---

[1] The full story of the underground movements in Israel has not yet been told. The government version is given by Ben Zion Dinur et al. (eds.), Sefer Toldot HaHaganah (The History of the Haganah), vols. I and II (Tel Aviv, 1954–64), which deals with the dissident groups in vol. II, part I, pp. 574–85 and vol. II, part II, pp. 1053–72. An account of the Irgun is given by David Niv, Maarchot HaIrgun HaZvai HaLeumi (Battle for Freedom: The Irgun Zvai Leumi) (Tel Aviv, 1965), 3 vols. Nathan Friedman-Yellin and Israel Eldad (eds.) deal with the Stern group in The History of Lehi (in Hebrew, Tel Aviv, 1962), 2 vols., privately published. Jacques Soustelle, La longue marche d'Israël (Paris, 1968), gives an informative and concise description of the historical development of the Jewish terrorist movements; see also Menahem Beigin, The Revolt (London, 1951).

long report which even today, as I have mentioned, remains one of the most illuminating, honest, and best-written documents on the Palestine question. It also puts forward the second proposal for the partition of Palestine (the first one had, in 1921, resulted in the detachment of Transjordan from Palestine) which would have given to the Jews complete autonomy over a limited area around Tel Aviv and Haifa. The Jews were divided but on the whole ready to accept; so was Transjordan.[1] But, in the last resort, Arab fears of the possible consequences of partition prevailed. I shall discuss later (see Chapter 5) the consequences of such a decision, which was later criticized by some Arabs themselves. In fairness to the Arabs, it may be worth recalling here the consequence the Arabs feared most. Officially this was Zionist expansion through immigration, but no less important, if less obvious, was the possibility of an agreement between Transjordan and the Jews which, with England's help, could make Abdullah a powerful, if not the most powerful, ruler in the Middle East. Then there was the apprehension the Arabs felt over the proposed exchange of 1,500 Jews living in the territory allocated to the Arabs, with 250,000 Arabs living in the territory allocated to the Jews. It is, however, important to note that as long ago as 1937, the idea of the partition of Palestine was inextricably linked in Arab minds with the suspicion of a British scheme aimed at realizing, with the help of the Jews and of the Hashemite family of Mecca, a unified control of the Middle East which they had not been able to achieve immediately after the First World War.[2]

As far as the Jewish institutions, which we are now discussing, are concerned, the Peel Commission confirmed that they had reached a high level of efficiency and development in serving the social, economic, spiritual, cultural, and political needs and desires of a population which had grown in twelve years from 121,000 to more than 400,000 people. It summarized the situation in one sentence: 'Twelve years ago the national home was an experiment: today it is a going concern.' It noted that Jewish land ownership had increased by 100 per cent, and that on this land lived almost 100,000 Jews in 203 agricultural settlements, that the development of Jewish urbanism was 'impressive', with 150,000 Jews in Tel Aviv, a Jewish majority in Jerusalem, and 76,000 out of a total of 125,000 population in Haifa.

More important was the Commission's recognition of the strong

[1] H.M. King Hussein of Jordan, *Uneasy Lies the Head: An Autobiography* (London, 1962), pp. 99–100.

[2] P. J. Vatikiotis, *Politics and the Military in Jordan. A Study of the Arab Legion, 1921–1957* (London, 1967), pp. 50–1.

national feeling which now permeated the Jewish community of Palestine and which only a new partition of the country could possibly satisfy.[1]

To understand how such a feeling had grown and developed, it is necessary to describe the third and most important group of Jewish institutions in Palestine, the Socialist Zionist institutions, namely the kibbutz, the Histadrut, the Hagana, and the workers' parties. I shall attempt to do this in Chapter 4.

[1] *Palestine Royal Commission Report*, pp. 82–3.

Chapter 4

From National Home to Jewish State

What is a kibbutz? A collective farm where an old iron or cement water-tower still indicates the point where the first pioneers pitched their tents? Or is it a modern contribution to Jewish Messianism? Or a special Jewish brand of non-monastic monastery where agricultural and industrial products are processed by a collective aristocracy dedicated to the creation of a new type of the perfect society?

Perhaps one way of understanding the complex structure and meaning of the kibbutz is to look at its historical development and particularly at those events which took place in the collective society of Israel in the first period of statehood between 1948 and 1953. I shall do so in the first part of this chapter, which deals with three closely related subjects: the Socialist Zionist institutions in Palestine, namely the kibbutz, the federation of trade unions, the Yishuv defence organization, and the socialist parties; their attitude towards similar non-socialist, étatist Jewish institutions, in particular the right-wing, militant political organization, Jabotinsky's Revisionist movement; and finally the complicated relations between the Zionists, the British, and the Arabs which surrounded the process of the mutation and growth of a persecuted religious minority into a sovereign State.

The first kibbutz, Degania, was founded near the Jordan in 1909 (by a group of pioneers almost exclusively drawn from the Russians of the second *aliah*). One of its founders, Josef Baratz, has related the moving story of this first Jewish experiment in Utopia in Palestine and describes the combination of socialist, anarchic, nationalist, and Messianic ideals with the down-to-earth, day-to-day economic necessities of a pioneering existence.[1]

But there was another form of collectivism which was soon to join the first kibbutz enterprise. Vladimir Jabotinsky describes how he saw the idea taking shape in a dark room in a slum back in 1917 while listening to the prophetic words of Trumpeldor, at a time when the two

---

[1] Josef Baratz, *A Village by the Jordan: The Story of Degania* (London, 1954).

men were working for the creation of a Jewish army to participate in the military liberation of Palestine from the Turks.[1]

Trumpeldor was, like Theodor Herzl, a born aristocrat, one of the few Jewish officers in the Tsarist army (he had lost an arm in the Russo–Japanese war of 1905). He was later to lose his life in a Zionist version of Custer's last stand, against the Arabs in Northern Galilee.

Trumpeldor saw the kibbutz as a kind of permanent advanced agricultural base or depot for a corps of pioneers. Such a corps was to be in a state of permanent ideological and material mobilization, capable of fighting, ploughing, administering physical and ideological medicine to the emerging nation, an order of modern Jewish Knights, acting as the spearhead, the shield, the priests, the leaders, and servants of Zionist revival in the ancient homeland. It was called the 'HeHaluz' (meaning 'scout' or 'pioneer'), and it was as much an institution as a state of mind. Trumpeldor had in fact revived, in 1918, an older organization of the same name, which had been founded by young Jewish intellectuals in Russia in the wake of the 1905 revolution. Now their ideas spread through the Jewish communities of Eastern Europe. It was the result of Jewish enthusiasm for practical Zionism, of social upheaval, and a by-product—as Weizmann correctly surmised—of the military service in the Tsarist army by 600,000 Jews, mainly in pioneer corps.[2]

Between these two poles, farmers joining together chiefly to survive economically and physically in a hostile territory and the order of socialist pioneer knights of the HeHaluz, many other forms of communal and co-operative settlement found expression in Jewish Palestine.

The variations were as numerous as the ideological differences. There were the socialist working brigades, in the early twenties, which became more left-wing in the late twenties, and the militant nationalist Revisionist movement in the late thirties. There were religious kibbutzim and anti-religious ones. There were kibbutzim which believed in total expansion hoping to reach a point in which they might eventually become a town or large populated area, and there were others which purposely limited the number of their members in order to preserve a feeling of family life in the community.

The 'working battalions' of the nationalists and the communists never amounted to much. The Marxist formations played a more important role than the nationalists, in spite of the disagreements

---

[1] V. Jabotinsky, *The Story of the Jewish Legion*, pp. 103–4.

[2] C. Weizmann, *American Addresses* (New York, 1923), pp. 19–20. For a sociological analysis of HeHaluz, see Eisenstadt, op. cit., pp. 17–18.

between them. They aimed at economic self-sufficiency and wanted to be at the same time a quasi-military instrument at the disposal of the Zionist movement and an alternative to the land-based settlement. However they were in the end defeated by the impossibility of extending their basically élitist approach to the economy and to society as a whole and to the Jewish masses facing the realities of industrialization and urbanization. This was one of the dilemmas also facing the kibbutz movement. It aimed at including the whole of Zionist society in Palestine, but was hampered by a permanent tug-of-war between ideological radicalism, élitism, and practical economic necessities.

This dilemma brought about the dissolution of the first federation of kibbutzim in 1925 and influenced the development of the four main trends in socialist collectivism. The first and most important of these trends—later affiliated to the 'Aḥdut Haavoda' party (see p. 84)—was to become the 'Kibbutz Meuḥad' (United Kibbutz) with 58 settlements in 1965. The second and most radical trend—later affiliated to 'Mapam' (see p. 84)—was embodied in the 'Kibbutz Ertzi' ('Ertzi' from the word *erez*, meaning 'land') with 74 settlements in 1965. The third trend—affiliated to 'Mapai' (see p. 84)—was represented by the 'Iḥud Hakvutzot Vehakibbutzim' (Union of Kibbutzim and Kvutzot, plural of *kvutza*, meaning 'small collective settlement') which had 85 settlements in 1965, some of them up to a thousand strong and quite flexible in their ideological approach. The fourth trend was the religious one, which in 1965 controlled some twelve settlements (Hakibbutz Hadati) affiliated to the 'Hapoel Hamizrahi' and 'Poalei Agudat Israel'—religious parties which have so far had little impact on Israeli society (see pp. 86–7). Like the five collective settlements not affiliated to any political party, the religious kibbutzim were in fact created more to satisfy the needs of socialist individuals who wanted to live a religious life than to turn Israeli society socialist.

With the kibbutz, other forms of co-operative settlements were soon to be developed. The 'moshav' was a co-operative settlement, with each family organizing its private life, but linked with the others through common ownership of the land and of the means of production, and by the common marketing of products. They laid less stress on the élitist element and on ideological purity. The immigrants from Germany in the late 1930s established a mixed type of kibbutz and moshav system called the 'moshav shitufi', in which the community's ideological control over its members was greater than in the co-operative village. In this type of moshav economy and ownership are collective as in the kibbutz, but each family has its own house and is responsible for its own cooking, laundry, and the care of its children, as in the moshav, while work and pay are adjusted to individual circumstances. Furthermore, the moshav shitufi (of which twenty-two are at present in existence with a population varying from sixty to three hundred each) tends like the kibbutz to develop industry in addition to agriculture.

It has been correctly observed that the most important characteristic of the Socialist Zionist settlers was a 'fear of premature normalization coupled with strong ideological orientation'.[1] Ideological orthodoxy prevailed over agricultural activities even where this meant compromise. And this tendency was—with varying degrees of emphasis—shared by the rest of Israeli society: in the kibbutzim, in the co-operative settlements, in the socialist institutions, in the cities, and throughout the educational system, urban or otherwise.

In 1948 there were in Palestine 115 kibbutzim proper, and they were to grow to 230 in 1965. I shall explain later why their growth has slowed down with the creation of the State and why it has again accelerated with the military victory of 1967. However, in anticipation I shall mention here that many of the new collective farms created in the last seven years are, in fact, military agricultural camps established by a special army corps, the 'Naḥal' (Fighting Pioneer Youth) for purposes of defence and development of dangerous border areas. Their military population is a transient one, part of which remain on the spot after completing its military service, but without establishing a priori the kind of settlement which will be turned over to civilians. In other words, a Nahal farm can become a kibbutz, a moshav, or a moshav shitufi.

In 1948, when the total population of the State was about 650,000, the kibbutz population accounted for about 8 per cent of the total. Its total strength has since increased and in 1963 more than 80,000 people were living permanently in collective settlements. This was less than 5 per cent of the total population of the State, and one-third of the population of the 367 co-operative villages, which reached 124,000.[2]

It was in the pre-State period that the kibbutz movement developed its internal and external administrative and political institutions. Most of the trends and organizational grouping I mentioned developed during the third aliah. The institutionalization of the internal life of the kibbutzim goes back to a much earlier date, to the twenties when the pattern of communal settlement life was fully worked out. It provides for a general assembly of all the members, usually meeting on Saturday nights to approve the decision of the various kibbutz committees and annually electing its leaders: the kibbutz secretary, the directors of the

[1] Eisenstadt, op. cit., pp. 145–6.   [2] ibid., p. 120.

various branches of economic activities, the men responsible for social, cultural, and military matters. Socialization of the children was and remains a point of cardinal importance and discussion in the community, since they were to be the perfect unspoiled generation of the future. It is on this particular aspect of kibbutz society that sociologists have focused many of their studies of the kibbutz, where an experiment in socialization of children has been carried out with more vigour and perseverance than anywhere else in the world.[1]

Returning to history, one sees that economically the kibbutz led a very precarious existence till the creation of the State. In the 1920s and '30s outside paid work for private capitalists was one way for the kibbutz to make ends meet each month. But it was also because of the economic difficulties, already existing in the twenties, that the first workshops were established on the collective farms and mechanization was introduced. These two important steps were meant to save money, increase production, and ensure the technical independence of isolated farming communities. In fact they turned out to be the beginning of the evolution of the kibbutz agrarian society into a mixed agricultural/industrial system: a system which was in line with the Marxist ideology of the kibbutz, which always refused to let its members become 'farmers' but insisted that they retain the status, the dignity, and the conscience of the proletarian workers.

Another important step in the development and articulation of kibbutz economy was the establishment of 'service co-operatives'. As early as 1913 a United Committee of Palestinian Workers had prepared the way for the organization of the Jewish labour force in Palestine. The federation of trade unions (the Histadrut), established in 1920, immediately developed its entrepreneurial activities, which to this day balance and often outweigh its more radical side. I have already mentioned some of its subsidiary organizations like the Solel Boneh, the engineering contracting firm, Hasneh, the general insurance company,

---

[1] Y. Talmon-Gerber, 'Differentiation in Collective Settlements'; *Scripta Hierosolymitana*, vol. 3, 1956; *idem*, 'The Family in Collective Settlements', in *Transactions of the Fifth World Congress of Sociology*, vol. IV (1962); *idem*, 'The Sleeping Arrangements for Children of the Kibbutz' (in Hebrew), a report on research done for the Department of Sociology of the Hebrew University, Jerusalem, in 1956 (mimeographed). A. Etzioni, 'The Organizational Structure of the Kibbutz' (Hebrew), part A, in *Niv Hakevuzah*, vol. 6, no. 3 (1956); part B, in *Niv Hakevuzah*, vol. 6, no. 4 (1957). S. N. Eisenstadt, op. cit., pp. 165–9, 235–7, 252–3. And for a detailed study: Harry Viteles, *A History of the Co-operative Movement in Israel: A Source Book in 7 Volumes*: book I, *The Evolution of the Co-operative Movement* (London, 1966); book II, *The Evolution of the Kibbutz Movement* (London, 1967); book III, *An Analysis of the Four Sectors of the Kibbutz Movement* (London, 1968); book IV, *Co-operative Smallholders Settlements: The Moshav Movement* (London, 1968).

and so on. I shall deal in more detail with its role and organization later in this chapter. All that needs to be pointed out here is that the Histadrut was also responsible for the establishment of organizations which were more closely connected with the agricultural settlements. 'Hamashbir Hamerkazi' started as the central supply organization for Jewish settlements but in time became the main retail company of the country, covering up to 50 per cent of Jewish internal business at a time, supplying food but soon spurring on the industrial production of the Jewish community at large. 'Tnuva', the agricultural products co-operative marketing organization, soon became a leading factor in the development of Jewish agriculture. It rationalized and streamlined agricultural production, improved distribution services throughout the country, organized storage and a chain of vegetarian restaurants, protected prices and planned most of the food policy of the country. Solel Boneh, the construction company, became the greatest public works enterprise in the Middle East. None of these co-operatives were controlled by the kibbutz movement or were even part of it. They had been created as part of the Histadrut to serve the Jewish community of Palestine in general and the socialist one in particular. But they soon developed in terms of the 'strategy of survival' of the Yishuv, a strategy in which the agricultural settlements became advanced fortresses, Tnuva and Hamashbir their logistical suppliers, Solel Boneh their engineering corps, all contributing to the establishment of an unplanned but very efficient society, equally geared to economic and military challenges. Much has changed in Israel since then, but the fundamental idea that Jewish society should be in a perpetual state of mobilization is still very much alive, and the kibbutz still remains the typical unit in such a society.

The first real test of the efficiency of the kibbutz, and of its connecting net of articulated service institutions and its logistic supply channels came in 1933. From this year onwards the Yishuv was faced with the challenge of integrating the great immigration from Germany and soon afterwards of withstanding the economic, political, and military pressure of the Arab revolt. The challenge brought intense mechanization and irrigation to the kibbutz to increase autonomous Jewish production, just as urban industry was expanded to absorb the newcomers, and the growth of the basic infrastructure—shown in the development of Jewish-controlled electric power stations and of a Jewish port in Tel Aviv—was encouraged. Some figures from official British sources convey the extent of the forced advance of the Jewish economy during these crucial years, and on the agricultural 'front' in particular. Capital investment grew by 100 per cent from 1932 to 1933 and by 80 per cent from 1933 to 1934. The number of doctors grew by 209·9 per cent in the period from 1932 to 1936; engineers by 114·8; people in the liberal professions by 56·9 per cent.[1]

Tnuva, which in 1931 marketed £139,000 worth of agricultural goods, was already selling £600,000 worth in 1936 and made its first profit a year later. This was the time of the kibbutz's great leap forward.[2]

Between 1936 and 1947 the population of the kibbutzim increased by 100 per cent. The kibbutz—symbolized by the water-tower, the wooden stockade, and the few tents—spread over the whole country, occupying Jewish-owned but as yet uncultivated land in the heart of the Arab countryside, overcoming British and Arab administrative and military resistance. It became an integrated network of agricultural, industrial, and military production. Its workshops supplied both the needs of the farms and of the secret Jewish army. Its barracks sheltered agricultural workers who were also soldiers in a permanent state of alert. The first military factories sprang up in the most desolate parts of Palestine, and as searches by the British proved later, the kibbutzim were favourite places for hiding arms and illegal immigrants.

The two elements of Jewish collective society, the Utopian, harmonious, egalitarian conception of A. D. Gordon and Trumpeldor's chivalrous, aristocratic conception of a fighting knighthood, united in a perfect situational logic which made the kibbutz grow in a highly efficient state of schizophrenic ideology: total harmony at home and total conflict outside the village.

Gordon, the prophet of the Zionist religion of work, had written in 1911: 'Our national movement is fundamentally a cultural act; it is the aspiration to reconstruct our life in harmony with our spirit and according to our ways which is the essence of our civilization.' Work, that is action, becomes for him not a means but a supreme ideal, the condition necessary to 'weld the distance which has separated [the Jews] from nature'.[3] The result was the crystallization of a unique society, which in many ways recalled the ancient Greek city state.

The kibbutz was, in fact, a little state run by an *élite* drawn from an already select Zionist society. It lived according to the social and moral laws of total democracy; it resented and rejected any outside interference in its internal life. The kibbutz prided itself on not using locks on the doors of its houses; on not depending on rabbis and religion for its

[1] *Palestine Royal Commission Report*, pp. 157 and 223.
[2] See Haim Darin, *The Other Society* (New York, 1962), pp. 78–82 and 115.
[3] A. D. Gordon, *Kitvei* (Writings), vol. I (Tel Aviv, 1927), pp. 7–11 et seq.

morality and the stability of its members' marital life. If anything went wrong among its members, the kibbutz had its own internal tribunals, the hardest punishment being, as in ancient Greece, ostracism—the expulsion from the village. The collective farm population usually led a very hard life. But it liked challenges and possessed unlimited reserves of moral courage and confidence: its sense of superiority and of mission was unbounded.

The kibbutz planned its internal life as well as its relations with the external world. Common topics of discussion in 1939—when economic conditions were particularly hard—were not only the number of new houses to be built, but also the number of children a couple could have without placing too much strain on the community. Thus each collective settlement was an integrated microcosm of Utopian society and statehood. It ran its economy, its police, its underground army, its local government, its cultural and educational system. It was both a frontier fortress and a highly select ideological and intellectual club. It was a farm and a military camp, a laboratory for social experiment and a very efficiently run business.

Voluntarism was, of course, the source of the kibbutz's strength. Anyone was free to leave at any time. Furthermore, since the kibbutz was an organized community, it could afford, through the assistance which each member gave the others, to provide more men for service to the whole Jewish community of Palestine. Their availability and their civic virtues made them the natural and accepted leaders of the Yishuv. This gave rise, in later years, to the accusation of fostering particular interests and advantages through community service. But at the time, Jewish society in Palestine requested and was glad of the kibbutz's capacity to answer the call of public service.

The kibbutz became quite naturally an aristocracy of interests from having been an aristocracy of ideals. From a disinterested Utopian élite, it turned into a curious socialist plantocracy with more political and economic weight than any other group in Jewish society in Palestine—and later, in Israel. But it was a plantocracy capable of fulfilling many important needs. These needs were different in kind, but equally vital to the formation and development of the Jewish national home.

There were, first, the material needs which I have already mentioned: mutual economic help within the kibbutz community on the basis of the principle 'from each according to his ability and to each according to his needs'. Such a policy made it possible for thousands of inexperienced immigrants to face the challenge of physical survival, to find work, social assistance, and moral companionship in a very hard new environ-ment. Co-operative organizations in the towns and in the countryside also shared the credit for this.

The kibbutz also contributed to the production of much-needed agricultural and industrial goods for the whole Jewish community in Palestine; protected it from Arab boycott; cultivated Jewish land, even when it was economically difficult, thus making sure that it did not revert to its former Arab owners; and surrounded towns with chains of settle-ments capable of assuring supplies and some defence in case of necessity.

Defence and military organization was the second kind of need which the kibbutz helped to fulfil for the Yishuv. We have already mentioned the collective settlement as a strategic outpost for the urban Jewish settlement, as a military depot, as a military factory and repair shop, and as a training ground for Jewish underground forces. One should add that the kibbutz also had a prominent role in the formation of a very special type of military unit, the pioneers' shock troops—the 'Palmach' —and the selection and training of many commanders of the future Israeli army.

The Palmach's story goes back to the years of the Arab Revolt, which occurred in Palestine from 1937 to 1939. At that time, a young British artillery officer, Captain Orde Wingate, the nephew of the former Commander-in-Chief of the British troops in Sudan, and a fanatical believer in the written word of the Bible, set out to convince his superior officers that British security in Palestine could be provided with the active collaboration of Jewish military units. His efforts did not go very far, since he soon became involved in the complicated politics of the military in Palestine, to the point of being considered a traitor by his British colleagues.[1] But the few hundred men whom he organized into commando units called 'Special Night Squads' not only showed the fighting qualities of the Jews, but also the importance of commando tactics in the type of war then being waged in Palestine.

When Wingate left the country to take a leading part in the Abyssin-ian campaign, and later to direct and perish in the famous British Chindit expedition behind the Japanese lines in Burma, he also left behind him, in Palestine, a personal legend and a group of trained soldiers which included some of the future commanders of the Israeli Army, General Yigal Allon and General Moshe Dayan among them.

But Wingate did something more. Before his appearance on the Jewish military scene, the Zionist Organization had its own little army. But the Hagana, established in 1920 and supported by the Histadrut,

[1] See Christopher Sykes, *Orde Wingate* (Cleveland, Ohio, 1959).

was faithful to its name: it was prepared, for tactical and ideological reasons, to defend itself—never to attack.

During the Arab disturbances in 1936 one of the main points of contention between the Zionist Organization and its right-wing competitor, the Revisionist movement, founded by Vladimir Jabotinsky, was the military tactics to be applied against the Arabs.

The rise of terrorism put the official Zionist authorities on the horns of a dilemma: whether to continue the quite ineffective policy of *havlaga*, or find some other way besides terrorism to take the military initiative against the Arabs. The answer was proffered by Wingate. His special troops proved to have all the necessary qualities: courage, ingenuity, a heightened sense of political responsibility, socialist indoctrination, loyalty to the democratic cause which Britain was defending in the face of mounting fascism and Nazi aggression.

When in 1942 Rommel reached the frontiers of Egypt, and the British High Command began to think about the necessity of defending Palestine, the Jewish Agency proposed, and the British authorities accepted, a compromise typical of the climate then prevailing in Palestine: the Jews would organize their fighting partisan units in the kibbutzim, to be used in the rear of the Germans in the case of a Nazi invasion. The British were prepared to give them limited instruction and limited quantities of arms. They knew that the Jews had their stock of weapons and the Jews, for their part, understood that the British—at least for the duration of the war—would not ask them awkward questions about the armament of their special units.

So the Palmach was born, organized, and trained. It became a unique organization of hand-picked soldiers, working and living in the kibbutzim in the narrowly ideological atmosphere of the collective movement. When the War of Independence broke out in 1948, these troops formed the spearhead of the Jewish defence organization and were largely responsible for the military survival of the Jewish State.[1]

With the war of 1948 over, the existence of a compact and victorious politically indoctrinated army in the kibbutzim could not fail to pose a serious threat to the unity of the State. I shall return to this question when discussing the Israeli Army. Here we must move on to the third and most important contribution of the kibbutz movement to the Yishuv, namely its social example.

The kibbutz was the most faithful realization of the Zionist Utopia.

---

[1] Perlmutter, op. cit., ch. III, 'The "Academies" of the Future Israeli Army', pp. 32–45, is the best concise analysis of the subject. The Hagara High Command set up the first Palmach unit as early as May 1941.

It not only stood for the Jewish return to the homeland, but for the creation of a new, humane society. It built in Palestine a sample of that perfect, rational, harmonious world which the eighteenth-century Utopians had everywhere dreamt of, nowhere realized.

Later the kibbutz organization was thrown into a major crisis when the State of Israel, to which the kibbutz had helped to give birth, turned out very differently from the Utopian model desired by the collective society. But, in the period we are dealing with, the hard years of the construction of the national home, the kibbutz was at its best. It led the rest of the country, not only because it was a pioneer organization, but because alone among all the other social groups and institutions it was fundamentally élitist, willing to face and capable of facing the multiple challenges of the time. It was in fact a true collective aristocracy which fully responded to the needs of the people and the times. It could not fail to make an impact on the rest of Jewish society in Palestine out of all proportion to the numerical strength of its members.

This impact expressed itself in many ways: in terms of pioneering and soldiering; of radicalism and social experiment; of culture and invention. It was, above all, an example of frugality and social puritanism. Economically speaking, both the Jews living on the collective farms and those living in the rest of the country, were poor and in constant need of help. But while most of the population was poor out of necessity, the people of the kibbutz, like monks, were poor because they chose to be, claiming that all superfluous income should go to the community as a whole, and after the community to humanity.

They practised and taught simplicity in manners, frugality in life; they made the rich in the towns feel ideologically and individually ashamed. They made the whole Yishuv despise, or at least behave as if they despised, comfort, they made women forgo fashion, and they made the political leaders and bureaucrats shy of showing any personal advantage gained from their jobs while they were in fact much better off than the rest of the population.

In a certain sense, the puritan example of the kibbutz was similar to that offered by Protestantism to the fathers of the industrial revolution, or perhaps even more to the patriotic example given by the Samurai in the Meiji Restoration to the Japanese society of their time.[1] In any case, it helped to establish an élitist social pattern which, well

---

[1] See Masao Maruyama, *Thought and Behaviour in Modern Japanese Politics* (London, 1963), pp. 11–13, 134–5; and V. D. Segre, 'Israel: A Society in Transition', in *World Politics*, XXI, 3 April 1969, pp. 345–65.

after the kibbutz had ceased to be the central source of pioneering status in Jewish society, continued to make ostentatious use of riches and comfort despicable, or at least of secondary importance.

As a result, the process of rising demand for consumer goods and growing economic frustration was slowed down. This did not prevent the amassing of considerable private wealth, as we shall see in a later part of this book. Neither did it prevent, in the sixties, the largest share of national income from being distributed among the minority of Israelis born in Western Europe. But the development of this situation of economic inequality took place well after the State had already built the foundations of a solid industrial infrastructure capable of expanding and thus meeting the rising demands of the new immigrants. Even those who criticize the economic selfishness and privileges of the kibbutz in the State of Israel cannot deny that the Spartan way of life of the kibbutz's aristocracy spared Israel from the dilemma confronting most of the underdeveloped countries of the world today: the dilemma of choosing between industrialization imposed by authoritarian régimes and economic and industrial development left to private capital and initiative, which is more sensitive to its own private interest than to the national one.[1]

The kibbutz would not of course have been able to impose its way of life on the whole of society without the help of other larger and less select, but no less efficient, institutions. These were the Histadrut and the socialist parties.

If the kibbutz can be considered—especially in its glorious pre-Israeli period—as a collective aristocracy or, to paraphrase a term from W. H. Armitage's book *The Rise of the Technocrats*,[2] a Socialist Zionist plantocracy, the Histadrut was for many years a state before the State, and still remains today a state within the State.[3]

The Histadrut phenomenon is probably as unique in its way as the kibbutz. Like the latter, it was the product of the tug-of-war between Utopian Zionist socialism and hard competitive conditions in an underdeveloped colonial country. It was, from its inception, 'more than a trade union or a federation of trade unions. Working conditions and labour disputes were of some importance in its initial phases, but they were not predominant in or primary to its basic conception. The aim of

---

[1] David Patterson, 'The First Fifty Years of Collective Settlement in Israel', in *The Jewish Journal of Sociology*, II (1960), pp. 42–55. He discusses the social image of the kibbutz in Israel with rare insight.   [2] London, 1965.

[3] See A. Malkin, *Hahistadrut Bamedinah* (The Histadrut within the State), Beit Berel, 1961; P. Lavon, *Haarachim Veshinuyim* (Values and Changes), Tel Aviv, 1960; Eisenstadt, op. cit., pp. 38–43.

the Histadrut was more to create conditions beneficial to the development and organization of a new privileged working class than to protect
the interests of an existing underprivileged one.'[1] At the beginning, in
1920, it had only 4,433 members, in a Jewish society of some 100,000
people—less than 5 per cent of the total population. Forty years later
it could boast a membership of more than 700,000, just less than 30 per
cent of the population of Israel.

If the Histadrut has greatly increased its numbers and extended its
activities in a way certainly unforeseen in the early twenties, it has never
changed its basic principles. In fact, the Histadrut was created not
only as a federation of trade unions to meet the challenge of class war,
but as a national Jewish institution aiming at the realization of the
Jewish national home in Erez Israel.

To a great extent this was the result of one man's ideas and actions:
Ben Gurion's. The future Prime Minister of Israel became the first
Histadrut's General Secretary in 1920. From the very day he had
arrived in Turkish Palestine in September 1906, Ben Gurion, an active
member of the Poalei Zion (Workers of Zion) Party, had tried to
convince people that, whatever the organization or the policy, it had
to be Jewish, i.e. national, first and foremost. This was of course in
total opposition to the policy of the predominant Jewish workers'
movement in Eastern Europe, the Bund. But in this respect the
Marxist–Zionists, like Ben Gurion, were helped by the situational logic
created by immigration to Palestine. It was a prominent feature of this
immigration—as it is today—to concentrate ideological formulations on
problems of absorption into the new society, and to attempt to justify
and explain rather than shape and forge, ideologically, the waves of
immigrants.[2] In February 1919 Ben Gurion succeeded in reaching a
working agreement with another Marxist party—'Hapoel Hatzair' (The
Young Worker), which was less Marxist than his own group, but more
concerned with the idea of agricultural redemption of the Jews than
with the idea of Jewish national redemption. From the agreement
between the two groups the Histadrut was born in 1920. To Ben
Gurion it was the institution which was to make 'of the class we represent a nation'. But it was also a tool to implement—with facts, not
empty words—the Balfour Declaration.

In a sense, the Histadrut was a national 'church' of pragmatic
socialism. It had to 'convert' its own members, not to its ideology, but

[1] Eisenstadt, op. cit., pp. 138–9.
[2] ibid., p. 9. Also A. Perlmutter in an unpublished D.Phil. thesis, 'Ideology and Organisa-
tion: The Politics of Socialist Parties in Israel, 1897–1957' (Berkeley, 1957).

to the condition of the workers. The Jewish proletariat, made up of young idealistic students, merchants, and small tradesmen, were to be given the opportunity to act as proletarians. They had to have factories and wages before they could have capitalists to fight against. They had to survive physically in an hostile country before they could survive ideologically as a separate class. So the new workers' organizations decided to 'build' workers *and* factories at the same time; to provide capital *and* labour; to ensure military security *and* education; to provide social *and* cultural services. The Histadrut, which was a socialist 'church' by vocation, became a national 'church' by necessity. In the circumstances it could not be particular about its ideology. It inevitably became, as Ben Gurion wished, a combination of socialism and national Messianism.

Many of its basic ideas could be found in the writing of Jewish Socialist Zionists who never set foot in Palestine. Nachman Syrkin—as I have mentioned—was one of them. He thought that only Zionism—as a political and national solution to the Jewish problem—and not class struggle—could solve the Jewish question, since the Jewish social struggle should follow, not precede, the establishment of a Jewish State. The form of the Jewish State was 'the only debatable issue involved in Zionism'.[1] He recognized that contemporary political Zionism was striving towards the creation of a Jewish State based on the right of ownership and which 'in essence does not differ from the practical attempt of colonisation . . . yet it is inconceivable that a people will agree to the creation of an autonomous state based on social inequality, since this would amount to entering into a *social contract of servitude*.'[2] This phrase, which was underlined by the writer, also gives, incidentally, an idea of the extent of the involvement of eighteenth-century Rousseauian Utopianism in nineteenth-century Socialist Zionism. The contradiction between the ideas of the French Revolution—those of egalitarian Messianism—and the nineteenth-century ideas of class strife, was bridged by the belief that the Jews who 'were historically the nation which caused division and strife [would] now become the most revolutionary of all nations'.[3] Thus it was felt that tradition—the binding element of Judaism—should be incorporated into the workers' society, not rejected. Berl Katzenelson, a most outspoken partisan of Jewish socialist traditionalism, the editor of the Histadrut paper *Davar*, said as much in an ideological article published in 1934, and

---

[1] Nachman Syrkin, *The Jewish Problem and the Socialist-Jewish State* (1898); partly translated from the German and reprinted in Hertzberg, op. cit., p. 348.

[2] ibid., p. 345.   [3] ibid., p. 350.

which claimed that 'our movement by its very nature must uphold the principle of revolutionary constructivism'.[1] And, answering the needs of constructivism, the Histadrut became everything: an organization of workers through their trade unions, and a creator of jobs; a builder of factories and farms; a founder of banks to finance their activities, co-operatives to provide them with services, schools to teach the sons of the workers, papers to indoctrinate and inform its members, theatres and orchestras to amuse them, a military organization to defend them, social and medical services to care for them; and even, at a later date, a provider of rabbis for their religious needs.

Very soon the Histadrut became the greatest capitalist in the country, owing to the fact that it disposed of the richest source of Zionist investment: labour. Its economic strength was further increased by the large net of servicing and marketing co-operatives which it set up in order to gain maximum control over the Jewish community of Palestine. A current joke among Israelis, till not so long ago, was that no one could find the slogan 'Proletarians of Israel Unite!', in the Histadrut headquarters, because it had been stolen by the Manufacturers' Association of Israel. They, the capitalists, and not the workers, felt that they were the oppressed social class of Jewish Palestine.

In fact, even the most violent critics of the Histadrut recognize that without it the Jewish State and the Jewish economy would probably not have come into being.

The Histadrut took upon itself dangerous economic investments and industrial initiatives in the national interest that no private enterprise would or could have afforded. Because most of the economic development work of the Histadrut was done at the time of the British Mandate, which was indifferent to industrial expansion, the federation of trade unions took upon itself the burdens and responsibilities of a still non-existent national government. This was most evident in the case of the medical and social services of the trade unions (Kupat Holim) which continue, to this day, to provide the main social services for the population of the State of Israel.

But it was evident that, in the long run, the Histadrut would not have been able to face the contradiction implied by its monumental role as a socialist-capitalist two-headed Janus. I shall discuss this problem in a later chapter. Here I shall limit myself to a brief description of the organizational and personal links between the workers' organization, the workers' parties, and the Jewish Agency bureaucracy.[2]

The Histadrut was conceived as an open democratic organism to

[1] Quoted in Hertzberg, op. cit., p. 392.   [2] See also Eisenstadt, op. cit., pp. 40–1.

which every worker—including members of the liberal professions—could belong. At the top there is a General Council which elects an Executive Council. The candidates are elected on the basis of party lists (the parties fighting the elections inside each union) so that the distribution of the places at the top corresponds more or less to the effective strength of the various parties. Since 1930 Ben Gurion's new united party Mapai has been able to control without a break the majority of the Histadrut Executive Council seats although it never controlled more than 40 per cent of the country's votes.

The company which legally owned and in practice decided the entrepreneurial activities of the Histadrut was and still is a company called Hevrat Ovdim (Workers' Company), whose directors are appointed according to the relative strength of the various trade unions and parties. This means, in practice, that the majority party in the Histadrut could dispose of the tremendous purchasing, distribution, and investment powers of the socialist sector.

The party system was also the one by which Zionist bodies were controlled; in 1933 Ben Gurion's party canvassed 50 per cent of the total Zionist vote. It followed that during most of the time of the British Mandate, the socialist majority party, Mapai, controlled both the Zionist Organization (which meant the contacts with the Jewish pro-Zionist Diaspora and with the British through the Jewish Agency for Palestine) and the Histadrut. It was thus in a situation of a majority governmental party in spite of the non-existence of a Jewish government.

Their constant presence at the helm gave the workers' parties in Israel a sense of responsibility which was stronger than and sometimes even in conflict with their commitment to the interests of the working class. I shall underline here some of the main peculiarities of the Jewish workers' movement.

The first feature is that because the socialist parties were so strong and the capitalists so weak the communists were never important in Israeli politics. They were anti-Zionist, demanded a bi-nationalist state, and thus their programme was inconsistent with the whole national fabric of Jewish society. The communists never left the opposition and in the process became one of the most splintered communist parties of the world.[1]

A second unusual feature of Israeli socialism is that, because the workers' parties were for long periods (Mapai constantly) in power,

[1] There are today two communist parties in Israel: the Communist Party of Israel, founded in 1929 with one seat in parliament, and the New Communist List, mainly composed of Arab communists or Progressive Nationalists, with three seats in parliament.

their co-operation and disunity were subject more to personal than ideological animosity. The big issues debated by the Jewish workers, or on which unity broke from 1919 to 1965 were personal as well as ideological disputes. It took ten years, from 1919 to 1929, for Ben Gurion to unite 'Aḥdut Haavoda' (Unity of Labour Party), which he had formed soon after the war, and to come to an agreement with another organized group of Jewish labour, and a sprinkling of non-partisans to form Mapai, which has since dominated the political scene of the Yishuv and of Israel. But it has not remained united. In 1944 some members of Mapai broke away under the old name of Aḥdut Haavoda and in 1965 it was the turn of Ben Gurion himself to break from his own party, and form a new one, 'Rafi', not because of ideology, but because of his personal quarrel with Lavon. But the splinter groups had no greater stability. In 1948 Aḥdut Haavoda merged with a strong, left-wing collective pioneers' group, 'Hashomer Hatzair', and formed a new coalition of left-wing groups, Mapam (United Workers Party), only to break once more in 1954, when Aḥdut Haavoda became autonomous again, to rejoin Mapai in 1965, this time with another socialist 'prodigal son', Ben Gurion's Rafi—but without Ben Gurion, who insisted on representing Rafi by himself. This socialist 'musical chairs' is more apparent than real. The three main political sectors of Israel—the religious, the nationalist, and the socialist—have remained extraordinarily stable in their reciprocal control of the electorate. Important shifts of power are carried out within each sector, and not at the expense of a rival group outside the sector itself. This concentrates political life in Israel inside the party caucuses and makes election time very vocal, but real ideological differences are petrified to the point of monotony.

Elections are of course an important element in Jewish political life and one has to make distinctions between political groups according to official party labels and supporters. But the reason why this has never meant much to the remarkable political stability of the country is that political life has been dominated more by the necessity of constructing a State rather than by the different conceptions of how this State should be run.

Thus one must differentiate between two characteristic features of Jewish political organizations: they were all parties (i.e. vote-seekers) and movements (i.e. seekers of integrated and ideologically 'correct' ways of life) at the same time.[1] This meant, especially prior to the creation of the State of Israel, that the workers' parties—which were the strongest from the electoral point of view—were also the only ones

[1] See Leonard J. Fein, *Politics in Israel* (Boston, 1967), p. 68.

which could claim that they had the effective means to create the 'good' society. All the other political groups had ideas, ideologies, and a bureaucracy. Some of them even had paramilitary organizations, like the revisionist Beitar. But none, except the workers' parties, were able to build the very tissue of the Israeli society. This is what Ben Gurion meant when he proclaimed at the first Histadrut meeting, in 1920, that the new trade union federation was the class—the matrix—out of which the nation was to be born.

It is in the light of the confrontation of movements—not of parties—that one should look for some logic in the tangled thicket of the internal political struggle in pre-Israeli Palestine.

As I have already mentioned, Jewish political society was divided—and fundamentally still is—into three blocs: the socialist bloc, the religious bloc, and the 'national' bloc, which we shall call the 'étatist' bloc, not because of its desires to increase the control of the State over the country, but because its most distinctive characteristic is a passionate attachment to the idea of Jewish statehood, and to the good technical functioning of the State machinery, rather than to its moving ideologies. Each group has many party divisions and sub-divisions. But the compartmentalization of the Jewish electorate into three main blocs seems to be the chief explanation for the extraordinary stability of political life in Zionist society since the early twenties. The two political blocs in Jewish Palestine which competed for influence and power with the socialist bloc were the religious and the étatist-bourgeois-nationalist group.

In the religious sector of Jewish political life in Palestine, there were many groups and factions, the main line of division being the acceptance or the rejection of Zionism by Jewish Orthodoxy for the redemption of Israel. This was less a question of ideological choice than a search for a definition of nationhood. So far it has been easier for the religious Jews in Israel to define themselves in terms of what they refuse to see changed than in terms of what they want to add to a community which has switched from dispersion to national concentration. Jewish nationalism being equally rooted in the old religious tradition and in modern political ideology, the European distinction between Orthodoxy and secularism is misleading and one should perhaps speak of Judaist versus non-Judaist Jews.[1]

The concept of the Judaist Jew still remains very fluid.[2] On one side

[1] See Fein, op. cit., pp. 48 ff.
[2] See Aaron Antonovsky, 'Socio-Political Attitudes in Israel' (in Hebrew), *Amot*, vol. I, no. 6 (1963).

one finds the small, vocal, and relatively influential group of the 'Naturei Karta' (Defenders of the City), for whom the very existence of the State is an abomination. Then comes the 'Agudat Israel' (Association of Israel) Party, which remained outside Zionist politics till 1947 but joined on the eve of the War of Independence.[1] In doing so they forced the non-Judaist political groups in Palestine to maintain, after the creation of the State, the religious *status quo* which existed in Palestine under the British Mandate, and which gave the Judaist groups, especially in the municipal organizations, an influence superior to their numerical strength.

But it would be wrong to think that these concessions were extracted by the astute political manoeuvres of a minority group. Whatever the numerical strength of the Judaist Jews in non-Judaist Yishuv Palestine, no one contested the fact that they were truly representative of that body of national tradition in Judaism which had preserved Jewish identity and made Zionism possible. Paradoxically, the Judaist Jew is the only Zionist who remains so even when he declares himself anti-Zionist and fights the official Zionist institutions. Agudat Israel had always been deeply conscious of this and from it, it drew justification for participating in the government of the State. The party was founded in Poland in 1912. It established a 'workers' branch'—Poalei Agudat Israel—in 1924, whose primary objective was to counteract anti-religious sentiment among Polish workers.[2] The members of Poalei Agudat Israel were from the beginning more involved in social struggles, and gradually came to distinguish themselves from their parent party, Agudat, which remained a middle-class movement. The distinction, in action rather than in thought, grew up with the establishment in 1934 of the first rural settlement by Poalei Agudat Israel, which eventually created fifteen villages—collective and co-operative—and one agricultural school, taking full advantage, in this, of the facilities—money, land, organization—offered by the non-Judaist Zionist Organization. In politics, Poalei Agudat Israel participated in coalition governments even when Agudat Israel remained in opposition.

It was this kind of 'co-operation with reserve' which to some extent also characterized the Zionist religious parties. 'Mizrahi', which in Hebrew means 'oriental' but in fact is an acronym of *merkaz ruhani* (spiritual centre), was founded in 1902. With the development of Zionist youth movements after the First World War the workers'

---

[1] See Moshe Prager, *Beit Yaakov*, vol. v, no. 62/63 (1964), on the agreement signed on 19 June 1947 by Agudat Israel and the directorate of the Jewish Agency.

[2] Eisenstadt, op. cit., p. 291.

branch of Mizrahi, the Hapoel Hamizrahi, was founded in 1929 in conjunction with religious Zionist youth movements such as the 'Benei Akiva' (Sons of Akiva, the great rabbi who inspired the revolt of Bar Kochba in the second century) and 'Tora-ve-Avoda' (Law and Work, a slogan reminiscent of the medieval Benedictine motto: *Ora et Labora*). The aim of these religious movements for the young and the workers was 'to base the new Jewish society in Palestine on the laws of the Tora, united with a socialist approach to labour relations'.[1] The consequent involvement of the Judaist Zionists in the social and political activities of the Yishuv had two main feed-backs. It increased the tendency to compromise in the religious parties and at the same time decreased the influence of the more rigid Diaspora religious element over the Palestinian one—through the fact that the Judaists of the Diaspora obviously did not fulfil the supreme Jewish commandment to return and build the Land of Israel.

The influence of the Zionist parties of the Diaspora over the Palestinian Yishuv had in any case been declining since the First World War, long before the Nazi holocaust had destroyed Eastern European Jewry. The Mizrahi party was no exception[2] and the trend reached its logical conclusion in 1956 when the 'Mafdal' (National Religious Party) was created from the absorption of Mizrahi into the Hapoel Hamizrahi. At all periods, however, the moral weight of the religious groups was great —since, as already mentioned, religious tradition has been the guardian of Jewish national identity throughout the centuries. But the political and social weight of the religious bloc in pre-Israeli Palestine was limited. Most of its adherents were town-dwellers with very little active political cohesion among themselves and no interest or experience in the manipulation of political power—except for the safeguard of their religious rights. And these were far better guaranteed under the Mandate laws which identified the communities in Palestine with their religious affiliation.[3]

The position of the étatist sector was entirely different. It consisted of several groups, some interested only in the limited advantages of administrative manipulation of the instruments of power. But their adherents belonged mainly to the urban, small, and middle bourgeoisie. Without being ideologically anti-Marxist, they resented the workers' parties' supremacy, although never sufficiently to break away from them on the fundamental issue of the common drive to build a Jewish national home.

---

[1] ibid., p. 239.   [2] ibid., p. 42.
[3] See Moshe Burstein, *Self-Government of the Jews in Palestine since 1900* (Tel Aviv, 1934).

On the right of the étatist bloc, there was however a large organization —the Revisionist Movement—which seriously challenged the Socialist Zionist enterprise both ideologically and institutionally. If the Histadrut was the realization of Ben Gurion's idea of socialist Jewish statehood, the Revisionist movement represented an attempt to realize Vladimir Jabotinsky's idea of Jewish national statehood.

His greatest mistake was to forget that the Jews who were ready to carry out dull, day-to-day work in Palestine were not heroes in shining armour, but dedicated, stubborn, and ideologically conservative human beings overwhelmed by the human problems of personal survival. Jabotinsky was restless with them and was pushed by the realities of the situation more and more into the right-wing opposition. We have already mentioned the role of Jabotinsky in the creation of the Jewish Legion, the Beitar paramilitary movement, the Revisionist Party, and his break with the Zionist Organization in 1935.

The Revisionist Party was characterized not so much by its urban, bourgeois structure, which it had in common with other Zionist parties —for example, the Religious Zionists and the General Zionists—but by its opposition to the idea of Jewish nation-building through pioneering and colonization. Its youth organization, the Beitar (founded in Riga in 1923), was far more concerned with military organization and foreign policy than with social problems.

This opposition can be traced to the debates of the Fourteenth Zionist Congress held in Vienna in August 1925, when Revisionist and practical Zionism clashed over almost every point on the agenda. For the practical Zionists, headed by Weizmann, Palestine had to be taken 'as it was, with her dunes, her rocks, with her Arabs and with the Jews as they came'. All the rest was irrelevant and Zionism would 'stand or fall by our work and only by our work'.[1] For the Revisionist Jabotinsky the aim of Zionism was to achieve a Jewish majority in Palestine. To do so, 40,000 immigrants a year were required. Such an enterprise could not be carried out only by the enthusiasm of private individuals: without government there could be no state colonization. He asked the Congress to fight not for pioneerism but for land reserves, fiscal legisla-iton, and above all for Jewish military protection of the Zionist enterprise.[2] In theory he was probably right and the subsequent extraordinary development of the Zionist enterprise under the Government of the Jewish State proved it. In fact Ben Gurion, with all his hostility towards Jabotinsky's conception of 'étatism' became, after the establishment of

[1] Speech at the Fourteenth Zionist Congress, Vienna, quoted in Dante Lattes, *Il Sionismo*, vol. II, p. 269. [2] Lattes, op. cit., pp. 270-1.

the State of Israel, the main supporter of the idea of Jewish *mamlachtiut* (statehood). In a later chapter we shall see how this idea became, in the sixties, one of the issues of the 'Lavon affair'. But historically and socially Jabotinsky was not right, because a State is not created by laws or international agreements but by the people who make it and who express their will and abilities through hard daily work, not speeches. These Jews simply did not exist in Palestine in the twenties, and Weizmann recognized the fact. This was not perhaps very diplomatic on his part in view of Arab opposition and increasing British second thoughts on the Jewish national home. But neither Revisionist political logic, nor terrorism, nor elections brought the Revisionist movement and its successor in Israel, the Ḥerut Party, any nearer to power. It was to be the pathetic experience of the Zionist Right, which had proudly declared that it had been 'born for government', never to be admitted into any Jewish government until the 1967 June crisis, when only the Arab menace made their entry into a unified national government possible.

Of the other bourgeois parties the General Zionists were the oldest. The term 'general Zionist' was first used in 1907 without political connotations to denote all those Zionists—and they were the majority[1] —who attended the Congress without political affiliations.[2] But to be apolitical in a politically Messianic society like Zionist society, meant in fact a political choice. So the General Zionists became a party— 'Mifleget Hamerkaz' (Central Party)—and was soon considered by its opponents to be a right-wing, reactionary group. In fact its political support was essentially urban, its attempt to 'penetrate rural areas' weak, and its programme mainly a defence of private enterprise against government interference. The party was officially organized in 1931, not out of any ideological ideal, but as a reaction to the creation in 1930 of a powerful workers' party, Mapai, from several workers' parties. This betrayed the negative approach and policy of the General Zionists, and their new party showed all its organizational and ideological weakness when it proved to be unable to agree on any clear policy concerning the mass immigration of German Jews into Palestine after 1933. As a result, the General Zionists split into two factions, A and B, which were reunited in 1944 but never became a decisive force in Palestine because the majority of the urban, middle-class population never developed class consciousness. This middle class gave 85,000 votes to the General

---

[1] See Eisenstadt, op. cit., p. 42. The General Zionists held 73 per cent of the seats in the 1923 Zionist Congress, 57 per cent in the 1931 Congress, and only 44 per cent in 1933.

[2] See Moshe Kleinman, *Haziyonim Haklaliyim* (The General Zionists), Jerusalem, 1945.

Zionists in 1950 when it felt endangered by what seemed to be socialist despotism but soon switched its preference to the Herut Party, which had a more militant anti-socialist policy. Eventually the General Zionists combined with the small German immigrants' Progressive Party to form the Liberal Party. In 1965 the Liberal Party combined with the Herut Party in an electoral alliance called 'Gahal' (Liberal Herut Bloc).[1] The Progressive Party was formed in 1948 from the union of two middle-class pioneering Zionist groups, mainly from Germany, 'Haoved Hatzioni' (Zionist Worker) and 'Aliah Hadasha' (The New Immigration). The Progressive Party was the only non-Messianic party of the Yishuv, seeking a middle way between old British liberalism, socialism, and Zionist Messianism. It was mainly interested in the organization of the administration and played an important role in the fight against the politicization of the bureaucracy.[2]

On the whole, however, because of the lack of organized participation of the Zionist bourgeoisie—secular or religious—in the colonization of Palestine the Jewish community of Palestine grew to political responsibility and statehood mainly around the complex institutions which Zionism and socialism had brought into existence. It was a strange combination of outdated ideologies, stern local economic and military realities, and acid parochial and personal recriminations. These factors alone would have been sufficient to twist and stretch ideas, principles, tactics, and values to breaking-point. But the fate of the Jewish national home was further complicated by the fact that it did not unfold in a political vacuum, accessible only to the logic of Zionism. It developed in one of the most critical regions of the world, in an area singled out by history and religion, in which the Jews were now confronting the British and the Arabs over the most difficult problem imaginable: the evolution of a persecuted religious minority into a sovereign State.

Referring to this evolution, Arthur Koestler wrote: 'Judaism is a freak of history'.[3] And a Jewish freak, even if supported by the strongest ideological passions and historical claims, could hardly be more intelligible and acceptable to the British and the Arabs than to the majority of the Jews who, to this very day, have neither become Zionist nor Israeli.

·   ·   ·

[1] See Joseph Badi, *The Government of the State of Israel. A Critical Account of its Parliament, Executive, and Judiciary* (New York, 1963), pp. 51–6.
[2] ibid., p. 50.
[3] Arthur Koestler, *Promise and Fulfilment, Palestine 1917–1949* (London, 1949), p. 3.

The problem of reciprocal understanding, the problem of communication, was and still is today the most difficult problem in the whole Palestine question. I shall try to describe briefly the extraordinary psychological climate in which the three communities of Palestine—the British, the Arab, and the Jewish—nervously coexisted during the thirty years of the Mandate.

It was a climate of passion and distrust, of hope and frustration, of world-wide political strategies and Machiavellian tactics to undermine each other's positions. It was a climate of social and political neurosis by which men and institutions could not fail to be influenced and often contaminated; in which people met, regardless of their national alliances, quite freely during the day, in buses, offices, markets, and places of work, and at night took pot-shots at each other. A climate of passion and devotion—religious, ideological, national, and even cultural, in which men opposed and mistrusted, rather than hated, one another. But it was also a climate in which men and women felt the caress of history in their daily lives and a direct relationship with the glories of Christendom, Judaism, and Islam. It was a climate of ready acceptance of hardship which the perpetual blue skies, the brilliant nights over the desert, the horrors of the old, eroded stones, and the sound of the wind through the newly planted arbours made worth while for people to live in—and to die for. In such a climate, could relations between the three communities have been different?

British–Zionist relations certainly could have been different if the Jewish national home had become part of the British Middle Eastern imperial interests and policies. By the end of the First World War the idea of a great Arab pro-British Empire was not, after all, less far-fetched than the idea of a Jewish State.

The British candidate for head of the Arab Kingdom, Hussein, the Sherif of Mecca, was a local chieftain without authority in the Arab world, soon to be dispossessed of the little political hold he had in his own Arab sheikdom of Mecca and Medina by another local bedouin leader, Ibn Saud. In 1924 Hussein had antagonized the British so much, that they refused to take sides in the mounting quarrel between him and Abdul Aziz Ibn Saud, the Wahabi leader of the barren Nejd of Arabia. When, in the wake of the Turkish abolition of the Caliphate in March 1924, Hussein proclaimed himself Caliph of all Islam, his claim was disputed by Saud, who conquered Mecca and expelled its ruler to end his days in Cyprus. As for the sons of Hussein, Feisal, leader of the Arab revolt, was without doubt an outstanding and accepted Arab leader, but his authority outside Arabia was disputed. When he tried to negotiate with the French for a political compromise over Syria, he was soon to fall out with some important members of the Damascus Arab Congress, who called him a traitor.[1] Feisal, of course, remained the hero of the national revolt, in the eyes of the Arabs, but it was only with the help of the British that he managed to impose his authority on the recalcitrant cities of Mesopotamia, which became the Kingdom of Iraq under him in 1924.

If, in spite of criticism and regional antagonism, the popularity of King Feisal remained untarnished, tension between the Hashemite dynasty and the nationalists (including the separatist Kurds) remained a permanent feature of Iraqi policy. The conflict between dynasty and people became absolute after 1955, with Nasser gaining the enthusiasm of the masses for his policy of rejection of any pact with the Western powers. The tragic fate of the Iraqi dynasty and of the Nuri Said government in 1958 is well known.

The other branch of the Sherif family, whom the British helped to govern first Transjordan and then Jordan, had no better luck. Abdullah, Feisal's brother, another leader of the Arab Revolt, was murdered by a Palestinian nationalist in Jerusalem in 1951. His son Talal went mad and his grandson, Hussein, is by his own admission the most threatened monarch in modern times.[2]

Thus the British dream of governing a united Middle East through a number of moderate Arab kings of their choice turned out to be at least as impractical as the idea of having a Jewish national home in Arab Palestine. The great difference, however, was that at the time, the number of English people who believed in the possibility of a pro-British monarchic Middle East was much greater than the number of those who believed in the realization of a pro-British Jewish State in Palestine.

One of the latter was Colonel Richard Meinertzhagen, who held a prominent position as Chief Political Officer for Palestine and Syria on General Allenby's staff; another was Wyndham Deedes. At least one Zionist leader, Jabotinsky, considered Meinertzhagen's role to have been decisive in 1919–20 in balancing British anti-Zionist influences in Palestine at that time. And, if we are to believe Meinertzhagen himself and his diaries, he even tried to make the idea of a Jewish State consonant with British imperial strategy in the Middle East.

On 25 March 1919 he was invited to lunch by the British Premier Lloyd George (to whom he was attached as a Middle East expert at the Versailles Peace Conference) and asked to prepare a memorandum on

[1] Zeine N. Zeine, op. cit., pp. 130–1.   [2] See *Uneasy Lies the Head.*

the future of Sinai. The answer had a streak of prophecy in it and claimed, among other things, that the Peace Conference would be laying two very dangerous eggs: Jewish nationalism and Arab nationalism.

In 50 years' time, both Jews and Arabs will be obsessed with their nationalism ... A National Home for the Jews must develop sooner or later into sovereignty; Arab nationalism will also develop into sovereignty from Mesopotamia to Morocco. Jewish and Arab sovereignty will clash. The Jews, if the immigration programme succeeds, must expand and that can be accomplished only at the expense of the Arab who will do his utmost to check the growth and power of a Jewish Palestine. This means bloodshed. The British position in the Middle East is paramount; the force of nationalism will challenge our position ... With Jewish and Arab nationalism developing into sovereignty and with the loss of the Canal in 1960 (only 47 years hence) we stand a good chance of losing our position in the Middle East ... Previous to 1906 the Turkish–Egyptian frontier ran from Rafa in the north to the neighbourhood of Suez ... In October 1906, Egypt was granted *administrative rights* [my italics] in Sinai up to a line drawn from Rafa to the head of the Gulf of Akkaba, Turkey expressly retaining the *right of sovereignty*.[1]

Meinertzhagen thus proposed to the British Premier to annex Sinai in order to create a buffer zone between Palestine and Egypt; to give Britain 'a strong foothold in the Middle East with access to both the Mediterranean and the Red Sea'; to create a strategic base and 'with Jewish consent the best harbour in the Mediterranean' in Haifa.[2]

The plan was rejected because President Wilson did not like the idea of British annexation of any territory, even uninhabited. But the main objection came from Meinertzhagen's colleagues in the British Intelligence Service in the Middle East, who fought tooth and nail for their dream of Arab independence under the British, an invisible British empire in the East.

From the moment the Jews failed to claim a place in British imperial strategic considerations, a Jewish national home was only a nuisance as far as Britain was concerned. But back in 1919 no one in London had been able to estimate how much of a nuisance, since very few people believed that a Jewish State could, in fact, come into being.

The British were not the only ones to think that the idea of Jewish political independence was wishful thinking and that the most the Jews could achieve in Palestine was the creation of a community chiefly concerned with the spiritual, religious, and cultural revival of Judaism in the land of its birth.

[1] Col. R. Meinertzhagen, *Middle East Diary, 1917–1956* (London, 1959), pp. 18–19.
[2] ibid.

On the whole, the Jews were even more sceptical than the British about the future of Zionism. This could be seen in the objections which leading British (and later French) Jews raised against having the concept of Jewish sovereignty mentioned in the Balfour Declaration and in the Palestine Mandate—as well as in the status of the Jewish Legion. The official version in the letter dispatched by Balfour to Lord Rothschild only spoke of a vague national home, leaving its meaning open to all possible interpretations. The opposition of French Jewry to Zionism was even stronger.[1]

The doubts about the feasibility of a Jewish State in Palestine were not only common among the Jews of the Diaspora. Even among the population of Palestine one could find groups violently opposed to the idea of Jewish independence. There were, first of all, the Orthodox groups (of some of which, such as the Naturei Karta, we have already spoken). Then there were the liberals, people like the philosopher Martin Buber, the American-born rector of the Hebrew University, Judah L. Magnes, and Professor S. H. Bergman, who worked desperately for Jewish–Arab co-operation on the basis of moral and human understanding. Their organization, 'Brit Shalom', later the 'Ihud' (Union), was small but influential and highly critical of the policies of the Zionist Organization.[2] It never achieved any positive result either on the Jewish or the Arab side, but it at least kept alive the opposition to a purely Jewish State.

More important, however, was the opposition to Jewish national independence from the Left. Communists and Marxist radicals, like the members of Hashomer Hatzair, fought not only the idea of a Jewish State, but even the idea of Jewish independence. Hashomer Hatzair (The Young Watchman) was an interesting example of a highly ideological and socially self-defeating Zionist group. It was the oldest Zionist youth organization, created in Poland in 1913 as a radical scouts' group. It was the Jewish version of the German *Wandervögel* youth organization of 1901 and of the older (1897) 'Narodnaya Volya' Russian socialist agrarian revolutionary movement. It was imbued with a spirit of revolt against society, against symbols of accepted authority, and with a passionate hope for the rejuvenation of society through youth. The social origins of its members were, and still remain in present-day Israel, middle-class with a large percentage of members coming from broken homes and for whom 'the atmosphere of this ideo-

---

[1] See Leonard Stein, op. cit., pp. 484–501, 526–9; Weizmann, op. cit., pp. 204–5.
[2] See Judah L. Magnes and Martin Buber, *Arab-Jewish Unity. Testimony Before the Anglo-American Inquiry Commission for the Ihud (Union) Association* (London, 1947).

logically intensive movement and the thorough and efficient organization of its members' life appear to be a substitute for a stable home life.'[1] From all this stemmed a consistent, sometimes almost pathological hostility to any political and psychological identity with the values and symbols of religion, nationalism, and the Establishment. The theoretical programme of the movement was laid down at a conference in 1924 in Danzig and carried out by its members after the movement was revived in Palestine from 1929 onwards. Chaim Brenner, the anarchist secularist and immensely gifted novelist who was killed in the disturbances of that year in Jaffa (see page 39), had a great influence on them. But their strength within the Zionist movement came, in spite of their small number, more from their psychological approach than from their ideological convictions. They were the real heirs, in Palestine, of that Russian intellectual movement of the beginning of the twentieth century in which 'the essential thing was to offer oneself without calculation, to give all one has for the sake of the light within (whatever it may illuminate) from pure motives. For only ideas count.'[2] And this was also their greatest political and moral weakness. Because in the inevitable intellectual segregation of a colonial community of farmers, even a collective and socialist one, their ideas were never confronted with a real challenge from other equally powerful ideas, local or imported. And so, like many Russian intellectuals at the turn of the century, the members of the Hashomer Hatzair often became obsessed with their own ideas simply for the lack of others to satisfy their intellectual needs. For them the idea of a national Jewish State which was not communist was as revolting as was the idea of a Jewish State not created by divine intervention for the Orthodox Jews. They demanded a Jewish–Arab bi-national State and they knew that this really meant no State at all. In 1942 some kibbutzim had second thoughts even about raising the national blue-and-white Zionist flag and insisted that only the red flag could symbolize their political allegiance. Such an attitude was by no means general, but it was a significant one. There was also strong opposition to the singing of the Jewish national anthem, 'Hatikvah', and violent discussions about the 'nationalistic' content of the Jewish workers' song 'Tehezakna Yadenu' ('May Our Hand be Strengthened'). In fact, some people believed that only the 'Internationale' was the proper musical expression of faith in Palestine.

The left-wing opposition to an independent State had been apparent in the socialist camp since 1937. The members of the socialist parties

[1] Eisenstadt, op. cit., pp. 238, 242.
[2] Isaiah Berlin, 'A Marvellous Decade', *Encounter*, June 1955.

were divided according to three different types of political strategy. Ben Gurion wanted a Jewish State, even if only in part of Palestine and even if it had to be a 'capitalist' one. Berl Katzenelson, the Mapai's ideologue, wanted a prolongation of the Mandate, by an international authority if not by Britain, because he thought that the Yishuv was not yet ready for independence. Finally, there was Itzchak Tabenkin, the ideologue of the Kibbutz Meuḥad movement, who wanted independence, but only for a State firmly ruled by the collective movement. He believed that building the kibbutz society, not political independence, was the aim of Zionism. He had criticized Ben Gurion in 1935 for coming to an agreement with the Revisionists to share with them the immigration permits granted yearly by the British authorities to the Jewish Agency. He rejected equally the idea for the partition of Palestine advanced by the Peel Commission, as he thought that the proposed Jewish State would be 'Tel Aviv's State', namely a bourgeois, urban State, not a kibbutz State. He advocated instead a 'last frontier concept [of independence] whereby the size of the future State would be determined entirely by the scope of a border settlement and not by political bargaining'.[1]

When Ben Gurion succeeded in getting unanimous backing from the 600 Zionist delegates gathered at the Biltmore Hotel in New York for unlimited immigration into Palestine and for the creation of a 'Jewish Commonwealth', once the war was over, the most radical elements of the Mapai decided to break away. The so-called 'B' faction seceded under the leadership of Tabenkin and took with it many of the kibbutzim and the great majority of the commanders of the Hagana's shock troops. Politically, the break has not been mended to this day and it has produced some extraordinary evolutions on the Zionist Left. They are mainly identified with the political and organizational vicissitudes of Mapam.

Historically, this party came into being in 1948, from the union of Hashomer Hatzair, the Aḥdut Haavoda dissidents from Mapai (because of the 1942 declaration in favour of the creation of a Jewish national State), and the left-wing group of the old Poalei Zion Party (Poalei Zion Left) which had broken with the parent party after the Russian October Revolution. Poalei Zion Left championed close cooperation with Russia and pushed their internationalist approach to the point of preferring Yiddish to Hebrew. (Paradoxically, but psycho-

---

[1] Declaration adopted by the Extraordinary Zionist Conference, 'The Extraordinary Zionist Conference of the American Emergency Committee for Zionist Affairs, Stenographic Protocol', New York, 9–11 May 1942, pp. 480–3.

logically understandable, this was also the linguistic policy of the most Orthodox religious groups.)

The union was, however, a short-lived one. In the wake of open Soviet hostility towards Israel and Zionism at the beginning of the 1950s, Mapam disintegrated. Some of its members joined the Communist Party, others went back to Mapai, and the Poalei Zion–Aḥdut Haavoda became again an autonomous political group. In 1968 they merged with Mapai. So did Mapam in 1969, after having led a politically schizophrenic life for fifteen years relying almost exclusively on the Hashomer Hatzair group which threw away many of its anti-nationalistic objections after the 1967 war. Politically and ideologically speaking the whole of the Mapam operation amounted to a *Brothers Karamazov*-like political drama, passionately enacted in the tea-cup of colonial Israeli political society. However, militarily speaking it was a momentous decision which, during the War of Independence, twice brought the Jewish community of Palestine to the brink of armed rebellion, as I shall show later.

Curiously enough, the left-wing radicals, who were, of course, pro-Russian, anti-capitalist, and anti-British, were indirectly supported in their opposition to Jewish national independence by the most authoritative leaders of the Zionist Organization. Dr. Chaim Weizmann, the future first President of Israel, was very anxious not to break away prematurely from the British Empire, on which, he believed, the future of the national home still depended to a large extent. This attitude was not new in Zionist political thought. Max Nordau, Herzl's great disciple, believed that a Jewish State should also be an outpost of European influence in the Middle East.

Weizmann's loyalty to Britain was the main source of friction between him and Ben Gurion and led to furious internal squabbles within the Zionist movement, and in the Mapai leadership.

Historically, this was to be the first of the many disagreements between the believers in the 'civilizing mission' of European imperialism and opponents of colonialism in the period after the Second World War which preceded the granting of independence to colonies in French Africa. There is much more in common between Dr. Weizmann's attitude to Britain and that of Ivory Coast President Houphouet-Boigny, who stubbornly fought to keep his country within the French Union, than would appear at first sight. It is also a proof of how anglicized the leadership of the Zionist movement had become since the issue of the Balfour Declaration. We are told how Ben Gurion never forgave Weizmann for having agreed to the British idea of a 'temporary' halt to Jewish immigration to Palestine in 1936, in order to help England to overcome the Arab rebellion in Palestine.[1] True or not, it is certain that Ben Gurion fought bitterly against Weizmann in 1942 to have his idea of an independent Jewish Commonwealth pursued by the Zionist Organization, in the middle of the War. His success was considered by the Palestinian Zionists to be a slap in the face for the continued official British opposition to any form of Jewish independence after the War. And it also marked a momentous change in the political geography of the Zionist movement.

Until 1942 the British Zionist Organization was the most influential Zionist political group in the world. After that date the centre of Jewish policy switched to America. One of the political merits of Ben Gurion was to have understood as early as 1942 that European Jewry was doomed, that Britain was losing her grip on her overseas empire, that America—traditionally opposed to British colonialism—was becoming the new leader of the world, and that New York and Washington—not Warsaw and London—were the new centres of vital importance for the future of Jewish independence.

Such were the divided feelings among the Jews and the Zionists about the future of their national enterprise, that it is not surprising that many British officials and politicians dismissed or underestimated the potential of Jewish nationalism and became increasingly impatient with what they considered to be the impossible British policy towards Palestine and its Jewish national home.

The British Mandate officials were not anti-Jewish, although a growing trend towards antisemitism could be found in the lower echelons of the Palestine security forces and among many British officials' wives. But they were deeply disturbed and irritated by the incongruity and hesitations of a British policy in Palestine, which, as the Peel Commission's report had indicated, left unsolved the main political (and for many British also the moral) question of whether and for how long Britain should help the Jews to become a majority in Arab Palestine. They might have understood a clear-cut policy in favour of the creation of a Jewish State conceived as a pro-British Jewish military base, helping to guard the vital road to India and to create an alternative to the Suez Canal. That would have made sense. But to be bound by an international treaty to co-operate with a 'Jewish Agency' for the creation of a national home which nobody, even the Zionists, could define, was more than they could take. The British administration in Palestine

[1] See Michael Bar-Zohar, *The Armed Prophet. A Biography of Ben Gurion* (London, 1967), pp. 57-8.

resented the confused policy of the London Government and they vented their resentment on the Jews, who were the cause of it, and, on top of that, such a political and social nuisance as well.

To many British officials who did not speak Hebrew, who knew little about the Jews, and who were totally unfamiliar with the society of Eastern Europe from which most of the Jews of Palestine had come,[1] the Zionists appeared quite impossible; Koestler has described vividly the British resentment towards the Jews for their 'lack of manners', for their 'insolent pretension' to teach the British both their colonial history and their Christian religious morals.[2]

The British administrators knew how to rule natives, how to train colonial troops, how to build roads, how to impose British justice and taxes. But to build a Jewish national home, with the 'co-operation' of Russian and Polish Jews, who believed in the redeeming powers of socialist Messianism and Tolstoyan Utopianism, was too much for them. The idea must have been anathema to the most unpopular of the British High Commissioners of Palestine, H. McMichael, a nephew of that paladin of British imperialism, Lord Curzon, imbued as he was with the ideals and prejudices of the British colonial role, and probably without any of the qualities needed to cope with difficult political situations. It did not help matters that many leading British officials in Palestine considered themselves members of the great orientalist family of British political specialists in the Middle East. Many Zionists even suspected the first Jewish High Commissioner, Lord Samuel, of being a crypto-Arab-sympathizer. That there was some truth in their allegations is borne out by statements made by people like Ronald Storrs, the first British Governor of Jerusalem, who cried: 'Tramways in Jerusalem? Never.' But what made the Zionists difficult for the local British officials to bear was the contrast they made with the Arabs.

On the one hand, the British saw a bunch of agitated Utopians; on the other, vast crowds of calm, proud, dignified traditionalists. On the one hand they were confronted with continuous demands for change, with acid but often unjust criticism, with boring and irritating moral arguments. On the other they met with outward appreciation, respect, and understanding, especially from the pro-British Arab notables. The Jews were garrulous, over-educated, and lacking in charm and manners. The Arabs were perhaps pompous, mainly illiterate (as colonial natives should be), and gracefully mannered. Thus the British lived in a state of perpetual psychological defence where the Zionists were concerned;

[1] Burstein, op. cit., pp. 13–17.　　　　[2] Koestler, op. cit., pp. 12–15.

they felt at ease and superior with the Arabs. Arab–Jewish relations were less complicated but equally negative.

The two communities had reciprocal, clear-cut reasons for their feelings of hostility, which made theoretical justification of the fighting and the hating easier. Both were bent on proving their political and historical rights to the same land, with contradictory statements that were very similar in nature and sources. There was an almost complete lack of communication between them.

The Jews had bad communications with the British, but at least there was communication. With the Arabs, with the exception of some economic contacts in the cities and between 'experts', life went on as though the communities lived on two different planets. The Jews dressed, ate, spoke, behaved differently from the Arabs. Their conception of society, honour, feminine beauty, music, and the very meaning of life was different. It was not a question of a European dislike for oriental life, as has been so often intimated. It was something very different and perhaps more dangerous: it was indifference.

The Jews built their society as if the Arabs did not exist. This was probably the only way of doing it, since only the total concentration of the whole Jewish community on Jewish national tasks could achieve some measure of success. The Sephardi Jews of Palestine, whom I have already mentioned, had never been able to create anything comparable to the Zionist realization of a Jewish national home, probably because of their assimilation into the Arab way of life and society. And their dwindling political role in Zionist Palestine made co-operation with the Arabs even more difficult.

In spite of several sincere Jewish efforts to come to a mutual understanding, such as the negotiations with Arab moderates in 1934,[1] the gulf between the two communities remained unbridged. The very limited appeal which programmes of co-operation—such as the one proposed by Martin Buber—had on the Arab and Jewish communities was a proof of the impossibility of establishing fruitful relations between the two communities rather than of the contrary.

The depth of the conflict could be measured by the opposing statements made by Jewish and Arab leaders in front of the Anglo-American Commission for Palestine in 1946 and the United Nations Commission in 1947.

The Zionist leaders proved—figures at hand—the considerable advantages which the Arab community had gained from the Jewish immigration. Before the arrival of the Jews, they said the price of a

<hr />

[1] Bar-Zohar, op. cit., p. 54.

dunum (one-tenth of a hectare) of land varied between £5 and £15. It had risen to an average of £80 in 1944. After centuries of stagnation, the Arab population of Palestine had grown from 600,000 souls in 1922 to 1,200,000 in 1944. This was not only due to the improved health conditions brought about by the Jewish medical work but also to a considerable immigration of Arabs into Palestine from nearby territories, mostly seasonal but some permanent. This was what the Jews believed, anyway, and what the British constantly denied—both being aware of the difficulties of checking population movements along frontiers which, like so many colonial boundaries, were a recent product of the new European administration in the former Ottoman Middle East. They were attracted by higher wages, better social conditions, and better opportunities created by Jewish investments and initiative. In fact, during the same period, the population of Egypt had grown by only 25 per cent and in Iraq the average salary of an Arab labourer was one shilling per day, compared with an average of five to twelve shillings in Palestine. The British authorities had done little, said the Jews, to help bring about such a state of affairs. The budget of the Mandatory administration was financed 70 per cent by Jewish taxpayers, who formed less than half of the population, and 30 per cent by Arab taxpayers. But the Arabs got more than 80 per cent of the budget expenditure, especially in the fields of education and health. This meant that the Jews were in fact paying for the Arabs' social improvements and providing most of the Palestine Government's revenues, which had increased by 100 per cent in eight years, from 1931 to 1938: a unique example of economic progress in the British Empire.

On top of this, the Jewish Community claimed to have spent a lot of money on providing non-governmental social services which indirectly benefited the Arab population as well. In the year 1934–5 the Jewish Agency spent £350,000 in medical services, while the Mandatory administration spent for the whole population £166,000. From 1922 to 1935 the Jews spent £403,000 on fighting malaria and draining the swamps. The Mandatory administration spent in the same period and for the same purposes only £85,000; the Arab community, as a community, nothing.[1]

The Jewish contribution to the development of Palestine and to the welfare of its Arab inhabitants was so evident that all the British Royal Commissions sent to Palestine to investigate the tension between the two communities were forced to recognize it. But it was one of the points of the debate which enraged the Arabs most.

[1] *Palestine Royal Commission Report*, pp. 230 ff.

The Secretary-General of the Arab League, Azzam Pasha, is on record as having declared in front of the Anglo-American Commission in 1946:

The Zionists . . . claim to have a special civilising mission to accomplish, through which they introduce elements of progress into a backward region. But this has always been the contention of the nations which wanted to colonize and dominate. . . . The Arab answer to it is simply 'NO'. We are not a nation of reactionaries, we are not a backward people. Even if we were a bunch of total ignoramuses, the difference between ignorance and knowledge is a question of ten years of schooling. We exist. We are reviving our nation. We are giving birth to as many children as any nation. We have brains. We have a great heritage of civilisation and of spiritual life. We are not going to be dominated either by great nations or by small ones, nor by dispersed nations.[1]

The dichotomy could not have been greater. The fact that the Jews were not supported by any European State, and often hindered in their efforts by the British administration, made Arab understanding of their frantic efforts for physical survival more difficult. Looking at the Zionist enterprise from without, the Arabs saw a well-oiled, foreign steamroller moving towards them. They did not want to come into contact with this 'invader' and they had no interest in its way of life. They transformed the complicated Jewish and Zionist motivations and problems into a simple confrontation of historical rights in which everything was to be either black or white (and decided by an imaginary international court of justice) according to a logic which did not take into consideration either the forces of hope and despair which were driving the Jews on, or the political and moral weaknesses on the British and Arab sides. What confronted the Arabs in Palestine was not, in the last resort, a powerful, internationally supported, aggressive Jewish colonial movement, but a mixture of strength and despair with which the Arabs were not able or prepared to compromise. There were moments in which Jews were so desperate about their situation and the situation of the Jews of Europe, that they were quite ready to jeopardize their political future for the sake of saving the lives of some of their brethren in Europe. In 1937 they were prepared to accept the Peel partition plan which would have made Israel a small part of Palestine.[2] In 1946 even the extremist terrorist movements in Palestine declared themselves ready to stop their activities if Britain would allow the immediate immigration of 100,000 Jewish refugees, as the American Government recommended. Arab and British intransigence prevented this happen-

[1] Quoted in Koestler, op. cit., p. 33.   [2] Weizmann, op. cit., pp. 473-6.

ing, although it is difficult to put all the blame on the Arab leaders. After all, they were following the example of all the nations of the world (with the exception of Guatemala), which decided in 1940 to refuse admittance of Jewish refugees into their territories.[1] But the refusal of the Arabs to allow more Jews to immigrate into Palestine was motivated by a tangle of different reasons.

Basically, the Western world—the United States included—rejected the pleas of Jewish immigration into their territories because of anti-semitism, derived partly from ancient antagonism between Church and Synagogue, partly from the more recent hostility of Western middle classes towards Jewish immigrants who could be absorbed only by the middle classes of Europe and America.[2]

The Arabs, for their part, had no feeling of religious antagonism towards the Jews. They did not oppose the Zionists on grounds of class, since the Zionists wanted to create a 'normal' Jewish society in Palestine, with workers, farmers, and a limited middle class. Thus Arab resistance to the Jews came not specifically from Arab workers nor peasants who might have feared Jewish competition, nor from the Arab entrepreneurial class, although professional hostility and fears of economic displacement were certainly felt by all these groups. It came, rather, from a combination of ideological and psychological resistance by the Arab masses, bourgeoisie, and aristocracy to the general social and political change brought about by the Jews; a change about which little was or could have been done, in spite of good intentions, to dispel the Arabs' deep-rooted fear of having one day to face a new political and social situation foreign to them and in which they would play a second-ary role, if any.

Palestine was, from all points of view, an integral part of the Arab world, and more particularly of Southern Syria. It had never, unless in the periods in which it lived under Jewish or the Crusaders' control, had a history or a political personality of its own. Its population was closely related by ethnic origin, culture, religion, history, and language to the rest of the Arab Middle East. In 1946 the non-Jewish population consisted of about 1,200,000 people, of whom just over a million were Moslem, 66,000 bedouins, and 145,000 mostly urbanized Christians; 65 per cent of the non-Jewish population were farmers, 20 per cent formed the middle class, and about 15 per cent the upper crust.[3] This

[1] A. Tartakower and K. R. Grossmann, *The Jewish Refugee* (New York, 1944).
[2] Sir John Hope Simpson, *The Refugee Problem: Report of a Survey* (London, 1939), pp. 536 ff.
[3] Rony E. Gabbay, *A Political Study of the Arab-Jewish Conflict: The Arab Refugee Problem (A Case Study)* (Geneva, 1959).

statistical break-down does not, however, give a clear idea of the real political and social implications.

The vast majority of the Moslem population, with the exception of the Moslem urban proletariat, consisted of farmers with little or no land of their own. It has been shown how their resentment against the Jews had arisen, well before the establishment of the Jewish national home, from the fact that they often found themselves dispossessed by the sale of the land on which they lived (but did not own) to the Jews, with little or no compensation from their Arab landlords.[1] Furthermore, they belonged to a traditional society opposed to rapid modernization, compact behind its religious and family leaders, and fearful of change and innovation, especially when brought by foreigners, as in the case of the European Jews. Hostile feelings towards Zionism could, therefore, easily be kindled in their minds, for reasons independent of direct economic or social competition with the Jews.

It was the urban upper class which held the power in Arab Palestine. This was not a unified social group and its prominent families, the Husseinis, the Dajanis, the Khalidis, the Nashashibis, the Abdul Hadis, were urban, often non-resident in Palestine, and drew most of their income from land and real estate. There was bitter opposition and rivalry between them. For some of them Jewish immigration started an unexpected economic boom while the economic preoccupations of the Arab landed gentry had been evident since the time of the Paris peace negotiations over the future of the British Mandate in Palestine. The Italian delegate to the Versailles Conference, Count Theodoli, was closely connected with the Sursuk family, the big landowners of north Palestine, and was influenced more by his family connections than by his Government's instructions in his diplomatic attitude to the problem of the embodiment of the idea of the 'Jewish national home' in the British Mandate over Palestine.[2]

The Arab landed gentry was also the undisputed political monopolizer of Palestine Arab politics. As such, it could not fail to be involved in the general struggle of the Arabs for political independence, a struggle which in Palestine was more acute than elsewhere in the British-controlled Middle East because of the Zionist presence.

[1] Mandel, op. cit., p. 84; Gabbay, op. cit., p. 27. The Arab claim of Arab farmers' dispossession by the Jews was proved largely exaggerated when a 'Register of Landless Arabs' was opened by the Mandatory Government in 1931, with only 664 applications recognized as valid out of 3,271 submitted. See *A Survey of Palestine*, prepared in December 1945 and January 1946 for the information of the Anglo-American Commission of Inquiry, 2 vols. (Jerusalem, 1946), pp. 295–6.

[2] Weizmann, op. cit., pp. 457–8.

Arab political leadership in Palestine was also hampered by the fact that some of the leaders shared the economic advantages of Zionist colonization and yet were forced to fight it for political, social, and psychological reasons. It had also to face internal contradictions and the political competition of an urban Arab bourgeoisie, which, in many Middle Eastern countries under Turkish rule, had experienced long-standing competition with merchants of the Jewish minority.

The Jews were quick to discern the advantages offered by the Mandate's administrative law concerning the organization of religious communities. The 'Knesset Israel' (Community of Israel) and its institutions became the cradle of Jewish democracy quite apart and independently from the religious feelings of its members.

The same opportunity was of course open to the Arabs. But they never made any serious attempt to build on it. Many of the Palestinian politicians regarded themselves as part of the general movement of Syrian Arabs politically bound to the old Damascus Arab Congress's opposition to the League of Nations' mandates and paid dearly for their faith in a Greater Syria. To these politicians, the idea of a separate Palestinian community meant little or nothing, and seemed a disguised acceptance of the disruptive British imperial policy. Arab politicians finally organized themselves into an Arab Congress of Palestine in 1928. But the activities of the Congress were constantly hindered by rivalry between the leading Palestinian families.[1]

The Jews on the other hand, had political parties organized on a solid ideological and national basis, well integrated with the other national institutions and disposing of an effective control over the population; they showed, in spite of their political divisions, a deep sense of national responsibility.

The Arab parties were all blown-up family affairs, without real roots in the population of Palestine, each one concealing behind some pompous name the rather shaky loyalty of its own clannish clientele.[2] Internal Arab politics were often carried out with the same ruthlessness that the Arabs used against the Jews and using the same armed bands of 'patriots'. The period of the Arab insurrection against the British administration and against Zionism (1935–9) was also a period of bloody quarrel between the Husseinis, and their pro-German leader, the Great Mufti of Jerusalem, Haj Amin el Husseini, and another leading family, the Nashashibis, an aristocratic and pro-British family of Jerusalem.

More important, however, was the fact that the Jews built up, in their

[1] Gabbay, op. cit., pp. 15–17.   [2] ibid., pp. 21–2.

almost total psychological, economic, political, and cultural isolation, a social tissue of great human and moral strength. Because they realized how weak and how dependent on themselves they were, the Zionists created a community which, in spite of its internal divisions, had a consistency in its aims, undisputed social equality, and a deep sense of political responsibility, devotion, and efficiency. Because they were few, the Jews had to be and behave as an *élite*. Because they were 'stranded' in the Middle East they had to be united. Because they had no political protection from any State or government in the world, they had to develop their own protective system.

The opposite was true of the Palestinian Arabs. Because there were many of them, they never cared much for their inner social strength. Because they thought constantly in terms of Arabism and never in terms of Palestine, they relied too much on the political and military help of other independent Arab States which finally proved to be less efficient and less interested in Palestine than the Palestinians hoped it would be.

Few of the Arab political meetings over Palestine turned out to be more disastrous for the future of the Palestinians than the Arab Conference[1] which was convened at Bludan from 8 to 10 September 1937 and which *inter alia* rejected the Peel Commission's recommendation of the partition of Palestine, reiterating the Arab opposition to further Jewish immigration, and officially trusting the political fate of Arab Palestine to the hands of the other sovereign and bickering Arab States.

The British were impressed by this show of Arab unity, especially in view of the growing dangers of Italian and German penetration into the Middle East. They convened a round-table Jewish–Arab conference in London in February to March 1939, which had no other result than to confirm the diametrically opposed views of the Jews and the Arabs and establish for the Arabs the diplomatic principle, which they have since continued to observe, of refusing to sit down with the Jews to discuss the problem of Palestine.

Under the stress of events in Europe and with total disregard for Jewish survival in Germany, the British Government announced in May 1939 a new policy in a White Paper, which was in fact the acceptance of the Arab leaders' request for an end to the Jewish national home. The British 'Order 6019' of May 1939 (as the White Paper was officially known) prohibited the sale of land to the Jews in most of Palestine, limited immigration to a final 75,000 people in five years,

---

[1] *Great Britain and Palestine, 1915–1945* (Report prepared for the Royal Institute of International Affairs, London, 1946), p. 104.

after which an Arab–Jewish State would be created in Palestine on the basis of a 1 to 3 relationship of the two communities' populations.

The British believed they had at last solved the thorny problem of Palestine. In fact they had only sparked off the revolt of what was probably the most faithful 'colonial' nation of the Empire, opened the road to Jewish terrorism, and transformed the Palestine question from a more or less localized dispute into an international problem of world magnitude.

It took, however, another eight years for the old conflict to explode in its new form: eight years of dreadful incubation of Jewish nationhood which saw the destruction of 6 million Jews in Europe and the frantic and unsuccessful attempt of some of them to reach the shores of Palestine; eight years in which the British had to quell a pro-German revolt in Iraq—in 1941—and in which the war effort and pro-British enthusiasm of the Jews contrasted with the divided attitude of the Arabs; eight years during which 30,000 Palestinian Jews volunteered to fight for the British Army against Italy and Germany, from Abyssinia to the Po Valley, from Dunkirk to Yugoslavia, and in some of the most daring—and unpublicized—military operations of the war;[1] eight years during which the British stuck to the declared policy of the White Paper of 1939, less out of conviction than because of the deep divisions of opinion which the issue of Palestine and Zionism created in the War Cabinet, where some members—like Winston Churchill—were opposed to the policy set out in the White Paper, and some—like Lord Halifax—were in favour of it: a division of opinion which was, paradoxically, also to be found in the Labour Cabinet after 1945 in spite of that Party's unanimous and declared opposition to the White Paper before it came to power; eight years in which Palestine paradoxically enjoyed peace and the Jewish Community earned a great deal of money through war services, developing industries, agriculture, military experience and organization, national solidarity, and a confidence which turned out to be invaluable in the later fight for independence.[2]

I have already recalled how in 1942 the Zionist Organization, led by Ben Gurion, officially called, for the first time, for the establishment of

---

[1] See Pierre Van Paassen, *The Forgotten Ally* (New York, 1943).

[2] The cost of manufacturing supplies for the armed forces has been calculated at between £35–40 million. During the war years production in the Jewish sector of Palestine increased by 27·2 per cent. While the average annual increase of factories and workshops in Jewish Palestine was 101 from 1925 to 1935, 291 new industrial enterprises were created in 1941 alone. *The Jewish Plan for Palestine. Memoranda and Statements Presented by the Jewish Agency for Palestine to the United Nations Special Committee on Palestine* (Jerusalem, 1947), pp. 408, 409–29.

an independent 'Jewish Commonwealth' at the end of the War. It was the logical outcome of the earlier Zionist decision, taken at the time of the announcement of the White Paper policy in 1939, 'to fight the British as if the Nazis did not exist and to fight the Nazis as if the White Paper did not exist'.

It was a long, tenacious fight, which finally led to the British decision to disengage themselves from Palestine and turn over their responsibility to the United Nations, and to the Jews proclaiming their independence and the Arab States declaring their first war against Israel.

Chapter 5

The War of Independence and Its Consequences

The first Palestine war is usually divided in two periods: from December 1947 to the proclamation of the State of Israel on 14 May 1948 and from May 1948 to the signature of the first armistice agreement between Egypt and Israel on Rhodes on 2 February 1949.

On the battlefield the difference between these two periods was not great: there were almost as many casualties in the five months preceding the proclamation of the State as in the five months following. Some of the crucial battles for the survival of the Jewish State were fought before its official proclamation. However, there were other significant differences.[1]

From December 1947 to May 1948 the war was fought mainly by Arab and Jewish Palestinian military formations with the British Army and the Mandatory administration still officially responsible in the country. After 15 May or, as far as Israel was concerned, from 28 June (the date of the creation of Israel's Defence Army, I.D.A.[2]), the war was fought by regular troops on both sides: those of the Arab States which invaded Palestine after the Arab Palestinian forces had been routed and the new Israel Defence Army which superseded the older partisan military formations and was reinforced by a number of Jewish and non-Jewish volunteers from all over the world. These volunteers contributed their full share to the Jewish victory, especially in the airforce, and provided Israel with its first General in the person of Colonel Marcus, an American Jewish Westpointer.

For the first three months of violence the conflict looked like a series of isolated incidents with a lot of sniping on the Arab side and increasing reprisals from the Jewish side and little intervention from the British forces still officially responsible for the security of Palestine. By the end of January the Arab Liberation Army, commanded by the Lebanese Fauzi el Kaukji, backed by the Military Committee of the Arab League, had begun operations.

[1] On the War of Independence see *Toldot Milhemet Hakomemiyut* (History of the War of Independence), Historical Department of the Israel Defence Army General Staff (Tel Aviv, 1959), and Netanel Lorch, *The Edge of the Sword: Israel's War of Independence, 1947–1949* (New York, 1961). For a non-Israeli view, see Edgar O'Ballance, *The Arab-Israeli War, 1948* (London 1956).

[2] Also known as I.D.F. (Israel's Defence Forces).

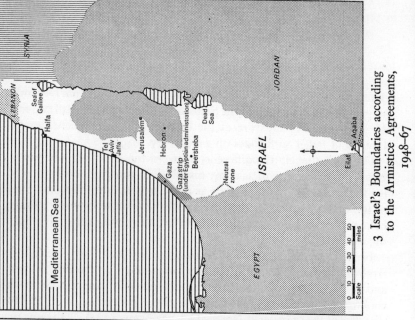

3 Israel's Boundaries according
to the Armistice Agreements,
1948–67

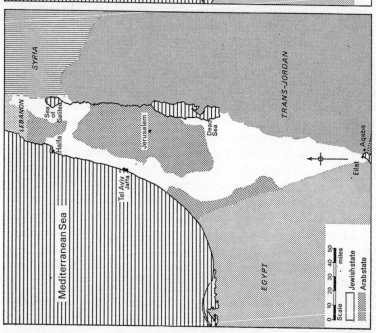

2 The United Nations' Proposal
for the Partition of Palestine,
November 1947

The Jews held out in the Jordan Valley, in the northern Negev, and in the suburbs of Jerusalem with grim determination; the collective settlements had received orders to fight to the last man. But the Arabs were not only on the offensive; they showed how vulnerable the Jewish communications system was. They had sealed off the Jewish quarter of Jerusalem from the rest of the Yishuv by March 1949. On 31 March Operation Nachshon was launched to save the whole City from imminent disaster. When Kastel Hill, overlooking the road to Jerusalem, was taken on 9 April, the tide of war began to turn. On that day three things happened: the siege of Jerusalem was temporarily lifted and reinforcements went through; Abdul Kader, a nephew of the Mufti of Jerusalem and the best Palestinian field commander, was killed and from that day onwards the Arab command in Palestine passed into non-Palestinian hands; the Arab population of the village of Dir Yassin on the outskirts of Jerusalem was massacred by men from the I.Z.L. and Stern Group. The last started a flight of Arabs from Israel that quickly became an exodus.

Kaukji's army was beaten in the Valley of Jezreel (at Mishmar Ha-Emek) and near Haifa (Ramat Yochanan) by the end of April. Haifa fell into Jewish hands on 22 April. On 1 May Jewish assault troops tried in vain to storm the British police fortress commanding the Safad area in Upper Galilee. Their failure might have turned into a major disaster if the village of Ramot Naftali, the key point in the defence system of Upper Galilee, had given way before a resolute Lebanese attack. The Arabs were as exhausted as the Jews from the two battles. On 10 May they evacuated the town of Safad and all Upper Galilee without a fight. On 12 May Jaffa fell but the Arabs, supported by the Arab Legion of Transjordan, achieved two major successes in the Jerusalem area. They took the Jewish quarter in the Old City of Jerusalem, including the Wailing Wall, and on the day of the declaration of the independence of the State they wiped out a group of villages at Etzion in Judea.

It was a costly war. From 30 November to 1 February the *Palestine Post* listed 204 Jewish dead and 512 wounded.[1] From December to April the Jewish casualties were given as 1,256 dead and 2,102 wounded, but this second account was far less accurate than the previous one, since it did not list many of the men who fell in battle and others who disappeared behind Arab lines in sabotage or commando operations. For the Arabs it was also a period of considerable loss of life: 3,569 dead and many more wounded.[2]

[1] *Palestine Post*, 2 February 1948.
[2] Rufus Learsi, *Fulfilment. The Epic Story of Zionism* (Cleveland, 1951), p. 368.

As for the British, they also lost more than a hundred men, but the most remarkable thing about them was that they lost their nerve. A few British soldiers and policemen, some of them with pro-Nazi leanings (e.g. Captain Ferran), were even directly involved in anti-Jewish terrorist operations, such as the bombing of the Jewish Agency headquarters in Jerusalem on 13 March, of the offices of the *Palestine Post*, and probably of a big apartment building in the centre of the city, in which forty sleeping Jewish citizens lost their lives and 130 were wounded, on 23 February.

The Attlee Government ordered inquiries, and anyone who rereads the British press of those days will be surprised by the passion with which the Palestine situation was described. No wonder: for victorious Britain it was the first colonial battle which she was to lose after the Second World War, and the British authorities seemed determined, like de Gaulle in Guinea in 1960, to leave chaos behind them and to make the Jews pay for their political effrontery.

In spite of the United Nations' requests, the Palestine Government refused to let representatives of the United Nations Organization into the country before the end of the Mandate. No orderly transition of power was carried out; police stations in areas allotted by the United Nations partition plan to the Jews were handed over by the British police to the Arabs—possibly according to a pre-arranged plan but probably out of sheer panic—only to be recaptured a few hours or days later by the Hagana after a bitter fight. The British Navy kept a tight control over access to Israel from the sea, still refusing to allow Jewish refugees or military supplies to come into the country. In February the British Government took an unprecedented step in the economic history of the Empire: it dropped Palestine from the sterling area, freezing more than £120,000,000 in London, most of it belonging to the Jewish community. It was to turn out to be an unwise decision for sterling, which thus lost control of several billion dollars subsequently mobilized by Israel. But one understands why Nuri Said, the Iraqi Foreign Minister, could write to the Baghdad parliament, after his meeting with Foreign Secretary Ernest Bevin in London on 16 January 1948: 'It became clear to us that Britain viewed with favour the Arab aims regarding Palestine.'[1]

British Policy in the Middle East was beset, however, with unexpected difficulties and contradictions. In spite of Bevin's support for 'Arab aims' in Palestine, the Portsmouth Treaty (15 February 1948) for

---

[1] Quoted in Jon and David Kimche, *Both Sides of the Hill: Britain and the Palestine War* (London, 1960), p. 60.

renewed British–Iraqi military assistance, encountered such opposition in Baghdad that the Iraqi Government collapsed and the country was faced with civil strife. From that moment, Iraq was out of the Palestine War. On the other hand (and while British 'astrologers' explained in the British popular press that the Jewish national home was doomed to defeat, because of the presence of Taurus—the Golden Calf—in the 1948 constellation),[1] British soldiers in Palestine were happily selling arms and ammunition to both Arabs and Jews. Even the departure of Sir Alan Cunningham, the last British High Commissioner, from Haifa, could not be carried out according to plan: because British soldiers had sold the Hagana two tanks, the General refused to attend the farewell party organized by the Jewish municipality in his honour.[2]

On the Arab side, inter-Arab animosity was as intense as Arab hostility towards the Jews. The Arab army had been plagued from the beginning by political and personal rivalry. From the beginning (September 1947) the Political Committee of the League of Arab States was opposed to the idea of an army of Arab volunteers under Kaukji. Animosity between the Lebanese officer and the Palestinian Arab Higher Executive Committee, headed by the exiled Mufti of Jerusalem, Amin el Husseini, ran very high. The Palestinian commander of the Jerusalem Front and the commander of Gaza region, both followers of the Mufti, refused to obey the orders of the Arab League's Supreme Commander. There were at least two bickering commanders in Jenin and several military factions in Tulkarem, almost opposite Tel Aviv. General conscription was never endorsed and, in the words of Musa Alami, 'the Jews proceeded along the lines of total war . . . we worked on a local basis without unity'.[3]

On the political level divisions among the Arabs became apparent soon after the United Nations' resolution to divide Palestine into two States, passed on 29 November 1947. On 12 December 1947 the Arab prime ministers met in Cairo to decide on their common policy against partition and to hear the report of the chairman of the Arab League Military Committee, the Iraqi General Ismail Safuat Pasha, who correctly described the military inability of the Palestinian Arabs to stand up to the Jews by themselves. He called for immediate military intervention by the Arab States.

But the 'peripheral States', Saudi Arabia and Egypt, refused categorically. All the Egyptian delegate was prepared to agree on, was to

[1] *Jerusalem Post*, 22 January 1948.

[2] R. M. Graves, *Experiment in Anarchy* (London, 1949); and Major R. D. Wilson, *Cordon and Search* (Aldershot, 1949).

[3] Musa Alami, 'The Lesson of Palestine', *The Middle East Journal*, no. III (October 1949).

arm the Palestinians and some non-Palestinian Arab volunteers. This suited the Arab Higher Executive Committee of Palestine, headed, as mentioned above, by the Mufti of Jerusalem, Amin el Husseini, who, above all, feared Transjordanian occupation of Palestine—which was exactly what King Abdullah was trying to achieve. As for Iraq, it contended that Arab intervention could take place only after the British had left.

So Arab Palestine was left with two uncoordinated armies: the Arab Higher Executive Committee's army, made up mainly of the Mufti's men, which Abdullah of Transjordan was out to destroy since it was the only Palestinian Arab organization of any importance, and the Arab Liberation Army, made up of volunteers, paid and armed by the Arab League under Ismail Safuat Pasha as Commander-in-Chief, and Fauzi el Kaukji, the Lebanese adventurer, as commander in the field. Both were ramshackle armies and no match for the Jewish Hagana.

But the Arabs lacked political as well as military unity and they had no clear idea of the future of Palestine. The Jews knew they wanted a Jewish State—at any cost. The Arabs in Palestine were more interested in not having a Jewish State than in having a Palestinian Arab one. This was also the issue on which the other Arab States were divided, with no one wanting the shaky inter-Arab balance of power unsettled by a new, independent, Arab unit—or by the conquest of Palestine by any one of its neighbours. And the incorporation of part of Palestine was the aim of Abdullah of Transjordan.

The King was the main opponent of an autonomous Palestine. He made no secret of his intention to get rid of the Arab Higher Executive Committee as soon as possible. He organized his own administration for Palestine and wrote to the *Manchester Guardian* on 9 January 1948, that since 'the King has long wished to rule over Greater Syria, the establishment of the National Administration for all Palestine would be a useful step in this direction'.

Abdullah felt that he could count on British help and approval, especially after Bevin's diplomatic fiasco in Iraq. He had revamped his military treaty with London in March 1948 and believed that the conquest of part of Palestine could be the first step on the way to the formation of a larger State which, he hoped, might eventually grow into a British-supported Greater Syria.

On 11 February 1948 the Arab League, under strong Transjordan pressure, shelved the project for a unified Arab Command. On 29 April Abdullah let it be known that his army intended to cross the Jordan and occupy Jericho, in Palestine, even before the end of the British Mandate.

The King declared: 'We are at war with the Jews', but later tried to deny this statement, which created concern in Cairo, where no decision had yet been taken to intervene militarily in the Palestine War. The causes for these hesitations are to be sought in the meeting of the Arab League which opened in Cairo on 10 April 1948 and lasted twelve days. As the conference went on news of the Arab Liberation Army's setbacks kept coming in. The Jordanians wanted to intervene as soon as possible but the Lebanese, and above all the Egyptians, were opposed to any military initiative on the part of the Arab States before the end of the Mandate for fear of a British reaction. Furthermore, King Farouk of Egypt told the Arab delegates on 12 April that 'under no circumstances' would he consider either the partition or the permanent occupation of Palestine by any Arab army. He feared above all a military initiative on the part of King Abdullah of Jordan, whose desire to annex Palestine was well known. So the King had to wait to give the British commander of his army the order to march into Palestine, although the Transjordan parliament approved the measure on 26 April. On 30 April the representatives of the Arab League met once more in Amman and Abdullah was still able to tell the delegates that he was sure of a quick victory once his army crossed the Jordan. But the fall of Haifa and Jaffa radically changed the situation and the King was induced to make a last attempt at direct settlement with the Jews. In a secret meeting with Mrs. Golda Meir, the present Israeli Premier, then Mrs. Meyerson and Head of the Political Department of the Jewish Agency, on 10 May the King tried to persuade the Zionist leaders to postpone the proclamation of the State. He would take over Palestine, annex it to Transjordan, and he offered the Jews good treatment and parliamentary representation.[1] It was too late; time was running short, and the Arab masses were impatient. Joseph O. Goodwin, the Associated Press correspondent in Damascus, wired on 10 May that 'the only Arab alternatives are all-out war or revolution at home'.

Two days later, Abdullah came out officially against the Arab Higher Executive Committee, which, according to him, had only brought misery to the population of Palestine (he went so far as to call the Committee leader, Amin el Husseini, 'our common enemy' in front of the Jewish Agency's envoys, who met him on 27 November 1947). It was

[1] See Marie Syrkin, *Golda Meir: Woman with a Cause* (London, 1964), pp. 198–201; also Christopher Sykes, *Crossroads to Israel*, pp. 371 and 375–6. Although no final or formal agreement was reached between Abdullah and the Zionist authorities, it can be claimed that the King respected his own side of the deal in so far as he did concentrate the attacks of the Arab Legion mainly against Jerusalem, which, according to the U.N. partition plan, was to remain an international city outside the territory of the Jewish State.

his Arab Legion, commanded by a British officer, Glubb Pasha (General Sir John Glubb), which was going to save Palestine from the Jews' aggression and Arab irresponsibility. There was no choice for the other Arab governments, if they wanted their share, but to follow his example. So on 15 May the Transjordan, Egyptian, Syrian, and Lebanese armies were ordered to cross the Palestinian frontier in defiance of the United Nations' resolution, and take upon themselves the 'responsibility for restoring order and justice' in Palestine. The Saudi Arabian and Yemeni contingents left for the Palestine front, but never arrived there. However, the Syrian, Egyptian, Transjordan, Iraqi, and Lebanese armies went to battle. They amounted to 23,000 men, together with 2,000 Palestinians of the Arab Liberation Army, against whom Israel deployed 19,000 men and women.[1]

The first Jewish–Arab war had officially begun. Many military studies have been made of this conflict. I shall confine myself here to reminding the reader of some dates. From 15 May to 2 June the Arabs (especially the Egyptians) advanced practically unchecked into Palestine, mainly into Arab-held territory. On 30 May the Jewish quarter of the Old City of Jerusalem fell to the Arab Legion, giving Abdullah—for the first time since his exile from Mecca—the possession of an Islamic Holy Place, the Mosque of Omar, the place from which Mohammed was believed to have ascended into the sky.

The Security Council managed to impose a truce of four weeks, which the Arabs used to co-ordinate their final military and political onslaught against the Jewish State, and which Israel used to amass military supplies.

The United Nations' Mediator, Count Bernadotte, flew to Palestine and started working on a new plan of partition: the Jewish State would get western Galilee, but would abandon claims to the Negev. On 11 July, following the Arab rejection of an extension of the truce, the Israeli Army launched its first great offensive: Lydda and Ramleh in the centre, Nazareth in the north, were taken. Angry demonstrations broke out in Amman. In nine days of fighting the Arabs lost 5,000 men and were forced to accept a second truce on 22 July.

From that time on, fighting became sporadic in the north against the remnants of the Arab Liberation Army and the Syrians, and in the centre—especially in Jerusalem—against Transjordan. But Israel's main effort was now directed against the Egyptians.

On 22 October Beersheba, the capital of the Negev, fell. Count Bernadotte, who tried to obtain an Israeli withdrawal from Jerusalem

[1] J. and D. Kimche, op. cit., p. 162.

and from the Negev, was murdered, allegedly by the Stern Group, in Jerusalem on 18 November, while Colonel Dayan and Colonel el Tal of Transjordan reached a quick truce in Jerusalem. The Hashemite kingdoms—certainly Jordan, and to a certain extent also Iraq—were not displeased by the defeat of Farouk's army and by the distress of the most powerful member of the Arab League. This attitude eventually contributed to the collapse of Hashemite power in the region, since it had a direct bearing on the 'Young Officers'' revolt in Egypt and else-where, a military revolutionary trend which under Nasser's leadership put an end to all Jordanian or Iraqi hopes of leadership in the Middle East.

At the beginning of December the Chief of Police in Cairo, Selim Sidki, was murdered; on 28 December the Egyptian Prime Minister, Nokrashy Pasha, was in turn shot dead, although the Egyptian Government had not yet told the people the full truth about the Palestine defeat. Ben Gurion decided to press his advantage. At the end of December the Israeli Army attacked on a wide front in the Negev, reached Eilat, and then crossed into Sinai. British troops landed in Aqaba, directly facing the Israelis. The British fleet was put in a state of readiness and the British Government delivered an ultimatum to Israel through the American Ambassador in Tel Aviv, warning that it would be forced to intervene under the 1936 Anglo-Egyptian military defence treaty. It was unwise for Britain to offer military assistance which the Egyptian Government had not asked for and which was deeply re-sented by the Army in Cairo. On 12 December, after Israel had shot down five British fighters, the United Nations' Acting Mediator felt obliged to warn both Britain and Israel against going to war.

The situation verged on the absurd when, in a sudden anti-climactic move, Egypt accepted the negotiation, at Rhodes, of an armistice agree-ment. There was nothing else for the British Foreign Secretary Ernest Bevin to do, except to admit defeat by throwing open the camps of illegal Jewish refugees in Cyprus and allowing them to go to Palestine.

On 24 February 1949 Egypt and Israel signed the first armistice agreement at Rhodes; those with Transjordan (3 April), the Lebanon (23 March), and Syria (20 July) soon followed. The first round of the Israeli–Arab war was thus concluded.

The Jews had established their State, added to it some two thousand square kilometres of territory over and above the area originally allotted to them by the United Nations' partition plan, and shared with Trans-jordan the City of Jerusalem. They had had some 6,000 dead and 8,000 wounded, 2 per cent of the community which had gone into war with a population of 650,000. (To grasp what this means, one has only to think that if the United States had the same proportion of casualties in Vietnam, it would amount, for a population of 180 million, to 4 million dead and wounded.)

They had to withdraw from north Sinai, leaving the Gaza Strip in Egyptian hands, but they were firmly established in Eilat, astride the strategic land bridge between the Mediterranean and the Red Sea. More important, from the Arab point of view, they had become a buffer between the Arabs of the Nile and those of the Euphrates.

The number of Arab losses is not known. King Abdullah came out of the war best, with his desert State transformed into the Hashemite Kingdom of Jordan, covering Transjordan and two-fifths of fertile Palestine, and with a population which jumped from 400,000, mainly bedouin, to 1,200,000—800,000 of them embittered Palestinians, refugees or not. The Lebanese were glad to see the Israeli troops retreat without discussion from the area occupied in the Litani valley, but Syria never forgot that it was the only Arab State which had succeeded in penetrating into Jewish-held territory. Before they would retreat from it, the Damascus Government demanded the demilitarization of the area west of the Jordan formerly occupied by its troops, thus creating a situation which was soon to become a source of unending friction between the two countries. Iraq, Saudi Arabia, and the Yemen simply disappeared from the Palestinian military scene, too preoccupied with their internal problems to bother about signing an armistice agreement. But they could not avoid sharing the bitter loss of national pride and prestige common to the Arab nations.

If the Arab governments had told their people before the war exactly what the situation in Palestine was, they might have had a rational explanation for the defeat. They could have pointed out that, on the whole, the military forces on both sides were equal in numbers—19,000 Jewish soldiers against 23,000 Arabs; that if, initially, armaments were superior on the Arab side, later they were equalized; that the Israelis had had the advantage of shorter lines of communication and the support of a far more industrialized and educated population.

But there could be no rational Arab explanation of this type. The Jews had been described as the 'scum of the earth', poor fighters compared with the chivalrous Arab soldiers. Antisemitic propaganda had reinforced this stereotyped image of the Jew all over the world; the Arabs accepted it and added to it the feeling that, since the Second World War, their power had grown considerably. They believed that they had overcome British and French imperialism and that they had become the new great force in the Middle East, because of their oil and because they occupied a strategic area which was vital to the West in its war against Communism. All this added to their confidence based on considerable—but only potential—force. To be beaten by a despised community of Jewish refugees was unthinkable, unacceptable, hence impossible. Therefore scapegoats and face-saving excuses—not analysis of the defeat—were sought, although there were some courageous and objective Arab critics of the situation.[1] But on the whole the grievances which the soldiers brought back from the Palestine front and the recriminations over the responsibility for the defeat were to poison the political climate of the Middle East for years to come.

More important, however, in this context is the meaning of the war for the Jewish community of Palestine, and its consequences.

In 1947 the Jews took up arms against the Arabs in order to achieve two objects: their survival and the creation of a politically independent state, in line with their national aims and interests.

The first aim was easier to define than the second, since there was general agreement about it among the Jewish population. Only the Jews' ability to defeat the Arabs in battle was needed to achieve it.

The second aim, namely the kind of state to be created, was more complicated and remains a central theme of discussion among Israeli politicians and intellectuals. The question was whether the new republic should be a Jewish State, an Israeli State, or a Marxist State. During the 1948 war, this question involved the Jewish military organizations as much as the parties, in a series of political reactions, which could—but fortunately for Israel, never did—turn into military *putsches* and civil wars.

Two of the military's attempts to influence the future character of the State came from the Left, one from the Right—and all took place at the most critical hours of the Jewish fight for survival against the Arabs. It is certain that on these three occasions (as, later, in May 1967) the external threat to the Jewish community saved it from perhaps fatal internal political divisions.

To take the crisis on the Left first: it was a crisis of ideology, power, and discipline, which had really started long before the proclamation of the Jewish State, in those confused days of 1942, when Ben Gurion proclaimed his determination to establish a 'national, independent Commonwealth', and his left-wing comrades opposed even the idea of having a Jewish national flag.[2]

[1] Musa Alami, op. cit.
[2] For a summary of the military crisis, see Bar-Zohar, op. cit., ch. 16: 'The Revolt Which

I have already mentioned how in November 1942 the 'B' Faction of Mapai broke away from Ben Gurion's party, taking with it the main military leaders of the kibbutz shock troops, the Palmach (see page 76).

In 1947 the Palmach was the backbone of the Hagana. It numbered 2,200 highly trained soldiers as against 7,000 men in the field units, and 27,000 in the militia. The majority of commanders belonged to the 'B' Faction or to the even more extremist Hashomer Hatzair Marxist kibbutz movement. The commander of the Hagana, Israel Galili, now Minister of Information, was also a 'B' Faction man. His first serious clash with Ben Gurion, as a military leader, came in 1946 when Ben Gurion advocated the immediate purchase of heavy arms, tanks, and airplanes for what he considered a certain war.

Galili, like most Israelis of that time, thought, on the contrary, in terms of communal warfare, and believed that small arms, which were easier to obtain and cheaper to buy, would be sufficient to cope with the situation. And it was during these early technical debates that Ben Gurion probably decided that Galili was not the man for the job and that a crisis of personal confidence became a crisis of political confidence.

The conflict burst out into the open at the beginning of May, when the Jewish Provisional Executive was formed, and the question of the Defence Minister's competence was raised. Ben Gurion wanted direct control of the Army through a military High Command. Galili wanted a division between the Minister and the General Staff of the Army. The battle dragged on for days and at one stage the Hagana commanders, siding with Galili, gave Ben Gurion a virtual ultimatum by presenting him with their collective resignations. It was, without doubt, the gravest hour in Ben Gurion's and the State of Israel's political life; and it is to Ben Gurion's credit that he managed to neither resign nor accept his generals' resignations, but, by skilful manipulation, outmanoeuvred Galili. He was fortunate, in this hour of difficulty, to have, paradoxically, the right-wing terrorist military formations to strengthen his position by offering to join a national army.

However, the agreement with the military formations of the Right did not last long. The commander of the Irgun, Menahem Beigin, laid the foundations for a new civil war by sending on 20 July a ship loaded

---

Failed', and ch. 20: 'Ben Gurion Resigns'; see also Soustelle, op. cit., pp. 166–80 and 288–97. Confirmation from a high official source is given in Zeev Sharef, *Three Days* (London, 1962), pp. 182–94.

with arms and ammunition to Israel from Europe, braving the United Nations' embargo on weapons.

It is not known exactly what went wrong between Beigin and Ben Gurion. Beigin has always claimed that there was an agreement between the Irgun and the Hagana over the arrival of the ship in Israel. Ben Gurion's supporters contend that the Irgun wanted to change the terms of the agreement by sending a substantial part of the arms to their units in Jerusalem.

At the time Jerusalem was not yet considered part of the Jewish State, and the idea has been advanced that Ben Gurion feared that the Irgun would establish a separate State in Jerusalem. Beigin has denied the accusation. In any case, when the ship—the *Altalena* (Jabotinsky's *nom de plume*)—arrived in Israel, Ben Gurion ordered one of his army brigades to seize the arms by force. The ship escaped and sailed for Tel Aviv where she tried to land men and weapons in front of the city seashore-promenade, while Irgun troops and their supporters sealed the roads to the coast.

Ben Gurion gave orders to the Army to fire. It was a terrible moment in Israel's history, with Jews fighting Jews, some of them refugees just out of German concentration camps, and some being killed on the ship, within sight of the 'Promised Land'.

Large numbers of the population along the coast had to be evacuated. In the streets crowds of supporters of both sides argued bitterly with loaded weapons in their hands. Civil war seemed imminent. It was avoided, at the very last moment, through the intervention of Menahem Beigin who, in a dramatic speech on the radio, bitterly attacked the Government but ordered his troops not to resist. The Irgun's military force was broken and its men were quickly incorporated into the newly formed national army, in which—it is fair to recall—they were not subjected to any discrimination.

In July a third political crisis broke out, once more on the Left. Once again Galili and the army commanders tried to insert a political wedge between the Defence Minister and the High Command. The Palmach units strongly resented being incorporated into a non-political army. They might have enjoyed wide military support, since out of twelve army brigades, nine were commanded by left-wing officers.

This time Ben Gurion used different tactics: he handed in his resignation and forced the Government to choose between him and Galili. With considerable military victories to his credit and having shown undisputed leadership during the Irgun crisis, the choice was inevitable. The military commanders backed down and on 7 July

Galili, stripped of all authority, returned to his kibbutz. He was excluded from power for the next nineteen years.

Out of these crises, from the Right and from the Left, two new parties were born: the Irgun became the nationalist Herut Party; the 'B' faction and the Hashomer Hatzair, together with most of the Palmach leaders, joined a new left-wing organization, Mapam (United Workers' Party), which in the first election established itself as the second largest party in the country; but it was a short-lived success. What, on the contrary, was to last for years was the personal antagonism between Ben Gurion, Beigin, and Galili, an antagonism which punctuated all the subsequent stages of Israeli parliamentary life, finally contributing to force Ben Gurion out of power in 1964.

The War of Independence, which divided the Arab States so deeply, united, through military necessity, Israeli political society. With the Jewish military victory over the Arabs, Ben Gurion's conception of Socialist Zionism triumphed. In ideological terms this meant that Israel was not a State, in the sense of Herzl's liberalism or Ahad Haam's 'spiritualism'. Neither was it an élitist Marxist State, as the kibbutz plantocracy demanded. It was to remain, on the contrary, a very pragmatic political society, unattractive to those who looked for political Messianism, moderate, and ideologically inefficient. It was a society better symbolized by the efficiency of the new army, than by Ben Gurion's nebulous ideas of 'national redemption'.

This army was in any case far more than a fighting organization. It was conceived as and became a school for citizenship, a highly efficient machine for fighting Arabs and for integrating the immigrants. It dried up most of the vitality of the party-controlled youth organizations of the country by establishing its own pre-military service in the schools; it robbed the kibbutzim of their role as frontier forts and even stole some of their pioneering tasks by establishing a special *élite* corps of fighting farmers—the Nahal—which later became the main source of border settlements.[1] From being a source of pride and an object of affection for the population as a whole, the Army soon became a symbol of social honour. But it never became a caste, or a separate social hierarchy within the country. It had no officers' messes, no batmen, no glamorous uniforms, not even medals. Such amenities being, of course, incompatible with the pioneering, egalitarian traditions of the

---

[1] Nahal units also became the pattern for combined civic and military service in many developing countries to which Israel supplied technical aid; see L. Laufer, *Israel and the Developing Countries: New Approaches to Co-operation* (New York, 1967), pp. 30–1 and 67–70.

Yishuv, but reflecting also the concern felt by the civil authorities for any form of crystallization of the military establishment—a feeling which was also expressed in the refusal of the Minister of the Interior, I. Gruenbaum, to accept the interior portfolio if it included responsibility for the police. He wanted a 'clean' Ministry and to this day Israel has a separate Ministry for police and prisons. The Army took upon itself the strict observance of religious rules—kosher food, observance of the sabbath rest, etc.—although most of the soldiers, and even more of the officers, were not religious. It adapted itself quickly to the dietary requirements of the religious minority, so that unity was not subjected to strain. Above all, the Army was, of necessity, an example of efficient organization. In a country where socialist ideology had made seniority and social security the fundamental principle of social and economic promotion, the Army adopted the principle of meritocracy and internal mobility by retiring generals at the age of 45.[1] The Army was the most important, the most original, and the only new Jewish institution to come out of the War of Independence. As such, it was more than a military organization: it was the outward expression of the true nature of the new State—a nation in arms.

But what of the other institutions of the Jewish community of Palestine, now that they had been turned into institutions of an independent State? They also, as we shall see, sustained a powerful shock, but they succeeded in braving the change to statehood with very few alterations to structure and personnel. The executive of the Jewish Agency became the Israeli Government; the Vaad Haleumi became the Knesset (the Jewish parliament); the old system of collecting charitable donations abroad became the new system of collecting donations for the State; the multi-party and electoral system of the old Jewish community was copied in the new multi-party and electoral system of the State; even the old Turkish civil code, which Britain had maintained, remained the law of the country, with political agreements between the secular and the religious parties to maintain the *status quo*.

The social forces were the most obvious forces at work in the new State. The creation of the State of Israel had brought about not only a new political entity, but also the sudden displacement of almost one and a half million people, some 500,000 Arab refugees and 1,000,000

---

[1] Perlmutter, op. cit., is the best work so far published on the Israeli Army. It is valuable for its original content and the important bibliography in English and Hebrew. See also his important article 'The Israeli Army in Politics: The Persistence of the Civilian over the Military', in *World Politics*, vol. xx, no. 4, July 1968, pp. 606–43.

Jewish immigrants, of which a large number can be counted as refugees. Both displacements were unexpected, unplanned, and basically un-wanted—at least in the unexpected, disorganized way in which they took place. And both were destined to have the same revolutionary consequences as the first Jewish–Arab war.

The Jewish refugees belonged to two categories: the displaced per-sons who had been waiting since the end of the Second World War in camps in Europe to find a haven in Palestine, and the Jews from the Arab countries. While everyone in Israel expected the Jews in the first category, nobody knew much about the intentions of the second group. As it happened, the enthusiasm created by the re-establishment of a Jewish independent State—combined with the fear of Arab violence, as a reaction to their defeat in Palestine—spurred the masses of Jews in the Arab world to come to Israel. In fact, no one can compare the Arab violence against the Jews in the Islamic world with the horrors of the mildest Russian pogroms. Still the Jews' new feeling of insecurity was strong enough to make them set out on the path of the return to the homeland.

There were, however, other, secondary, reasons. In the Yemen there was a particularly difficult economic situation and the Jewish relief organizations were able to offer the local rulers an attractive condition for the 'passage' of the Jews from the highlands to the coast. In Iraq the Jewish community—one of the oldest in the world—suffered heavily in social and political status first from the disappearance of Turkish, and afterwards of British rule, two administrations which had leaned heavily on the Jewish minority which provided them with a bureau-cracy for their indirect rule. In Libya the Arab violence against the Jews in 1946, the suffering of the last years of Italian and German occupa-tion, had destroyed the confidence of the local community in future Jewish–Arab relations in that country. But common to all these Jewish immigrants from Arab countries was a strong national feeling linked with their religion.

The Jews of the Islamic world—like any other minority living in the Arab countries made no distinction between nationality and religion. They lived under the *millet* system and *millet* in Islam means both a religious minority and a nationality. Furthermore, they had not been touched by the philosophical doubts of the European Renaissance, or the Reformation, the Western fight between State and Church—in a word, by the impact of modernism. Some of the Jews in Arab countries were members of the local intelligentsia, well educated and acquainted with the Western ideas. In Egypt, for example, Jews had been active in the indigenous liberal, as well as in communist, groups.[1] But they were a minority of the minority not the masses. Furthermore, both the Jewish intelligentsia and the Jewish masses belonged to a colonialized society whose main social and political preoccupation was not—as for European Jewry—individual assimilation into local society, but modernization of the whole society on Western lines. Whichever way a Jew looked for progress, equality, and social advancement, he soon realized that they were not to be found by assimilation into Arab society, which remained closed to minorities because of the religious-national character of Islam and because in many cases the Jews felt themselves more at ease with European civilization than with the traditional indigenous one. This does not mean that in Islamic society of the twentieth century there was no place for non-Moslems. In fact, the reason for the support of Arab nationalism, by the Middle-Eastern minorities, Jewish or non-Jewish, was due to the fact that at least some trends in Arab nationalism were in favour of political secularization of society.[2] But these trends were intellectual trends often linked with imported European ideologies and therefore alien to the prevailing national sentiments which remained deeply rooted in Islamic tradition.

Thus, for the Jewish masses, immigration to Israel represented many things: escape from danger; accomplishment of a national and religious hope; escape from social and economic stagnation in the Arab world; a Jewish version of a minority anti-colonial rebellion. But it was also *all* Zionism had never envisaged, since it neither had roots in Enlightenment, nor was it an escape from assimilation or antisemitism, nor class strife, nor Utopia of any kind. And, above all, it was not a response to Zionism, its ideologies, thinkers, and institutions, for the simple reason that the vast majority of oriental Jews had never heard of Herzl and Aḥad Haam, just as the Jews of Poland and of the Pale of Settlement never took much interest in the Arabized masses of Jews.

From 15 May 1948 to the end of that year, 101,805 Jews immigrated to Israel; in the next year 239,424; in 1950, 109,720; in 1951, 174,014. Then immigration dropped to a mere trickle—23,408 in 1952—for reasons I shall discuss later. Of these immigrants, 50·3 per cent were from the West, mainly Europe; 49·7 per cent were from Asia and Africa. From 1952 onwards, the proportion changed radically: 21·9 per cent from the West against 78·1 per cent from Asia and Africa between 1952

[1] Walter Z. Laqueur, *Communism and Nationalism in the Middle East* (London, 1956), pp. 33 ff.
[2] Typical was the involvement of Christian personalities like Michael Aflaq, the founder of the 'Baath' Party in Syria, in secular Arabism; see Gordon H. Torrey, *Syrian Politics and the Military, 1945–1958* (Columbus, Ohio, 1964), pp. 275 ff.

and 1954; 31 per cent from the West and 69 per cent from Asia and
Africa between 1955 and 1957, when immigration to Israel picked up
again. The Jewish population of Israel—which out of every 100 persons
in 1948 numbered 35 people born in Israel (mainly of European
parents), 10 born in Asia and Africa, and 55 born in Europe—in 1965
had a population of 40 per cent Israeli-born (mostly of Afro-Asian
parents), 29 per cent born in Asia and Africa, and only 31 per cent born
in the West.[1]

As to the Arab refugees, their plight has been the object of so many
studies that I shall only underline some generally accepted conclusions.[2]

They left their homes driven by a mixture of fear and lack of responsible leadership. The question of Israeli responsibility for the refugee
problem has been the subject of passionate debate during the past
twenty years, with each side blaming the other. In fact, the responsibility is probably equally divided; the Israeli authorities were worried
by the Arab flight and even tried to stop it in the beginning, although
later, after the Israeli–Arab clashes, they were relieved to see Jewish
territory cleared of potential enemies. In any case, by evacuating the
territory of Israel and not being allowed to come back, the Arabs
allowed the new State to create a Jewish homogeneity which had not
been forecast by the Zionists. Their departure, together with the special
'Jewish' immigration laws proclaimed by Israel,[3] put an end to the idea
of a pluralist Zionist society which had been current among the Jews of
Palestine since the time of Herzl, and added conviction to the Arabs'
accusation of 'Jewish racialism'.

The Arab refugees did not change their social environment with their
flight as the Jews did. They remained within the borders of the Arab
society, but estranged from it. It became their 'national duty' to remain
'uprooted', to wait for their return to their country of origin. Even when
they found jobs and new sources of income, they remained refugees,
backward-looking, whose world stopped at the moment of their flight.
This was undoubtedly the greatest psychological difference between
them and the Jewish refugees who came to Israel and who looked, with
a few exceptions, passionately towards the future.

[1] *Statistical Abstract of Israel 1961* (Jerusalem, 1962).

[2] Gabbay, op. cit., is one of the most informative books on the subject. For an Arab point
of view see Sami Hadawi, *Palestine: Loss of a Heritage* (San Antonio, Texas, 1963); *Colloque
de juristes arabes sur la Palestine: La question palestinienne, Alger, juillet 1967* (Algiers, 1968),
pp. 136–47. For an Israeli point of view, see Deborah Kaplan, *The Arab Refugees, An
Abnormal Problem* (Jerusalem, 1959), and Marie Syrkin, 'The Arab Refugees, a Zionist
View', *Commentary*.

[3] The Law of Return, 1950, which recognizes the right of Jews freely to immigrate to and
live in Israel.

Still, the Arab refugees had to live, and in some places, like the Gaza Strip, the help they received from international organizations gave them a higher standard of living than the nearby farmers. By sheer weight of numbers, they brought change and innovation to the countries in which they lived. This was particularly true of Jordan, where the Palestinians, on both sides of the river Jordan, were the majority of the population without having a corresponding share in political control, which was still in the hands of the Hashemite dynasty and the merchant class which surrounded it. So, as well as being a constant source of political tension for twenty years within the Arab States, they also fermented social upheaval all over the Middle East. The Palestinians already enjoyed a standard of life and education higher than that of most of the Arab States before 1948. Now, through the educational efforts of the United Nations, they supplied thousands of skilled technicians, teachers, and artisans to all the near-by States, but in particular to the oil-producing States of Arabia. They became the only Arab Diaspora in the Moslem world and thus powerful carriers of ideas, change, and tension.

Their position with regard to Israel was ambivalent. They were a perpetual danger around the frontiers of the Jewish State and their armed infiltrations caused continuous tension and at least one major war (in 1956). But, curiously enough, because they were used as a political and military threat against Israel by the other Arab States without being integrated politically into the Arab States themselves, their collective personality became increasingly—although negatively— shaped by Israel and Zionism. While the national image of the Jewish refugees in Israel developed totally independently of Arab or Palestinian influence, the national image of the Palestinian refugees was more the outcome of their relation to the Jewish State with which the Palestinians were allowed no direct contact, than a result, for instance, of their relations with Egypt.

In political terms the creation of Israel meant the appearance of a new sovereign State at a vital point of the Middle East, in the midst of an Arab nation still searching for its own identity and for the appropriate political, social, economic, and religious institutions to express it in the contemporary world. Soon after the cessation of the fighting, it became clear to the Arabs that peace with Israel could not be envisaged because their relations with the new State could not be defined in the simple terms of a balance of power. That type of balance existed, of course, as far as military forces were concerned. The armistice agreements confirmed it. But the military confrontation was the simplest aspect of the Jewish–Arab conflict. The real difficulty, for which no solution was to be found in twenty years and in successive wars, was the coexistence of two peoples, which were not only nations-in-formation, and therefore in a state of great fluidity, but to a certain extent nations which were also classes to their respective Western and Middle Eastern political and social environment. There was one big difference, however: the Jews were increasingly losing while the Palestinians were increasingly acquiring some of those behavioural characteristics which Weber attributes to 'pariah' nations.[1] On one hand there was a strong, westernized non-Arab State, which had mastered the secret of building a nation; on the other hand there was a traditional Middle Eastern society modernizing itself at a different speed, frantically trying to create in an idealized Arab unity—Pan-Arabism—the forces and the institutions of a supranational State out of a still politically incoherent nation. In other words, the question which had to be solved before sitting down at the conference table was how modern, and uncontrollable, Israel could be assessed in terms of inter-Arab politics.

The psychological consequences of the first Arab–Jewish conflict were no less important and more obvious than the political ones. They have been analysed at length by those who believe that an Israeli effort to heal the Arabs' wounded national pride must precede any serious hope on their part of persuading the Arabs to talk about peace. The Arabs themselves speak continuously of 'lost national dignity' which has to be recovered before they can meet the Israelis. The meaning of 'honour' and 'national dignity' seems, however, to be quite different for the two sides in conflict.

The Israelis admitted, without prompting, that something had to be done to soothe Arab susceptibilities. They thought in terms of economic compensation—payment for lost Arab property, joint co-operation for the development of the Arab Middle East, international guarantees of non-aggression, and open, possibly extra-territorial, access to the sea for the Jordanian Arabs.[2]

The Arabs thought, and probably still think, in terms of *restitutio in corpore*, the handing back of land and houses, and of the return of the Jews to their lands of origin. As is common in Mediterranean countries they thought of honour as something that one recovers by making the offender lose materially or symbolically, totally or partially, something of his own.[3] Victorious Israel was not ready to do this.

---

[1] Max Weber, *Ancient Judaism*, trans. H. H. Gerth and D. Martin (Glencoe, Illinois, 1952), pp. 3–5.   [2] Abba Eban, *Voice of Israel* (New York, 1957), pp. 93–122 and 216–37.

[3] J. G. Peristiany (ed.), *Honour and Shame: The Values of Mediterranean Society* (London, 1965).

Turning to the economic consequences of the war, they were felt more in the impact and the misery of the Arab refugees than in direct Arab military losses. After all, in the 1948 conflict, the Arab States had not lost an inch of their own territory and Jordan and Egypt had added some to their own. The Arab refugees were a real burden to the Arab economies,[1] in spite of considerable international help[2] and in spite of the fact that, in a decade, they would become a considerable asset to the countries which integrated them. But in the early fifties, the potential value of the refugees was not evident to anyone in the Middle East. The Arab refugees seemed to the Arab governments a heavy economic and social burden, much as the Jewish refugees seemed a heavy liability to the Israeli Government. It was one of the tragic consequences of Arab–Jewish political and emotional hostility that the Arabs were never able to admit the fact (which the Israelis soon did) that refugees were a powerful element in social and economic development. Official Arab policy regarding the Arab refugee problem remained one of total refusal to integrate them in the other Arab countries and, in the countries in which Arab refugees were in fact integrated, of non-recognition of their contribution to the development of the Middle East, even where their contribution was an obvious one.[3] This negative policy was inspired by the natural desire to utilize the refugees as a political, emotional, and military weapon against Israel and as moral pressure on world opinion. In time, it turned out to be an equally powerful factor in the increase of the refugees' consciousness of their own special position, in the promotion of a Palestinian political conscience, and in the creation of the 'Palestinian personality' (as the Arab governments called it); a situation in which the Arab refugees, without losing their hostility to Israel, grew more and more resentful of the control of other Arab States, particularly of Egypt and Transjordan, over the non-Israeli part of Palestine.[4]

From the very beginning, Arab refugees brought political and social instability to the Middle East; they were a focal point for international concern and a major source of friction between Israel and its neighbours. In fact, it was the refugee problem which put an end to any

---

[1] Gabbay, op. cit., pp. 163–219; Joseph B. Schechtman, *The Arab Refugee Problem* (New York, 1952), pp. 77–93.

[2] Deborah Kaplan, op. cit., p. 175.

[3] Quoted in *Colloque de juristes arabes sur la Palestine*, pp. 121 ff.

[4] The antagonism of the Palestinians to the Arab governments has been expressed with particular violence since 1967 by the representatives of the Palestinian guerrilla organizations, especially Dr. George Habbash's Popular Front for the Liberation of Palestine, which stresses the need for Arab revolution even before the liberation of Palestine.

hope of transforming the armistice agreements into peace treaties. The direct bearing of the refugee question on the settlement of the Middle East crisis became clear during the unsuccessful meetings of the Palestine Conciliation Commission in Lausanne in 1949. The Israeli Government has constantly claimed that the methods adopted by the Commission in dealing with the problem of the two sides in talking to each other—namely its acceptance of Arab insistence on collective rather than bilateral discussion (as was the case in Rhodes for the armistice talks) constituted the major reason for the failure of the talks.[1] Whatever the importance of diplomatic tactics in Middle Eastern politics, they do not seem to have been so decisive as claimed in some Israeli sources. The Arabs' inability to assess correctly the political role of a non-Arab State in inter-Arab politics was in any case certainly a greater, or at least not a lesser, obstacle to peace than the difficulty which the Arabs had in assessing Israel's social impact on Arab society.

Many Arab and non-Arab students of the Middle East agree on the fact that Israel is an element 'foreign' to the region. The Arabs and most of the 'progressive' States of the Third World simply identify Israel with the West, with American imperialism and European colonialism. Influential voices have been heard in Israel claiming that the State was and must remain westernized and avoid Levantinization. Statements of this sort were to be widely quoted by the Arabs to confirm their theory that the Zionist State was a foreign body, an 'unnatural, hybrid, cancerous' growth in the homogeneous social and political tissue of the Arab Middle East. Convenient for propaganda, this oversimplified description of the nature of the Jewish State led many of its enemies into dangerous misconceptions. Israel was not so much 'foreign' as a 'stranger' to Middle Eastern Arab society, stranger in the sense given to this word by Georg Simmel in a well-known essay written almost a century ago.

To use Simmel's definition, Israel was not a 'foreigner' who comes today and goes tomorrow so much as a stranger 'who comes today and stays tomorrow'.[2] The Jewish State with its declared and deeply felt historical and religious attachment to Palestine, its enforced isolation (there are no other Jewish States or autonomous Hebrew-speaking communities in the world) from the family of nations, including the Western ones, and its increasingly Arabized population was far less 'transitional', far less 'crusading' than many people both in the Middle East and outside it were led to or were ready to believe. This miscon-

---

[1] Walter Eytan, *The First Ten Years* (New York, 1958).

[2] Quoted in K. H. Wolff, *The Sociology of Georg Simmel*, ch. 5 (Glencoe, Ill., 1950).

ception of the nature of the Jewish State was to be the primary source
of Arab military and political miscalculations about Israel. It also
caused repeated misjudgements on the part of the Great Powers of
Israel's ability to carry out political, diplomatic, and military initiatives
of her own.

Things might perhaps have been different if the people dealing with
Middle Eastern affairs had remembered that, unlike the 'foreigner', the
stranger 'like the poor and like the sundry "inner enemies" *is* an element
of the group itself',[1] and if they had realized that at least part of the
Jewish State's amazing capacity for survival was due to the fact that
Israel was objectively outside and organically inside the Arab world, not
only geographically but politically, economically, socially, and ideologically—'the "inner enemy" which belongs to the group'. Israel became
part and judge of the Middle Eastern drama at one and the same time.
The impact of Israel's broadcasts in Arabic were, for instance, significant proof of her ambiguous position in the Arab world, just as at
various stages of the bitter inter-Arab strife for leadership over the
Middle East Israel was indirectly responsible for the strengthening of
some Arab governments against others.[2]

The inside role of the Israeli 'outsider' in the Middle East was naturally
no less maddening to the Arabs than its military superiority. Israel's
presence underlined regional, ethnic, and political splits which governments and theoreticians believing in the inner unity of the Middle East
tried to suppress or dismiss as unimportant. It accelerated modernization in an area where traditionalism was strong and the population
resented change at the pace set by 'strangers'. It served as a focal point
for that trend of Arab escapism which wished to ignore rather than face
the disagreeable realities of the Arab world. No outsider could have had
the same influence.

The terms demanded by both sides for a Jewish–Arab agreement
were too far apart to be bridged by diplomatic tactics and political
Machiavellianism. To the victorious Israelis, the minimum they considered themselves entitled to was Arab recognition of their *right* to live
according to their standards and beliefs. To the Arabs, the minimum
they felt they should demand—in accordance with their potential
strength, their strategic and economic value to the Great Powers, their
interpretation of the United Nations' decisions, their conception of
national honour, and, last but not least, in relation to the political

---

[1] ibid.
[2] Yehoshafat Harkabi, *Emdat HaAravim Besichsuch Yisrael-Arav* (The Arab Position in
the Israel–Arab Conflict), Tel Aviv, 1968, especially pp. 307–13.

isolation and the then apparently limited powers of retaliation of Israel—was the renunciation by the Zionist State of its own conception of statehood, as well as of the territory added by war to the original area of Palestine allotted by the United Nations to the Jewish State in 1947. Considered from these subjective points of view, the fight could only go on.

Chapter 6

The Years of Survival

The word 'revolution' can be derived from both 'revolt' and 'revolve'. Originally it indicated only axial or orbital movement; later, when people started to attempt analogies between natural and social forces, it came to mean social upheaval as well. In the case of Israel, the word 'revolution' in both senses can be applied to the period between 1949 and 1957—the period between the two first Jewish–Arab wars, namely the War of Independence and the Sinai Campaign. It was a time of upheaval, because the new State, in its own contradictory, hesitant, intriguing way, was attempting like any ex-colonial territory to define itself in terms of opposition to, or at least diversity from, its 'metropolitan' parents—namely the Zionist movement, the Jewish Disapora, and Anglo-Saxon influence.

It was a time of revolution in the sense of rotation, because the upheaval never succeeded in creating a break between Israel and its traditional Western Jewish origins. The State of Israel's attempt to assert itself against the 'metropolitan' influence of Judaism was balanced by an equally strong need for the Diaspora's increased support due to the strain imposed on Israel by the mass Jewish immigration into the new State and by the Arab siege.

It seems to me that, contrary to many statements to this effect, setting the Israeli State free from its 'metropolitan' Jewish and Western dependence was not one of the achievements of the Jewish colonial revolt. The achievement was rather to place it in an enlarged orbit: a political, social, economic, and cultural rotation—equally bound by the old centres of attraction and repulsion—namely the Jewish Diaspora, the Western world, the Arab world, Eastern European (communist) antisemitism.

Much confusion was thus created. Old anti-colonial, revolutionary symbols, institutions, slogans, and men remained to interpret, express, and manipulate a situation which had changed in extent but not in its basic attitudes. But the same words and ideas, about colonialism, the liberation movement, anti-imperialism, *inter alia*, began to assume different meanings in Israel and in other emerging societies, at a time when the channels of political, ideological, and religious communication between Israel and Western and Eastern Europe were not clear. With the communist world they were soon totally blocked. Once more, Jewish nationalism found itself operating under the stress of a desynchronized situation and of almost total isolation.

I have tried to show above how Zionism had striven to solve the Jewish problem by applying eighteenth- and nineteenth-century ideological and technological tools, borrowed from Europe, to the twentieth-century colonial agrarian situation in Palestine. Independent Israel was forced to face a different but equally conflicting situation: in the midst of an anti-Western, colonial world in revolt, where men were passionately attempting to build modern States out of incoherent nations, Israel was groping with the task of creating a nation out of a State which looked like a glorified, half socialist, half capitalist, Jewish ghetto.

One has only to read the speeches of Zionist leaders, such as Ben Gurion[1] and Louis Finkelstein,[2] or intellectuals like Carl J. Friedrich,[3] to realize how the combination of intense national emotion, extraordinary historical circumstances, and the Jewish predilection for historicist interpretation of current events led otherwise cool political minds to express themselves with Messianic lyricism, often descending to banality. However genuine, this Zionist reasoning suffered from the inevitable limitations—and vulgarity—of any human attempt to squeeze universal ideals into current politics. The greatest of modern Jewish Israeli writers, Nobel prizewinner S. Y. Agnon,[4] was one of the first although certainly not the only Israeli intellectual to feel and express the discrepancy between the values of universal Judaism and and those of Jewish nationalism. Martin Buber was another. But somehow they stood outside the social and intellectual realities of the State because for many years Zionist society was too much involved in building up its material structure to have time to spare for thoughts and doubts. In a sense Israeli society developed a gift for simplification at the expense of imagination, especially in the local social, political, and technological fields.

This does not mean that the various groups, factions, and leaders had no ideas and ambitions of their own—quite the contrary. But no one

[1] David Ben Gurion, 'The Spirit of the New Israel' in Moshe Davis (ed.), *Israel: Its Role in Civilization* (New York, 1956), pp. 18–30.

[2] Louis Finkelstein, 'The State of Israel as a Spiritual Force' in ibid., pp. 3–11.

[3] Carl J. Friedrich, 'Israel and the End of History', in ibid., pp. 92–110.

[4] For a complete list of Agnon's books and a study of his work, see Arnold J. Band, *Nostalgia and Nightmare: A Study in the Fiction of S. Y. Agnon* (Berkeley, 1968).

had the ideological and the political strength to make his own views on the nature of the new State accepted by a clear majority.

On the left of the political spectrum stood the Marxist parties, who theoretically had the power and organizational strength to put their ideology into practice. But in practice the distance between the Mapam-member, communist fellow-traveller, and former commander of the Hagana, Moshe Sneh (who favoured the immediate creation of an Israeli Popular Democracy), and an American-educated social democrat like Mrs. Golda Meyerson (later Meir), who paraphrased the *Haggada*[1] at the 1 May rally of Israeli workers in 1949 by shouting: 'Next year in a Socialist State', was greater than between Labour and Conservative supporters in England. At the other end of the spectrum stood the Orthodox parties, more united in their aim of transforming Israel into a theocratic State, but equally divided on the methods of achieving this goal. Some groups, for example, the Hapoel Hamizrahi, favoured and practised full co-operation with the other socialist parties; other groups, for example, Agudat Israel, kept their distance from the dangerous Zionist secularists. Equally convinced of their claim to be sole guardians of the truth, equally divided among themselves, and thus equally incapable of imposing their convictions on the country were the nationalist and 'capitalist' groups.

Eisenstadt has underlined the influence of this fragmented ideological identification on the Israeli *élites*. Their institutionalization became a process of 'selective entrenchment of protagonists of ideology in strategic parts of the social system who attempted to influence and control many of the important aspects of institutional structure'.[2] Because the pioneering myth had no counter-myth to struggle with in the Zionist society of Palestine, and because it quickly became an effective symbol of identity for large groups of the immigrant population searching for an identity, the belief that achievement was superior to speculation became widespread and popular. We shall see how one of the greatest crises in Israeli society, the Lavon affair, was in fact also a fight between those who believed in 'performance' and those who thought that performance alone was not enough.[3] But for both sides 'performance' remained of supreme importance. It expressed something of the 'protestant' ethic of action in Zionism, in the Weberian sense, and also the logic of a pressing local political and economic situation. In the Diaspora the Jew had remained conscious of his national identity, in spite

---

[1] The ritual recited in Jewish homes on the first night of Passover. It ends with the call, 'next year in Jerusalem!'   [2] Eisenstadt, op. cit., pp. 44–5.   [3] ibid., p. 327.

of the dispersed Jewish population, through his Messianic ideal. In Israel (as had happened to the Europeans who had gone to America) the Jews were becoming more and more conscious of their national identity because they were pressed together into the matrix of local nationalism by the problems of survival. In practice, no political co-operation could be achieved where ideology was concerned, but only in the face of pressing practical problems: the economic relations between the State and the Jewish Diaspora; the day-to-day problems of the integration of immigrants; the reaction of the State to its external enemies.[1] There was very little scope left for an active Israeli 'colonial' revolt against the Diaspora, although some intellectual movements, like the 'Canaanean' (which took its name from the Land of Canaan, pagan Palestine before the biblical conquest) upheld the idea of a total rejection of 'Jewishness' by the Israeli State in favour of its 'Semitic' integration into the population of the area.[2] The fact, however, that such a trend manifested itself more in artistic and literary than in political circles is a proof of the small following it achieved among the public in general, although the election to Parliament of one deputy of the 'HaOlam Haze' (New Force) movement, headed by the publisher Uri Avnery, in 1965 on a strong non-Zionist, secular, and Canaanean platform showed that this movement could move beyond the borders of literary circles and become a political force.

If one really wants to dig for some manifestation of an Israeli 'colonial' revolt, one must turn to the problem of immigration. Here the State was faced with a real conflict of authorities. On the one hand, it was economically necessary and politically convenient to let international organizations such as the Jewish Agency and the Zionist Organization organize, finance, and sponsor the migration of Jews from the Diaspora to Israel and their material integration into the State. On the other hand, the political leadership of Israel, which had come to the Government from the Directorate of the Agency, stubbornly refused to provide the Zionist Organization with a privileged status in the new State. Para-doxically, the discussions in 1953 about the legal position of the Jewish Agency and the Zionist Organization in Israel gave vent to the desire of Israeli politicians to assert their independence from the Zionist Organization. The representatives of the nationalist and middle-class parties were the only ones to demand that the Zionist Organization be regarded as the sole representative of the Jewish people at large. The left-wing and religious parties rejected this view. The Marxists did not want to make any concessions to organized Zionism because to them it

---

[1] ibid., pp. 306–26.   [2] ibid., p. 373.

represented American 'imperialist influence'.[1] The Orthodox denied, as they had always done, the right of a secular Jewish organization in Israel to represent the Jewish people as a whole. Thus, neither the political nor religious ideologies of the parties, nor the 'colonial' upheaval of the Israeli State against the vague, 'metropolitan' influence of the Diaspora, nor the Zionist Organization, could serve to establish a trend capable of driving the new State in a particular direction. The ideological stalemate and the absence of a real 'enemy'—the Arabs excepted—made the nation-building task of the bureaucracy easier and more purposeful. Israel became, politically, a flexible society, not because it had a tradition of liberalism, but because of the ideological impotence of its *élites* and the common need to react to contradictory external pressures gave the officials more responsibility and power than the theoreticians and intellectuals.

In spite of long experience of communal autonomous administration and some efforts to prepare appropriate personnel to take over the responsibility of government from the British, Israel arrived at independence with a very poor, uneducated, and inefficient bureaucracy. The reasons for this have been studied in detail and, over the years, serious efforts have been made to improve the situation.[2] But the Jewish State was not, and still is not, in a postition to apply fundamental remedies to the shortcomings of its administration.

To begin with, Israel was born not with one but with several bureaucracies, each operating according to its own Parkinsonian logic: State bureaucracy, trade union bureaucracy, the bureaucracy of the Jewish Agency and Zionist organizations, party bureaucracy, local bureaucracy, etc. Some increase in the size of the bureaucracy was inevitable with the swelling population and the growth in articulation of a modernizing State. It is however difficult to explain solely in terms of demographic growth the fact that the number of Jewish Agency employees increased from 759 in 1946 (when they performed many of the duties of a government administration as well as of an immigration agency) to 4,437 in 1951 (and they remained more or less at that level even after having been deprived of all government responsibilities). In 1947 in the Histadrut 6,000 administrative staff dealt with the 270,000 members of that organization. In 1964 this had risen to 24,816 staff for 1,388,000

---

[1] Leonard Fein, op. cit., pp. 103 ff., argues, with reference to the Jewish Agency and other non-governmental organizations, that 'some powers normally associated with governing have ceded to the State'. I think this is true of most of the Yishuv organizations such as the Histadrut, but not of the Jewish Agency, which saw its role and status in Palestine completely changed by the appearance of the State.

[2] Bernstein, op. cit., ch. 6, pp. 153–82, and Eisenstadt, op. cit., pp. 303–5.

members (and their families). Similarly the state officials, who numbered 3,000 when the State was established, numbered 15,880 one year later, 40,000 in 1956, and almost 60,000 in 1967. Not all the people employed in the tertiary—service—sector were paid officials but it is significant that by 1964 51 per cent of the employed population of Israel was engaged in service, and most of these were in white-collar jobs.

These jobs were distributed according to the numerical strength of their party—with the sole exception of the Army, and, to a lesser extent, of the diplomatic service. The bureaucratic sector was not only one of the least productive sectors, economically, of Israeli society, but also one of the most politicized. Politicization naturally led to inefficiency, partiality, and lack of public responsibility. Public service remained for many years the main source of income and status for a large part of the Israeli *élite*, which in an egalitarian society as existed in Israel was less able than other *élites* to fulfil its urge for social distinction and self-expression. At the same time, the State had to keep going, in spite of the ideological stalemate, its incompetent and overlapping bureaucracy, its lack of administrative experience; it had to cope with the economic and social problems created by mass immigration and the security problems caused by the Arab siege. Many of these problems found their practical solution with the aid of an unintended combination of bureaucratic activism and secrecy.

Bureaucratic activism *per se* is not an Israeli characteristic. In any state the 'Establishment' short-circuits to some extent the proper channels of authority in order to get things done more quickly or in favour of certain privileged groups or persons. In Israel, however, the phenomenon acquired particular importance because 'activism' became important in the choice and co-optation of policy-making personnel: it became an accepted state of mind in the higher echelons of the administration, where officials were often called on to solve problems on which parties and Government could not reach agreement.[1] As a matter of fact, many of the present cabinet ministers in Israel started or served some time as high officials, promotion from bureaucracy to government being helped by the high degree of politicization of the bureaucracy itself.[2] But bureaucratic activism had another important consequence.

---

[1] The best-known although by no means the only case being the military and political co-operation with France. It was a policy which was carried out with Ben Gurion's backing by the military establishment headed by the then Director General of the Ministry of Defence, Shimon Peres.

[2] The past and present Ministers of Commerce and Finance, Sharef and Sapir, were respectively Director General of the Ministry of Defence and Public Service Commissioner. The former Minister for Posts, Sason, was a diplomat who joined the Government without

To be effective its publicity needed to be limited, since publicity could cause jealousy and calls for increased public control. Thus it developed a club-like mentality which fed on an already existing deeply rooted tradition of secrecy in the behaviour of the political *élites*.

From the beginning, the leaders of the Jewish national movement had been engaged in semi-legal work and, out of necessity, secrecy had become second nature to them. The 'club' mentality was natural to people who knew the dangers of engaging in politics in Tsarist Russia —whence the majority of the leaders of Israel had come. Secrecy had also been necessary during the British Mandate, for the creation of an underground army and of an efficient autonomous Jewish administration. Secrecy was more than ever necessary and acceptable to those dealing with the security of the State—a large field of activity—for a country living in a situation of permanent military tension. But Israel was also an egalitarian society by vocation in which, quite independently of the state of emergency, secrecy became a status-symbol for all those who believed themselves more important because they knew more. To be 'in the secret' meant to be 'in' even when the secret was—as it turned out to be in most cases—an open one. There are probably few countries in the world where political gossip is so developed as in Israel. It may be connected with the mentality of the Jew, accustomed to living in a closely-knit community, but it certainly also answers a need for some form of social distinction suppressed by official egalitarianism. Gossip and secrecy served to distinguish those who knew more and thus could do more from those who 'were not in the know'. The ability to know and to act became a distinctive mark of the Israel *élite*, with secrecy reinforcing activism and vice versa, and both strengthening the power of a bureaucracy which was highly politicized, independent of ideological orthodoxy, operating by fits and starts through a network of personal contacts and family relations far more efficient than the machinery of the governments or of the parties.[1] It gave rise to strong accusations of

---

being a member of parliament. The present Deputy Minister of Finance was previously a Controller of Foreign Exchange.

[1] The late Prime Minister, Moshe Sharett, was related to the founder of the Hagana, Golomb, and to the Head of the Special Service, Avigur. The Minister of Defence, Moshe Dayan, and the former head of the Airforce, General Weizmann, are brothers-in-law, while General Dayan's father was for many years a representative of the powerful Co-operative Villages group. In the family of Dr. Ruppin, the ideologue and planner of Jewish colonization in Palestine between the two wars, one can find a former Chief of Staff, the President of the World Federation of Jewish Women, and several ambassadors. The late Aba Khushi, the 'boss' of the port in Haifa and for many years mayor of that city, has a political heir in parliament and in the Histadrut in the person of his son-in-law. The son of the Minister for Posts is a leading Arab expert and a diplomat like his father, as well as the Prime

partiality—in slang *protectzia*—of lack of democracy, but never of personal corruption. On the whole the upper echelons of the Israeli bureaucracy, although operating in a society still underdeveloped and agricultural, evolved very early into a modern technocracy, passionately devoted to action and to public service, standing on the borderline between political power and political influence, equally addicted to the euphoria of secrecy and gadgets which Lord Snow so well describes, in connection with Britain, in his *Science and Government*.[1] Of course they made many mistakes and, fought bitterly among themselves for power. But they also provided a strong impulse for the process of the transformation of Israel from a plantocracy into a technocracy, and provided a much-needed recruiting ground for the new political personnel, which the rigidity and sectarianism of the parties' organizations would never have been capable of providing.

The 'Establishment' in Israel was and still is largely synonymous with the veteran leadership of the second *aliah*. Out of 212 Jewish members of parliament who served between 1949 and 1964, 73 per cent were born in Eastern Europe.[2] In the Mapai party, which has dominated the political life of the Yishuv and the State since 1930, the Eastern Europeans made up 75 per cent of whom 25 per cent—and this included almost all the leaders—came to Palestine in the second *aliah*.[3] This trend becomes more evident when the second *aliah* is considered not only in a chronological context but also, as it should be, in a social and ideological context. In this light the role played by its veteran members, although greatly diminished by the biological imperative of age, looks even more central.[4] The second *aliah* included men like the late Premier Levi Eshkol, who came to Israel in 1913, the present Prime Minister, Golda Meir, who arrived in Palestine from America in 1921, and the Party Secretary, Pinchas Sapir,[5] who came in the thirties. They were all cut from the same psychological and ideological cloth. This explains many of their political ideas and their conflict with Israeli-born leaders like Moshe Dayan and the long—but now dwindling—concentration of power in their hands.

In the first Israeli Cabinet Mapai's seven Ministers had all been born

---

Minister's Adviser for the Occupied Territories. His son-in-law was for many years the Prime Minister's Political Secretary. In the late Chief Rabbi's family may be found the Director General of a Ministry, a Chief of Military Intelligence, and a Foreign Minister.

[1] C. P. Snow, *Science and Government* (London, 1961).

[2] L. J. Fein, op. cit., p. 151, quoting A. Zidon, *Beit Hanivcharim* (House of Deputies), Jerusalem, 1964.

[3] ibid., p. 151.

[4] ibid., p. 52.

[5] Minister of Finance since the 1969 elections.

in Eastern Europe in the eighties and nineties and had all come to Palestine before 1924. In the eleventh Cabinet, in 1963, Mapai's eleven ministers included six born in this century, two native Israelis, one immigrant from Iraq, and four Ministers who had immigrated to Israel after the thirties. The trend continued after the 1967 war when the new, Mapai-dominated Labour Party's thirteen Ministers still included only two native Israelis, two non-Europeans, and nine Central or Eastern Europeans (Foreign Minister Abba Eban being a British Jew of Eastern European origins). Of the eight other coalition Ministers, not one was Israeli-born or born outside Europe.

Up to 1948 the main sources of the power of the second *aliah* group were to be found in the close-knit society of the veteran immigrants, in the Yishuv acceptance of the identification of national identity symbols with the second *aliah* symbols of a Socialist Zionist Utopia—voluntary-ism, pioneering, and co-operation—and in the prominent positions achieved by participants in the second *aliah* in the course of the building of the national home. In 1948 Mrs. Meir, then Israeli Ambassador in Moscow, organized her embassy on kibbutz lines, with everyone sharing in the community's work and the Ambassador herself carrying the shopping from the market (something, by the way, her driver refused to do). Such a situation obviously could not last very long. Massive immigration, growing urbanization, industrial development, security, and educational requirements created new needs and new articulations of power. But it did not displace the central role of the second *aliah* veterans in Israeli society—especially in the political institutions. Here I should like to recall very briefly the facts of immigration and economic development in the fifties, two things which were to shake the foundations of the old Yishuv institutions and the powerful grip which the second *aliah* veterans had on them.

When the Second World War ended, the Palestinian Jews were the most flourishing community in the Middle East, and the Palestinian soldiers returning from devastated Europe were proudly conscious of the fact that they were, in many ways, better off than the majority of Europeans. This discovery increased their sense of mission, of self-assurance, and their awareness of belonging to a proud, devoted, idealistic colonial society, similar, in many ways, to the puritan New England of the seventeenth-century settlement. The Yishuv for the first time after many years of trial enjoyed the amenities of a relative economic prosperity and the satisfaction of sharing in the military triumph over fascism and Nazism, the two enemies from which the Jews have suffered most and against which Palestinian Jewry had contributed more than any other colony of the British Empire in proportion to its population.[1]

The situation changed abruptly with the War of Independence, out of which the Yishuv came victorious, but bled of its human resources (more than 6,000 men and women—1 per cent of the original population —had fallen in the fighting), destitute—the Israeli pound was devalued from $4 in 1948 to 55 cents in 1952—disrupted in its social structure by a wave of immigration which brought into the country in less than two years one destitute brother for every Jew living in Israel. Paradoxically, however, this influx did not change significantly the percentage of distribution of the population among the branches of production nor the share of each branch in the total national production. Half the Jewish population of Israel remained, as at the time of the Yishuv, employed in primary and secondary branches, with a 40 per cent share in national production. Agriculture employed a steady 15 per cent, services the remaining 35 per cent of the population, producing about two-thirds of the national product.[2]

In time to come, Israel was to realize that the immigrants' destitution was the State's greatest economic asset. The hundreds of thousands of Jewish refugees who poured into the new State brought with them their miseries, their skills, their passionate will to live and to rebuild, their open-mindedness and avidity for change, but also their different backgrounds and standards of education, all qualities and defects which made them easily adaptable to the most modern forms of production. The shortcomings were more obvious in the early fifties. The doubling of the population in less than one and a half years had forced the Government to impose a régime of austerity as strict as any in post-war Europe. There were no monetary reserves, no basic industry, insufficient agricultural production for the population's needs, no housing, and no modern communications systems. The most important and immediately available economic reserve was the abandoned Arab property—in which, by 1951, 25 per cent of the Israeli population was housed.[3] And it was the abandoned Arab land which, in spite of the havoc produced by the war, offered the Jewish economy an immediate basis for expansion.

This was made clear, not only by the increase in cultivated land— from 1949 to 1953 the acreage of Jewish farmland jumped from 400,000 to 890,000 acres—but from the ratio, in terms of production value, of

---

[1] Eisenstadt, op. cit., pp. 76–80.
[2] Eisenstadt, op. cit., pp. 94–5.
[3] For an evaluation of abandoned Arab property, see Gabbay, op. cit., pp. 345 ff.

agriculture to industry, which dropped from 2:3 to 2:2·5 between 1949 and 1954. After that, the ratio increased continuously in favour of industry and stood at 2:4·3 in 1964, in spite of an almost tenfold increase in agricultural production.[1]

Socially speaking, this curve shown by the ratio of agricultural-industrial production value meant the consolidation of the economic and political power of those groups who could best supply the State with much-needed agricultural goods, namely the collective and co-operative agricultural aristocracy which was also the political and social *élite* of Israel. It was a natural process which could not be stopped even by the most rigid political ideology. In fact, the collective settlements of the left-wing Marxist party, Mapam, which vociferously claimed immediate, total political equality between Arabs and Jews and the establishment of an Arab–Israeli Popular Democracy, were as eager as the other farmers to take possession of abandoned—and in some cases *de jure*, but not *de facto* abandoned—Arab land.

But the economic needs brought into being by the massive immigration bent the Marxist egalitarian social ideology of the Israeli agrarian aristocracy in another way. Since this closely-knit élitist society could not absorb thousands of newcomers without destroying its select social and ideological foundations (and since the new immigrants, totally unprepared for the collective way of life, also refused to renounce their individual way of life to join collective settlements), the Government asked the socialist farmers to employ as many salaried workers as possible. This, of course, was the very opposite of the theory of social equality and non-exploitation preached by egalitarian Socialist Zionism. But the necessity to provide work for the newcomers was stronger than ideology. So old and well-established agricultural co-operative and collective settlements not only engaged salaried workers, but used—especially the kibbutzim—their economic resources, their organization, and their political influence to create vast industrial plants.[2] In doing so, the collective agrarian socialist aristocracy turned into a technologically minded plantocracy, contributing not only to the tremendous expansion and mechanization of Jewish agriculture, but even to the increased industrialization of the State.

It was not so much a momentous change as the continuation of a trend, which, as we have already seen in the previous chapter, had contributed to the consolidation of Israeli society by combining the

[1] Ministry of Foreign Affairs, Information Division, *Facts About Israel* (Jerusalem, 1955/56, 1964/65, 1967/68).
[2] Eliyahu Kanovsky, *The Economy of the Israeli Kibbutz* (Cambridge, Mass., 1966).

agricultural and industrial efforts of an aristocracy with its exemplary simplicity and frugal way of life. But the growth of a collective vested interest in Israeli society contributed to another and later aspect of the conflict between plantocracy and technocracy, the 'Lavon affair', which marred the public life of Israel in the sixties.

It was a growth which also inevitably fed on the ability of the Israeli Government to mobilize and efficiently distribute the capital investments acquired from abroad for its survival. For the period 1949–57 these investments amounted to nearly 3 billion dollars, roughly a third of the total American contribution to the revival of the post-war economies of Europe, under the Marshall Plan.[1]

This can of course be only a very imprecise comparison, since it does not stress the differences existing between Western Europe and Israel. If it is true that, *per capita*, Israel received ten times more than Western Europe, it is also true that the Marshall Plan helped to revitalize the already existing and powerful European economy, which after two years of aid was already producing 20 per cent more than before the war. In Israel, foreign financial help disappeared for a long time into the bottomless pit of the basic requirements of the infrastructure and of military waste. Still, in terms of import surplus (especially capital import) in relation to G.N.P., Israel showed a capacity for capital mobilization twenty-three times greater than France and twenty times greater than Italy.[2]

The Jewish communities of the Diaspora made a significant contribution to the salvaging of Israeli economy. They poured in an average of 150 million dollars a year in donations, investments, and loans to help with the resettlement of the new immigrants. Between 1949 and 1959 Jewish sources provided 47 per cent of all capital imports to a total of 1,469 million dollars. They agreed, in 1951, to subscribe a Development Loan (which by 1965 had brought some 1,500 million dollars to Israel) in order to help the Israeli economy to take off with its own resources. This loan probably did more good to Israel than any other type of economic aid. It gave much-needed capital, it substituted credit for charity, and made more than a million Jewish and non-Jewish subscribers throughout the world sympathetically interested in Israel's survival. Politically, it was aid without strings, although it reinforced the influence of private Jewish investors on the then basically socialist-controlled economy of the Jewish State.

On the other hand, American economic aid, which between 1948 and

---

[1] *Statistical Abstract of Israel* (Jerusalem, 1961).

[2] M. Michaeli, in *Rivion Lechalkalah* (Economic Quarterly), Jerusalem, June 1961.

1962 amounted to about 831 million dollars, was obviously conditional on Israel's collaboration with the free world, although it was also based on long-standing American sympathy for the Zionist cause as well as the powerful influence of the large Jewish American Diaspora on American policy towards Israel.[1] The Israeli Government bravely tried for some time to steer a 'non-aligned' course between the two rival cold-war blocs. But by 1950, when Israel chose to back the United States' stand on Korea, it was clear that political ties with Russia and the communist world would have been of little immediate use for the solution of the pressing political and economic problems of the Jewish State. The U.S.S.R. had no influence in the Middle East at the time and communism was unpopular among the Arabs; it had no economic resources to spare for foreign aid; it soon became suspicious of the national influence of Israel over the important and influential Jewish population of the communist bloc and gave the green light to a renewal of traditional anti-Jewish and anti-Zionist sentiment.

The hostile attitude of the communist countries to Zionism, and the growing coolness between Israel and the U.S.S.R.—culminating in the 'Doctors' Trial' in Moscow, in the bombing of the Russian Legation in Tel Aviv in February 1953, and in the breaking of diplomatic relations between the two countries (re-established in July 1953), created an ideological crisis among Israel's socialists. Mapam broke up in 1954, and in the wake of the schism, group and personal conflicts in kibbutz society rose to a pitch where old-established settlements were expelling part of their membership. A death-blow was dealt by Moscow to the hopes of the Marxist groups in Israel of making Zionism and communism coexist. The ideological and political gulf between Moscow and Jerusalem was bound to weaken Marxist influence in Israel and increase the State's political leanings towards the West. These leanings were, in time, further strengthened by the German reparations to Israel.

The first demands for reparation from Germany were formulated by the Jerusalem Government to the four occupying powers in 1951. It called for a payment from the two Germanies of a total of 1,500 million dollars, but it fell on deaf ears, both where the occupying powers and the German authorities were concerned.

A new stage for negotiation was opened a year later, when the Allies decided to sign a peace treaty with West Germany and Chancellor Adenauer became convinced that something had to be done for Israel in order to change the Nazi image of Germany. He opened negotiations

[1] See Nadav Safran, *The United States and Israel* (Cambridge, Mass., 1963), especially ch. XVI, pp. 270–92.

which, through the active diplomatic mediation of Dr. Naḥum Goldmann, the President of the World Jewish Congress, began in Holland in
March 1952, and were concluded in Luxemburg on 10 September 1952.

I shall not go into the details of these negotiations. It will be enough
here to remind the reader that the agreement was meant to cover the
expenses borne by the Jewish Community of Palestine and by the State
of Israel for the rehabilitation of German nationals and other victims
of Nazism, not as a compensation for the killing of six million Jews,
for which there could obviously be no compensation; and on whose
behalf Israel—although she had granted symbolic citzenship to all the
Jews killed in Europe—was in no way entitled to speak.

The Reparations Treaty envisaged the payment to Israel over a
period of twelve years, of 750 million dollars in money and goods. The
payments started in March 1953; they were executed with meticulous
precision by the German authorities and used efficiently by the State of
Israel, which was represented in Germany by a special government
company. The German reparations undoubtedly saved Israel's economy
from total collapse in the difficult years after the big wave of immigration in 1949–51.[1] Arab protests did not deter Germany from fulfilling
its obligations nor did it cause any break in the relations between Bonn
and the Middle East.

There is no doubt, as I have mentioned, that German reparations
strengthened Israel both economically and militarily, and paved the
way to the normalization of relations between the two countries. They
also boosted Israel's exports to Europe; and contributed considerably—
as I shall describe later—to the Jewish State's efforts at co-operation
with Africa.

By 1962 Western Germany was Israel's third most important trading-
partner after U.S.A. and Britain with 62 million dollars' worth of
exports and 28 million dollars' worth of imports and with an unknown
share in investments not only in Israel but in many Israeli enterprises
in developing countries.[2]

But the main impact of Bonn's economic contribution to Israel was
to be felt in the political and social life of the State. Because of opposition to the treaty by the nationalist Ḥerut Party, which refused 'blood
money' from Germany, Israel came close to civil war. Ḥerut supporters
tried to storm parliament in the most violent political demonstration

[1] I have found much interesting information about the German reparations in B. Akzin
and Y. Dror, *Israel: High-Pressure Planning* (New York, 1966).

[2] *Facts and Figures* (Jerusalem, 1965), p. 86. For German co-operation with Israel in the
Third World, see Laufer, op. cit., pp. 44, 49, 254.

Israel had ever experienced. Two hundred people were injured on 9 January 1952 in Jerusalem; the army was called out to reinforce the police, and the political feud between Ben Gurion and what he called the 'fascist hooliganism' of the Ḥerut Party was established.

The political storm over the Reparations Treaty was quickly subdued by the economic benefits which affected both supporters of the nationalist party and the left-wing Marxists, who were equally opposed—but for different reasons—to Israel's relations with Western Germany. But the reparations were not Bonn's only contribution to the Israeli economy. More important were the personal compensations paid by the German *Länder* to individuals who had suffered under Nazism. This second type of German repayment benefited only a limited number (no more than 300,000) of Israelis—all of European origin, but those concerned have received, since 1958, some 1,500 million dollars, double what the Government received from the Reparations Treaty.

This money very quickly added to the financial and social problems of Israel. It accelerated inflation and widened the already deeply resented gap between immigrants from Europe and those from the Arab States, thus deepening a distinction which was already sorely felt in terms of cultural, ethnic, and social rivalry. In the period under review, these conflicts had not yet exploded: mainly because of the state of political and military insecurity which kept the Israeli nation mobilized and united in spite of its many internal political and social differences. The causes of this insecurity are linked with the difficult and still unsettled relations between Israel and her neighbours. But they obviously go beyond them and the Middle East.

When dealing with the Israeli–Arab problem one can argue that the relations between these two nations are inextricably involved with the struggle of the Jews to assert themselves as an independent nation. If so, the focus of any analysis of Israel's foreign policy should rest on the State's Jewishness as a factor of primary importance in the relations between the State and the Jewish Diaspora, but not in those with other countries.[1] It is true that some cases provide exceptions to the rule. One is the question of Jerusalem, in which religious and emotional considerations are important. Another is the anachronistic existence in Israel of the last of the Capitulation Treaties, namely the 1913 Treaty of Mytilene, signed between the Ottoman Empire and the Christian Powers of Europe and concerning the rights of Catholic religious

[1] I have discussed this problem in 'Pre-Risorgimento and Post-Risorgimento Zionism' in *The New Middle East*, December 1969; see also S. Rosenne, 'Basic Elements of Israel's Foreign Policy', *India Quarterly*, XVII, 4, October–December 1961.

institutions in Palestine. It is one of the paradoxes of Israel that this treaty—which is of very limited practical scope—is being upheld by France, the first of the European countries to fight for the separation of the Church from the State.

Another common argument is the one which describes Israel as the product of an international conspiracy. This is the current image in Arab, communist, and 'progressive' propaganda, strongly reminiscent of the Nazis' description of the Jews as agents of a pluto-democratic-communist international plot. The parochial and at the same time supranational interests of the State of Israel can provide grounds for accusations of all sorts of 'cloak-and-dagger' machinations connected with its establishment and its survival.[1] In fact, the foreign policy of Israel is easy to explain when looked at from three different sides of the Arab–Israeli struggle: the Israeli–Arab border relations; the Israeli–Arab relations as part of the inter-Arab struggle over the balance of Arab power in the Middle East; the Israeli–Arab relations as an aspect of the non-Arab interest in the Arab world.

The Israeli–Arab border relations are the most violent but also the least complicated part of the problem. These relations were—and still are—dictated as far as Israel is concerned by three basic necessities: the need to fill empty land within the State's borders; the need to ensure Israeli sovereignty over contested border areas; the need to overcome the Arab economic, political, and military siege. However, while the realization of the first two needs—namely the settlement of empty Israeli territory and the upholding of Israeli sovereignty over contested areas—could be achieved without Arab consent, the breaking of the economic, political, and military siege could not be accomplished by unilateral action. It demanded a measure of Arab agreement and of open or secret co-operation, which in turn required concessions which Israel was not prepared to make.

On the Arab side, frontier relations were dictated by similar considerations in reverse. Against Israel's empty spaces stood the overflow of Arab refugees which for human, economic, and political reasons pressed both on to Israeli territory and into the power vacuum created by Arab political evolution inside the host countries. Confronting the Israeli effort to assert Jewish sovereignty over demilitarized border areas was the Arab determination to erode as much as possible of the areas controlled by the enemy. Finally, running counter to the

---

[1] As Karl Popper says, in *The Open Society and its Enemies*, cloak-and-dagger activities have in them as much—if not more—irrationality and randomness as any other human behaviour.

Israeli need for peace, for Arab recognition, and for Arab economic markets, was the equally passionate need of the Arabs to 'contain' the Jewish State, to keep it in a situation of insecurity, of political incertitude, of perpetual economic crisis. Just as the Jews wanted to strike roots as quickly as possible in their new country, so the Arabs were interested in keeping the Jewish immigrant population as rootless and 'transient' as possible. The Arabs had fought and lost a war mainly in order to abolish the right of free immigration into Palestine for the Jews. Now they at least hoped to discourage further immigration by forcing Israel into a state of economic bankruptcy and physical insecurity. For the Arab governments and societies, which were basically still traditional and agrarian, any Jewish population increase could not be dissociated from the Jews' need for increased territory. Hence, to the Arabs, more Jews in Israel inevitably meant Jewish expansionism. They did not realize that military pressure along the frontiers and economic boycott would also lead to a powerful—and perhaps otherwise non-existent—incentive for Israel to engage in rapid settlement of its empty areas and to develop towards complete industrialization. They did not attribute any particular significance to the fact that in more than fifty years of organized Zionist immigration only 1 million Jews out of an estimated 16 million had come to Palestine nor to the fact that they tended to concentrate in a very limited coastal area even when disposing —as Baron de Rothschild's colonization society did—of large tracts of land in Transjordan.[1] This does not mean that agriculture was not important to the Israeli economy, nor that the Zionists renounced their claims to Palestine. But the extent of settlement was certainly dictated more by non-economic considerations than by the agricultural needs of the Jewish population. The major incentive for putting people along the frontiers was political and military, not economic. Ben Gurion was obsessed by the idea of a territorial security void within the State which might be filled with pockets of Arab populations. He saw the survival of Israel as dependent on its population's capacity 'to fill the land', and Arab armed infiltration considerably increased his concern. In fact he felt so strongly about this danger that in 1953 he decided to set an example by retiring from active political life in Jerusalem to become a shepherd in a new kibbutz in the heart of the Negev Desert, guarding the road to Eilat, exerting only an indirect influence on the affairs of the State. His example was not followed by many, although it undoubtedly gave encouragement to those new immigrants who were

[1] See Israël Margalith, *Le Baron Edmond de Rothschild et la colonisation juive en Palestine 1882–1899* (Paris, 1957), pp. 135–6.

not very happy about being settled along the frontiers, and it contributed indirectly to the development of the Negev. It is, however, doubtful that people would have gone to live in the harsh conditions of the border settlements, especially in the Negev and on the barren hills of Judea, had it not been for the unsettled security situation of the country. Even today, in spite of strong religious and emotional propaganda, and economic incentives, less than 1,000 Jews have taken up residence in the non-Jewish quarters of unified Jerusalem.

Harassed by Arab infiltration—which in the beginning was neither organized nor even well armed—the Israelis paid a very high price for their border settlements, which were built, for security reasons, in places unfit for agricultural development—like the corridor leading to Jerusalem. Border settlement assumed at times the proportions of a Sisyphean effort: villages were losing inhabitants as fast as they were getting them. The cost of such chronic instability of population was euphemistically entered in the Jewish Agency and government budgets under the heading 'consolidation of existing settlements'. But spending money on settling the frontier had at least one advantage: the State was not forced to enact laws forcing new settlers to remain in their border villages against their will. The Israeli frontier thus never turned into an area of punishment, and in time those who stayed put were caught up in the industrial development of the countryside or developed local industries to compensate for the insufficient agricultural revenues. This was the case of desert outposts like Arad, which grew from wilderness and Nabatean archaeology into a compact centre of natural gas and chemical industries; Lakish, a derelict Arab village north of Beersheba, which became an agricultural processing town[1] with 15,000 inhabitants; Beersheba and Eilat, which had only a few thousand inhabitants in 1955 and which became caught up in the economic, scientific, and transport revolution brought about by the development of the potash mines of the Dead Sea, by the establishment of an atomic industry, and by the development of tourist and naval facilities on the Red Sea coast. But even this type of development was in large measure a consequence of a security rather than an economic need. Without the closing of the Suez Canal to Israeli shipping Eilat would probably never have become a petrol harbour. And without the armament race, atomic research would never have been developed in Israel, at least to the extent that it has been in the Beersheba area.[2]

---

[1] Called Kiryat-Gat.

[2] For the strategic and political problems posed by Israel's frontiers, see Moshe Dayan, 'Israel's Border and Security Problems', *Foreign Affairs*, 33, no. 2, January 1955, pp. 250–67.

In the absence of security the frontier became all-important politically for both sides.[1] It is however significant that, as far as Israel
was concerned, there were no Arab 'infiltrators' until 1954—only
'marauders'.

The distinction was not only linguistic, but also political. Although
the Arabs crossed the frontiers in their hundreds, to work border tracts
of land, to steal from Jewish villages, and often to murder, usually
acting in co-operation with Jordanian national guards and Egyptian
intelligence officers, Israel was for a long time uncertain of how best to
deal with them. For at least three years, from 1949 to 1952, the Israeli
authorities took the view that on the whole the infiltrators were really
marauders, namely people who crossed the borders to collect crops
grown on their old farms and not yet harvested by the Israelis. They
were a nuisance and a danger, but they did not seem to operate according to any political and military plan. During this period Israel still had
considerable faith in the United Nations and believed that the best way
to deal with the problem was through the Mixed Armistice Commissions. Furthermore, most of the marauders came from Jordan and
during the first three years of its existence Israel hoped for a border
settlement and possibly peace with Jordan. Finally, the Israeli authorities were anxious not to overemphasize the real damage the marauders
were causing. This might have had a bad effect on the morale of the
new immigrants, and one finds very little information on border clashes
in the Israeli newspapers or radio broadcasts of the time. Most of the
information came from Arab sources. A typical and significant example
of the indecisive policy of the Israelis over border infiltration may perhaps be seen in the reprisal raid on the Jordanian village of Kibya.
There were scores of dead and wounded among the Arabs. There was
a Security Council meeting which condemned Israel; the whole country
talked about the raid. But the acting Prime Minister, Moshe Sharett, as
well as Ben Gurion, who was on leave and came back to Jerusalem to
broadcast a 'message to the nation' on 19 October 1953, disclaimed all
government responsibility for or even knowledge of the Kibya raid.[2]

The policy was soon to change with Ben Gurion's return to power in
1955. With him, and under the new military leadership of General
Dayan, the policy of reprisal became official and was constantly applied.[3]
And through this hard, bloody, and hazardous border guerrilla warfare,

[1] Nadav Safran, op. cit., ch. XII, 'National Defence: Threat, Response, Implication',
especially pp. 182–92, a thesis which the author has recently developed in *From War to
War: The Arab–Israeli Confrontation, 1948–1967* (New York, 1969).

[2] *Jerusalem Post*, 17–20 October 1953.

[3] Moshe Dayan, *Diary of the Sinai Campaign* (Eng. trans., London, 1966), p. 8.

the whole fighting structure and strategic conception of the Israeli Army changed radically.

Israel had from the beginning spent a large part of its national income on security. In the early fifties the Arab military threat, even after the 1948 defeat, looked impressive—at least from Tel Aviv. The fact that the Arabs had refused to transform the armistice agreement into a permanent peace settlement was of course understood as the best proof of their desire to reopen the conflict as soon as possible. The situation has not changed in this respect in the last twenty years and the Israelis continue to consider it as imperative that any settlement with the Arabs should be accompanied by a direct and formal agreement in which the opposite side formally accepts the existence of the Jewish State. But back in the early fifties the Israelis' feeling of insecurity was reinforced by their analysis of the balance of military forces. It was an analysis which linked military power with conventional ability to mobilize the largest number of soldiers and arm them with the largest number of weapons. In this confrontation of quantities Israel had no chance of victory. Egypt alone, which from 1952 onwards had been run by a military régime committed to refurbishing the military image of the State, had a population thirteen times greater than that of Israel.

Even if, in terms of real fighting forces, this might not have meant much, it could upset the already vulnerable economy of the Jewish State in terms of labour confrontation. For Israel an army of 40,000 men meant 7 per cent of the population unproductive. For Egypt an army of 160,000 men meant an impingement of only 1·5 per cent on the labour force. Israel was spending an estimated 29 per cent of her budget on defence which meant that, *per capita*, each Israeli spent four times as much as an Egyptian. The Egyptian Government had at its disposal a revenue for military expenditure two and a half times larger than that of Israel.[1]

One important contribution by General Dayan to Israel's security was to increase the efficiency of the fighting force of the Israeli Army without increasing its size. It was commonly believed that the ratio between 'teeth-and-tail' in the Israeli army was 50 per cent as against 28 per cent in the European armies and probably less in the Arab armies.[2] But a second and perhaps more important contribution by Dayan was to give the 'teeth' a combative spirit which was definitely missing before he took over the command of the Israeli Army.

Dayan was a staunch supporter of commando tactics, which he had first learned under Orde Wingate in the thirties. He had lost an eye

<hr />

[1] Safran, op. cit., p. 185.   [2] ibid., p. 195.

while scouting for the British forces in Syria during the 1942 campaign against the Vichy French. He first tested his ideas as a commander of mobile units in the Negev, where in 1950 he was asked to fight the increasing Arab infiltration in that then empty area. He did it by organizing a system of mechanized patrols, the predecessors of the highly mobile fighting units of the Israeli Army.

Dayan spent most of 1951 abroad on diplomatic and study missions and was not involved in the operation against Syria at Tel Mutilla in May 1951, which proved how low the morale and the fighting strength of the Israeli Army had dropped since the end of the war. This was to be expected, since most of the experienced military organizations of the Yishuv had been disbanded and the new units were largely composed of newly arrived immigrants who had no taste for war, but it was a shock to the Government and to Ben Gurion in particular. As a result Dayan was appointed second-in-command of the Army in 1952, under General Maklef who stayed on as Commander-in-Chief just long enough to allow Ben Gurion to overcome the widespread opposition to the promotion of Dayan to the highest Army command. It was in this capacity that Dayan witnessed, on the night of 23 January 1953, the paratroopers' attack on the Jordan village of Falama, a base of Arab infiltration, where ten members of the Jordanian militia beat off the attack with heavy losses for the Israeli side. The battle of Falama probably represents a turning-point in Israeli military tactics. It speeded the creation of Battalion 101, which under the command of Ariel Sharon (later one of the top commanders of the Israeli Army) established a pattern and standards for all other units of the Army. On 14 October 1953 it showed in the attack on the village of Kibya what Dayan's new fighting formation could do. The attack, for which, as I have mentioned, the Israeli Government has not yet had the courage to assume full responsibility, brought Israel to the verge of a clash with Great Britain and drew a strong condemnation from the Security Council. But it also officially launched Israel's new policy of reprisal attacks against infiltrators which would eventually lead to the Sinai war.

In December 1953 Dayan was appointed Chief of Staff by Ben Gurion a few days before the Israeli Prime Minister decided to retire to his Negev kibbutz, Sdeh Boker. In his new capacity as Supreme Commander Dayan immediately set about reorganizing the structure of the Army. He created two new military branches—training and intelligence—picking Colonel Rabin, the victor of the 1967 war, as Director of Military Training. All services were combed for able officers; all officers were asked to undergo paratroop or commando training; more than sixty senior officers were dismissed and as many military services as possible were switched to civilian contractors. Attendance of Israeli officers at military schools abroad was cut to a minimum on the assumption that the country should produce its own independent strategy. For this purpose a Military College was opened for the training of senior officers, while all reserve officers had their period of training extended. Most important of all, Dayan believed that the Israeli soldiers and commanders should learn in the hard school of border fighting. For this Arab infiltration offered endless opportunities. It was through them that Israel selected her future commanders, that the troops were toughened, and, above all, that the principle of attack became the standard policy of the military establishment. Israel, thus ran the doctrine, could not afford to fight, let alone lose, one single battle on its own territory if it wanted to survive.

This was the exact opposite of what was happening in the Arab armies. All Arab officers and governments spoke of attack but in fact spent most of their resources on defence installations and equipment. They relied more and more on numbers and guns while Dayan proclaimed the theory that 'Israel should be as strong as its means', meaning by this that it should develop its own autonomous military infrastructure. Since he knew he could not compete with the Arabs in quantity he decided to make the fullest use of Israeli technological and organizational ability in order to make any military action as unconventional as possible.[1] He pressed the Israeli Government to purchase jet planes; he asked for light, fast French tanks, whereas the Arabs went in for heavy British and later, in 1955, Russian ones; he put all his infantry on half-tracks to cross the desert, whereas the Arabs still marched their regiments or wheeled them around in trucks along the vulnerable roads. The Arab policy of armed infiltration played straight into Dayan's hands. On the political and diplomatic level the Israelis might have looked completely isolated. They were in fact under strong British and American pressure to make territorial concessions to the Arabs, who in the Western capitals looked 'sixty times stronger' than the Israelis.[2] But on the military level, Dayan

[1] Naphtali Lau-Lavie, *Moshe Dayan: A Biography* (Eng. trans., London, 1968), pp. 96–116.

[2] The new policy of the Republican Administration towards the Middle East was first laid down by the Secretary of State, John F. Dulles on 1 June 1953. It was spelt out, in what the Israelis thought was a clear indication of the State Department's new hostile attitude, by the Assistant Secretary of State, Henry A. Byroade, in two speeches on 9 April and 1 May 1954. The most obvious attempt to link a settlement in the Middle East with border concessions on the part of Israel was made by Sir Anthony Eden, then Prime Minister, in a speech at the Guildhall in London on 9 November 1955.

knew by the end of 1954 that Israel had regained the upper hand. The main reason was probably to be found in the fact that while the Israeli Army was being geared for war in the almost daily border incidents, the Arab armies avoided all military confrontation with the Israelis and preferred to send Palestinian refugees to carry out murderous, but from the military point of view incoherent, guerrilla operations. When the new Ben Gurion government succeeded the Sharett government in November 1955, it was already a war cabinet. At the end of the same month, well before the nationalization of the Suez Canal, Ben Gurion pressed his colleagues for a decision to launch a full-scale operation against Egypt. He asked Dayan when such an operation could be carried out. He received an official answer saying 'the sooner the better'.[1]

The Palestinian refugees were increasingly used by the Arab governments for hit-and-run raids, usually against civilian targets, but they had never been allowed to become a real army for fear that they might one day become strong enough to demand the withdrawal of the Egyptians from the Gaza Strip and of the Jordanians from the West Bank. This policy could hardly strengthen the Palestinians' fighting spirit, but the border clashes had an equally negative influence on the Arab armies' tactics and morale. The Syrians built, with foreign help, a formidable 'Maginot line' along the Jordan, and bombarded the Jewish settlements in the valley below without ever joining battle. The Jordanian Army manned some border forts, suffered casualties in the border fighting, but on the whole stayed well behind the borders, never evolving its old-fashioned British colonial tactics. The Egyptians carefully avoided military confrontation. In the fifties, as in the sixties, they built huge fortification systems in the Sinai, stockpiled weapons, and spent fortunes on ever more sophisticated types of military equipment. But at the same time, as mentioned above, they never tasted battle, leaving the Palestinians to do the infiltration and sabotage jobs. Such commando operations were responsible for the explosion of two wars in the Middle East; but the screening of the Arab armies behind them was largely responsible for the two Arab military catastrophes which accompanied them.

The story of Jewish–Arab confrontation along the borders has been fully recorded, mainly by the United Nations. The material is so abundant and freely available that it is unnecessary to deal with the subject in detail here, important as it is for a full understanding of the

[1] Dayan, *Diary of the Sinai Campaign*, pp. 12–15.

two Arab–Israeli conflicts in 1956 and 1967.[1] I would prefer to recall briefly another equally important cause for the escalation of Jewish–Arab border fighting: the problem of sovereignty over the demilitarized zones.

With the exception of the Lebanon, Israel had accepted the demilitarization of certain areas included in its own armistice boundaries with its other Arab neighbours. These zones were a source of constant friction, but the demilitarized areas along the Syrian border were the object of the most violent fighting.[2] There were many reasons for the particular sensitivity of the Syrians along the border. They alone among the Arab States which declared war on Israel in 1948 were in possession of Israeli territory at the time of armistice. They could thus claim that the Syrian Army had never really been defeated and that its evacuation of border areas—which then became demilitarized—did not mean the automatic return of Israeli sovereignty over them. Furthermore, though the demilitarized areas along the Jordanian and Egyptian frontiers had strategic importance—as in the case of the Jewish-held Mount Scopus, overlooking Old Jerusalem, or Nitzana, controlling the approach to three Sinai roads—they had little economic value. Little or no change was thus brought to them by the fast development of the Israeli economy. This was not the case with the demilitarized zone along the Syrian border, from which Syrian troops had withdrawn in 1949 in accordance with the armistice agreement. It was an area lying astride the River Jordan, north of Lake Tiberias, and in the heart of agricultural Jewish Galilee. The only point on the River Jordan from which the Israelis could divert the water needed to irrigate their southern desert—without having to pump it upwards—was located at a height of some 650 feet above sea level, right in the middle of a demilitarized zone. For Israel, this was a vital development area. For the Syrians, it was politically and economically important that it should not be developed.

The Syrian frontier thus remained an abscess of permanent tension for twenty years. It was the place where, back in 1951, the Israelis for the first time used their airforce in a reprisal raid which was to become a standard pattern in following years. On the question of the use of the Jordan's water, Israel clashed for the first time with the United States

[1] The most detailed work on the U.N.O. activities in the Middle East is Rosalyn Higgins's *United Nations Peacekeeping, 1946–1967: Documents and Commentary*, vol. 1: *The Middle East* (London, 1969). For the period 1954–6 see Lieut.-Gen. E. L. M. Burns, *Between Arab and Israeli* (New York, 1963), the best of the many accounts by U.N. officials connected with the Palestine problem.

[2] Shabtai Rosenne, *Israel's Armistice Agreements with the Arab States* (Tel Aviv, 1951).

and had to retreat under the threat of American economic sanctions.[1] It was also on a question relating to the use of the demilitarized zone along the Syrian border that the U.S.S.R. used, for the first time, its veto in the Security Council—against Israel and in favour of the Arabs —on 22 January 1954. It was because of the Jordan irrigation scheme that Syria launched its policy of 'total war' against Israel which, in the sixties, led to the third Arab–Israeli war. All these events are well known and have been analysed in detail.[2] What should be stressed is that, in the case both of Arab infiltration and of confrontation in the demilitarized zones, Israel could, and in fact did, carry out its policy in spite of Arab opposition. Infiltration was met with reprisals and border settlements; the Jordan Valley was put under cultivation and the water of the Jordan was brought to the south, not directly from the river but, more expensively, from Lake Tiberias, into which the Jordan flows. Thus, the Israeli policy of the *fait accompli* did succeed and the by-products of Arab hostility were to some extent even beneficial to the development of the Israeli military power and industry. The same cannot be said of the Israeli attempt to break the Arabs' economic and military siege.

There was little that Israel could really do about the Arab boycott.[3] The State remained completely cut off from Arab markets until after the war of June 1967, when goods from the neighbouring Arab States again began to flow into the Israeli markets and vice versa. Hopes of seeing Iraq oil flow again into the Haifa refinery evaporated very quickly. One after the other international airlines stopped their east-bound flights from Israel, making Lydda a terminal airport and Beirut a flourishing cross-roads. In spite of a Security Council decision to the contrary, taken on 1 September 1951, the Suez Canal remained closed to Israeli shipping and later to Israeli goods transported on foreign boats. In spite of formal Egyptian guarantees to allow free Israeli navigation through the Straits of Aqaba,[4] Jewish shipping was soon precluded from passing through them. The Arab League Boycott Committee made it hard for Western industrialists to invest in Israel and in the Arab States at the same time, and some of the most important European firms, including French and American government operators, were forced to stop their activities in Israel. Only after 1958, when

---

[1] This was in fact the only time the U.S. Government actually suspended its aid to Israel.

[2] N. Bar-Yaacov, *The Israel–Syrian Armistice: Problems of Implementation, 1949–1966* (Jerusalem, 1967).

[3] For a brief summary of the Arab boycott, see W. Eytan, op. cit., pp. 90–8; see also *Rivion Lechalkalah*, vol. I, no. 3, pp. 196–207.

[4] Egyptian *aide-mémoire* to the U.S. Government, 28 January 1950, quoted in Eytan, op. cit., p. 103.

Israel had become a relatively important market for European and American exports, could a 'counter-boycott' begin to be envisaged. Israel's diplomatic isolation in the non-Western world was for many years difficult to overcome. Because of Arab pressure, most of the Asian countries, India included, did not recognize Israel or did not establish diplomatic contact with her. Israel had to wait for the Sinai campaign and the breaching by force of the Straits of Aqaba—as well as for African independence—before she was able to establish close relations with the countries of the 'Third World'. As to the recognition of Israel by the Arabs, this appears to be as remote as ever even today, and no Israeli attempt to break the political and military encirclement of the Arabs has so far succeeded.

The second main factor influencing Israeli–Arab relations was Israel's impact on the Arabs' relations with each other. This was undoubtedly more conspicuous in the second decade of the State's existence than in the first ten years. From 1949 to 1958 the regional as well as the international impact of the Jewish State was very limited. One must have lived through the dramatic diplomatic experience of Prime Minister Sharett's meetings with the 'Big Four' Foreign Ministers in Geneva in the autumn of 1955, to realize the almost cynical indifference with which the representatives of Britain, the U.S.A., Russia, but not France, dealt with Israel's plea to stop supplying arms to the Arabs, and to try to do something about the armed Arab infiltration.[1] In fact, the question most often asked about Israel by diplomats at that time was not what the Jewish State could do but how long it could last.

Unlike most of the new States which had gained their independence since the Second World War (even those whose independence was contested by their neighbours, such as Mauretania, the Republic of Southern Yemen, Malaya), Israel had to work hard to be accepted even among those States who had voted for its creation. Many European countries, with a long and proud history of secularism behind them, suddenly became very conscious of being Christian when dealing with a Jewish State. Portugal and Ireland did not recognize the new State because they followed the 'lead' of Vatican diplomacy which, of course, was openly hostile to Israel. France, Italy, Belgium, Britain, and the United States felt 'very strongly' about a Jewish-occupied sector of Jerusalem and refused to recognize it as the seat of the Israeli Government. France, as we have seen, went so far as to make its support for Israel's admission to the United Nations conditional on Israel's acceptance of the last Capitulation Treaty imposed by Christian governments

[1] Eytan, op. cit., pp. 145-7.

on the Ottoman empire—the Treaty of Mytilene of 1913. Other countries, such as Greece, Ethiopia, India, and Iran, could only afford to have 'unofficial' or incomplete relations with Israel because of Arab threats.[1] Only in the sixties, after more than fifteen years of diplomatic struggles, did the Jewish State make a diplomatic break-through among the States of Asia and Africa.

Still, and in spite of these obvious limitations, the mere presence in the heart of the Arab Middle East of an independent Jewish State—however weak and apparently shaky—was enough to give Israel a role in inter-Arab politics.

We have already recalled the fear and the jealousy felt by some Arab States, and more particularly by Egypt, against British-supported Transjordan and how these fears and suspicions affected the Arab governments' decision to participate in the 1948 war. This hostility towards Jordan did not cool with the first Arab military defeat but in fact increased considerably. To this very day, Arab League meetings and other Arab conferences—to say nothing of the Arab press and radio—reverberate with perpetual reciprocal accusations of 'collaboration with the Zionist enemy'. And one can point to other examples of Israeli influence on inter-Arab politics.

The Israeli Government, for instance, welcomed the appearance of the 'progressive' military régime in Egypt and the fall of Farouk.[2] At the time this feeling was not shared by many Arab governments, especially Iraq. The Egyptians, for their part, knew how deeply preoccupied Israel was with the future of the Suez Canal and the huge military depots left by the British in the Canal Zone. They were afraid that Israel's right of free navigation through the Canal could be used as a pretext for prolonging British pressure in the Canal Zone, or that Israel might exploit the tense relations between Egypt and Britain in

---

[1] Although an Ethiopian Consulate has continued to function in the Israeli sector of Jerusalem since the time of the British Mandate, diplomatic representation has not yet been accorded to Israel. As for Israel, an Embassy was only opened in Addis Ababa in 1966, but close military, economic, and cultural relations started much earlier. Israel is recognized *de facto* by India but only allowed to maintain a consulate in Bombay. Close relations exist between Israel and Iran but formal diplomatic relations have not yet been established between the two countries.

[2] cf. Ben Gurion's speech before the Knesset, 18 August 1952. It has been a constant, if irrational, belief on the part of the old Israeli political establishment, reared in the socialist traditions of Europe, that a left-wing régime in the Middle East should be more 'pacifist' than a right-wing régime. All the moderate Arab leaders belong, as far as Israel is concerned, to the non-socialist, traditional camp. Because of their political weakness it is doubtful whether Israel could have reached any meaningful political agreement with them, but it is certain that they were looked upon by many Israeli leaders with less sympathy and consideration than the 'progressive' Arab leaders.

order to strengthen her position along the Negev frontiers. Thus, direct, high-level talks took place between the Egyptians and Israelis in Europe and elsewhere, in 1953, 1954 (and later), but they were broken off by Egypt as soon as an agreement with Britain was in sight. The first sign of change came in a speech from General Neguib to the Arab Armistice Delegations Conference in Cairo on 18 April 1953, when he declared: 'The existence of Israel is a cancer in the body of the Arab Nation, which ought to be exterminated.' This was the opposite of what he had said, on 30 August 1952, to the *Exchange Telegraph* correspondent in Cairo, namely that the Egyptian Army had no intention of taking revenge on the Israelis and that he had not yet received any report on Ben Gurion's proposal to conclude peace.[1] Egypt also refused to join the other Arab States in their decision to boycott Western Germany after the conclusion of the Reparations Treaty with Israel in 1952. The reasons for this change of attitude on the part of the Egyptians towards Israel have not yet been clarified. Following the fall of Neguib in October 1954, the attempt to assassinate Nasser in that same month, the mounting Western diplomatic pressure on the Cairo Government to join the Baghdad Pact, an anti-Russian defence scheme in which Egypt would have had to share the leadership of the Arab world with Iraq, the short honeymoon with Israel was over for ever. Border tension began to increase from the beginning of 1954. This increase was probably quite unintentional in the beginning and both countries were dragged into the increasing local conflict by Arab refugees and marauders crossing the borders, especially in the Gaza region. By 1955 these infiltrations were already co-ordinated and used for military purposes by the Egyptian intelligence and the Israelis claim that the *fedayin* (Arab guerrillas) were organized by the Egyptian Army well before the Israeli attack on the city of Gaza on 28 February 1955.[2] On the other hand, President Nasser always claimed that it was the traumatic effect of that attack (in which thirty-eight Egyptian soldiers were killed and thirty-one wounded, and the Palestinians in Gaza started clamouring for arms) that determined him to turn to the communist bloc to obtain arms to face the Israelis, who in his opinion were co-operating with 'Western imperialism' to force Egypt into the Baghdad Pact by exposing its military weakness.[3] With it also went the restraint which the Egyptian authorities had imposed on Palestinian infiltration into Israel from the Gaza Strip.

Ben Gurion is on record as having stated several times that Arab

[1] *HaArez*, 30 August 1952; *The New East*, vol. IV, no. 1, p. 27.
[2] *HaArez*, 25 January 1955, 22, 24, 27, 28 February 1955.
[3] *New York Times*, 14, 16 March 1955; *Al-Ahram*, 2 March 1955.

rivalry was more dangerous to Israel than Arab unity, since it could only produce an escalation of hate against Israel. Whether he was sincere or not is debatable, mainly because of a permanent contradiction in Israeli foreign policy which favours the development and modernization of the Arab Middle East on the one hand and desires to maintain the political *status quo* of the region on the other hand. It is because of her interest in maintaining the *status quo* in the area that Israel is being identified by the Arabs with Western colonialism (which is also interested in the stability of the Middle East) and accused of being reactionary by the Russians, who want the Middle East as unsettled as possible in order to have a chance of consolidating their influence there.

However the Israelis' wish to maintain the *status quo* in the Middle East did not bring them any closer to the Western powers, although they were also interested in the stability of the region. Furthermore, the transformation of the Jewish national home into an independent State did not decrease the 'nuisance value' of the Jews to the West. The Jewish question was, of course, still very much alive in many countries, especially in the communist ones. But to the people and the governments of the West it was becoming a secondary problem. The pressure of the persecuted Jewish masses in Eastern Europe having been relieved, as far as the West was concerned, by the physical destruction of 6 million Jews in Europe, it was sad but natural that this tragedy should be quickly forgotten and the problem of the Arab refugees put in its place, and used as a justification for the demand for compensation and concessions to the Arabs from the Jews. While it was possible for Arab and Israeli diplomats to argue about the reciprocal responsibility for the flight of the Palestinians, the hundreds of thousands of men, women, and children, who had become homeless and pawns in the Arabs' political game against Israel, added a tragic dimension of suffering and political instability to the conflict. They were also the most compelling argument in favour of a switch in focus of international conscience from Jewish problems to Arab problems.

To Britain, which in the fifties was still the ruling power in the Middle East, to the U.S.A., and to the great oil companies, Israel had very little to offer. It was looked upon as a cause of perpetual resentment of the Arabs towards the West, which they held responsible for the creation of the Jewish problem and which had helped to create the Jewish national home in Palestine. It had no economic resources; no known reserves of oil; no markets capable of absorbing Western products; no geographical or strategic value; no large investments to protect; no Christian minorities to defend. The small measure of political importance which the British attached to Israel could be measured by the lack of interest—often nearing disdain—which successive London governments, with one notable exception, the Labour Government of 1951,[1] showed towards the Israeli efforts to join in some way with Western defence plans in the Middle East.

These plans—which died almost as fast as they were invented by Middle East strategists—had two main and geographically divergent purposes. One was to 'contain' Russia or, as the Soviet leaders put it, to menace the U.S.S.R. at her softest spot—the Caucasus and its Moslem territories. The other aim was to keep the Middle East, with its Turkish and Persian periphery, under Western influence. This second aim was dictated by many Western strategic and economic interests: the need to perpetuate a unity of commerce, banking, overland communications, and the flow of oil across national boundaries; to ensure freedom of military movement; to guarantee politically and diplomatically a net of then vital military and air installations; and to control subversive anti-Western activities.

How much the Arabs resented the Western presence and influence in the Middle East could be seen from the recurrent explosions of anti-British feeling in almost every Arab country. In 1948, for instance, street mobs brought down the Baghdad Government which had dared to renew a defence treaty with Britain. From 1952 to 1954, Egypt stood in open defiance of Britain over the future of the Sudan and of the Canal bases; in 1953, the Mossadegh revolution in Iran jeopardized the supply of Persian oil to the West. Israel had no part in this turmoil nor in the acute inter-Arab strife for regional hegemony. But, even so, it represented an additional cause for resentment against the West, a physical obstacle in the path of Arab unity, an uncontrollable and alien catalyst of political and social change.

British and American strategists of the Middle East could claim, with a measure of conviction, that the Jewish State had brought additional instability to an area in which Western interests required stability above all, that it was an obstacle to the realization of Western plans for keeping the area within the 'free world's' sphere of influence, that, from a strictly political and economic point of view, its 'dislodgement' would certainly not be detrimental to the West, that its 'containment' was a

---

[1] Suggestions for a possible British–Israeli collaboration for the defence of the Middle East were put forward by General Sir Brian Robertson, Commander of British Forces in the Middle East, during a visit to Tel Aviv in spring 1951. They were followed by correspondence between Foreign Secretary Herbert Morrison and Ben Gurion and came to an end with the return of the Conservatives to power in autumn 1951. See Bar-Zohar, op. cit., pp. 182–3.

prerequisite for gaining Arab collaboration. The best use which could be made of it was to keep it as a potential threat to be used against the Arabs, should the carrot of political and economic co-operation be insufficient to drag the recalcitrant Middle Eastern countries into the Western camp.

The 1950 Tripartite Declaration, by which England, France, and the U.S.A. had pledged themselves to keep the *status quo* and the balance of armaments among the States of the region, looked to many Israelis and Arabs like a typical diplomatic trick with which to keep the Middle Eastern 'mad dogs' under control. In fact, there was no real collaboration between the 'Big Three' as far as Middle Eastern policy was concerned. The concepts of *status quo* and 'balance of armaments' were variously interpreted in London, Paris, and Washington. In this atmosphere of suspicion and gun-running morality, the scramble for arms became a recurrent factor in the diplomacy of the Middle Eastern countries.

It was because of arms that Egypt entered into the armaments deal with Czechoslovakia in 1955, that Russia was able to undermine Western influence in the Middle East, overcoming the deep-seated suspicion of the Arabs towards communism, that Israel became France's ally against the Arabs and that the Jewish State was spurred into an involuntary technological revolution.

The Tripartite Declaration was the first Western agreement over the Middle East in a long series of multilateral agreements which the French newspaper *Le Monde* described as the product of *pactomanie*, mainly because France was later relegated to being the back-seat driver. To Israel these defence schemes, with which she could not be associated, appeared as recurrent attempts by the Western powers to canvass Arab co-operation at the expense of Israel. Whatever the true intentions of the Great Powers, the Israelis were obsessed by the idea of an Arab-based Western military reorganization of the Middle East and by the fear of armaments being poured into the area: a situation which many Arab leaders explicitly declared to be a preparatory stage for a new war against the Jewish State.

Allegedly, as I have mentioned, it was because of Egypt's fears of an Israeli attack that the first Arab arms deal with Russia was concluded. Arab–Soviet relations after the Second World War had not been particularly warm. Russia had voted in favour of the partition of Palestine and had little sympathy for 'reactionary' ideas such as Pan-Arabism or Pan–Islamism,[1] but Moscow diplomacy had already lost faith in the

---

[1] See Walter Z. Laqueur, *Communism and Nationalism in the Middle East* (New York, 1956).

political value of Israel—to the Russians—in 1949.[1] Up to the death of
Stalin in 1953 the prevailing policy of the Soviet Union towards the
Middle East was based on the 1947 Zhdanov Doctrine, according to
which those States which did not take sides with Russia were considered
to belong to the imperialist camp. The Arabs, India, and Israel were
thus in the enemy camp: Israel more than the other neutrals, because
of the growing antisemitic tendencies in the last days of Stalin's régime.
In 1951 a prominent left-wing Israeli leader, Mordecai Oren, had been
arrested in Prague and accused during the Slansky trials of being an
American Zionist agent. His imprisonment was one of the major factors
in the breaking up of the pro-Russian Mapam party in Israel. In 1953 the
arrest of several Jewish doctors, accused of having taken part in a plot
against Stalin, heralded the 'Doctors' Trial', of marked antisemitic
nature, the proceedings of which were stopped by the death of Stalin. It
lasted long enough to bring relations between Russia and Israel to
breaking point. A bomb exploded in front of the Russian Embassy in
Tel Aviv and diplomatic relations were broken off. When they were
resumed in 1953, the Soviet Union was becoming increasingly suspicious of the Western attempt to organize Middle Eastern defence
schemes against her and was looking for a chance to circumscribe
Western influence in the area.[2]

During the twentieth Communist Party Congress in 1956 Krushchev
officially dropped the Zhdanov Doctrine and admitted the existence of
a neutral group of countries, neither communist nor socialist, but
pacifist, with whom the Soviet Union was ready to collaborate. The
Egyptians, who showed great dislike for the British-initiated Baghdad
Pact seemed to be the most interesting 'pacifists' of the lot. The Neguib–
Nasser régime, which in 1954 was still considered by Moscow to be a
'mad reactionary, terrorist, anti-democratic, and demagogic régime'[3]
became a 'staunch fighter against imperialism' to which as many
'defensive weapons' as possible should be sent.[4]

The need to thwart the military and diplomatic attempt by Britain

---

[1] As early as 21 September 1948 the Jewish writer Ilya Ehrenburg warned Soviet Jews,
in an article in *Pravda*, not to fall into the trap of believing that the solution to 'the Jewish
question' might be found in the military victory of the Jews in Palestine rather than in the
triumph of socialism over capitalism in the world. The U.S.S.R., he claimed, helped Israel
because Russia supported *all* struggles against imperialism. But, he added, Palestine
was no proper home for the Jews; it had already begun to be invaded by American
imperialism.

[2] Isaac Landau, 'Evolution of the U.S.S.R.'s Policy in the Middle East, 1950–1956',
Middle East Journal, May 1956, pp. 169–78.

[3] Quoted from *The World To-Day*, December 1955, p. 521, in Gabbay, op. cit., p. 490.

[4] ibid., p. 492.

and the U.S.A. to organize a united anti-Russian Middle East through the Baghdad Pact made it vital for the communists to support any anti-Western force in the area. Egypt was the obvious choice, and the Bandung Conference in 1955 also confirmed Nasser as one of the leaders of the emerging nations. It was there that, thanks to Chinese communist mediation, the first Egyptian–Russian talks about a possible arms deal between the communists and Egypt took place.[1] It was preceded and followed by more fighting along the Israeli frontiers and it was accompanied by the official organization of the Palestinian refugees into an army of saboteurs,[2] by the refusal of the Americans to finance the Aswan Dam, which brought about the nationalization of the Suez Canal, and, six months later, by the Franco-British operation at Port Said and the synchronized Israeli attack in the Sinai. The 'Suez affair' has been the object of many studies, and I shall deal here and in the next chapter with only some aspects of the Israeli involvement in it.

I believe that it is impossible to grasp the real motives for Israel's 'collusion' with France and Britain in the Suez affair without some understanding of the prevailing state of mind in Israel between 1952 and 1956. There are practically no documents—with the exception perhaps of a penetrating novel by a leading Israeli writer[3]—capable of retracing the unreality of the situation: the confusion, the anxiety, the hopes, and the despair, the rapid change in ideas, institutions, and moods of a population which had lost its geographical, social, and ideological points of reference. It was a situation in which the miracle seemed a more common commodity than day-to-day reality; in which a victorious army could not protect the population from growing enemy infiltration; in which the Government never knew if it would have enough money to reach the end of the year; in which embassies were sometimes so short of cash that they had to borrow from local Jewish personalities in order to pay the monthly salaries of their staff, and the Jewish community in Rome had to buy blank cartridges for the Israeli navy (three frigates) crossing the Atlantic to participate in fund-raising operations; in which the Jewish Agency officials could never tell the Government how many thousands, tens of thousands of new immigrants would pour into the State. It was a situation in which everyone had the impression of living in a confused twilight of ancient history

---

[1] Robert St. John, *The Boss: The Story of Gamal Abdel Nasser* (New York, 1960), pp. 196–212.

[2] Gabbay, op. cit., pp. 504–5.

[3] S. Izhar, *Yemei Ziklag* (The Days of Ziklag), Tel Aviv, 1958.

and future promise; in which everything seemed possible and still so unattainable. It was an endless battle for survival, and it took the single-mindedness of a Ben Gurion to move the new State and the new society out of its grave material difficulties and ideological confusion.[1] And the battle for survival meant a struggle for normality as well, both within and without the State.

The Arabs rejected, and still reject, the mere idea of a Jewish State.[2] But it was not easy for Israel to make even friendly States agree to it. If one looks at the history of the Israeli State, especially before the Sinai war, one cannot avoid being struck by the extent of the totally inefficient but consistent attempts at international interference in and control over the Jewish State: control of the frontiers by U.N. Observers; control of Jerusalem by Christian powers; the constant appearances of Israel before the Security Council, usually to be condemned; real dependence on foreign and Jewish international economic aid. Not a single country in the world to this day has recognized the Israeli frontiers. Many were for years doubtful of the very possibility of the existence of a Jewish State, while, paradoxically enough, everyone, Jews included, was critical of the incapacity of the State to meet the lofty expectations attached to a country which named itself Israel.

While this exceptionally difficult situation lasted, the Israeli leaders were bent on one policy: that of survival. This meant that, whatever the political or diplomatic price to be paid in the future, it was worth any practical aid in the present. France, from 1954 onwards, met exactly the prerequisites of this policy as a European power which was neither hostile (like Russia) to Israel, nor part of the Western Middle East defence plans; she was becoming increasingly involved in a struggle against the North African Arabs and Arab nationalism; in spite of her attempts to keep up good relations with Egypt, she was deeply disturbed by the nationalization of the Suez Canal; she offered Israel arms and scientific and industrial know-how unconditionally in exchange for an extension of French cultural influence in anglicized Israel, which the Israelis were more than happy to accept. When the Suez Crisis began, France offered Israel unlimited arms supplies; during the Sinai war, she gave naval and air cover to the menaced cities of Israel and diplomatic support in the United Nations; she provided, at a moment when American pressure against Israel might have brought the Jewish

---

[1] Significantly, 'Southward' was the title chosen by Ben Gurion for the traditional introductory article by Israel's Prime Minister in the *Israel Government Yearbook*, 1955-6.

[2] See most of the articles by Arab authors published in 'Le Conflit Israélo-Arabe: Dossier', *Les Temps Modernes*, 22e année, 1967, no. 253 bis.

State to its knees, a protective veto in the Security Council, arms, and large financial credits and investments. But, above all, France meant to Israel a helping hand at a difficult time, a friend in the midst of total political isolation. It is not difficult to understand why—in spite of the obvious danger of becoming associated with a colonial venture— Israel chose to collaborate with France over Suez, and it is not difficult either to envisage the effects of the shattering blow delivered by de Gaulle to a friendship which, for so many Israelis, looked almost like a family involvement, unless one recalls the situation which prevailed in the Jewish State during these dramatic years.

Thus, by the end of 1955 and the beginning of 1956, Israeli–Arab border tension, indirect Israeli involvement in inter-Arab affairs, and Great Power policies in the Arab world had turned a difficult situation into a crisis. On all three levels, for quite different reasons, tension increased relentlessly: on the Israeli frontiers because of the infiltrations; among the Arab States because of the Baghdad Pact rivalry; between the Great Powers because of the Cold War; between the Great Powers and the Arabs because of French involvement in North Africa, Anglo-French involvement in Suez, and Anglo-American strategic and economic involvement in the Middle East, and in general because of Russian determination to destroy Western influence in this area.

Could the second Israeli–Arab war in 1956 thus really have been avoided?

In spite of the mass of books and articles which have been written by close, distant, partial, and impartial observers, we do not yet have enough evidence on which to formulate a balanced judgement of what happened in Israel during this period. The most one can say, on the basis of authoritative statements, is that the Jewish State might have gone to war against Egypt without the close support of France and Great Britain as Ben Gurion's plan of October 1955 envisaged. Whether war could have been avoided, is another and more controversial question.

There is one thesis—mainly advocated by the Arabs and by anti-Israeli progressive and communist groups, but also, with variations, by progressive Israelis—based on the 'conspiracy theory'. It runs on these lines: Israel, being by nature and by circumstances an imperialist colonial country, must behave in a contradictory way, since she reflects the deeper contradictions of the camp which Israel, willingly or unwillingly, represents and is tied to. If from 1949 to 1952 Israel tried to make peace with Jordan (some French sources also claim that there were serious contacts with the successive Syrian dictators, especially

Zaim and Shishackli), this was an effort carried out in the framework of a longer term, mainly British, policy aimed at strengthening the authority of the pro-British Hashemite dynasty in Jordan and Iraq over the 'Fertile Crescent'. King Abdullah, who was prepared to come to terms with Israel as a preliminary step towards asserting his authority over 'Greater Syria' paid for his political dreams with his life. One Israeli author, Colonel Beer (Ben Gurion's trusted military adviser and for many years the army's chief historian, later convicted of espionage for the communists), believed that in Ben Gurion's insistence on coming to an agreement with Abdullah there was a clear indication of the Israeli Government's fundamentally reactionary, imperialist policy towards Arab nationalism.[1]

The question whether the violence of the Israeli reprisal action against Gaza in 1955 intentionally or unintentionally triggered off the Sinai war, is still an open one. The policy of retaliation, which the Israeli Army consistently followed, was dictated by tactical imperatives of security and hampered the crystallization of moderate trends among the Arabs and thus any long-range political strategy. One may, however, wonder whether the inner logic of a 'progressive' military régime like Nasser's, activated by the ambition of establishing Egypt's political supremacy over the Arab world—and perhaps beyond it—would have made the régime less hostile to Israel in the absence of an Israeli retaliatory policy. President Nasser, as I have mentioned, has often expressed the conviction that Israel's attack was part of a premeditated imperialist plot to force Egypt to join the Baghdad Pact by showing her weakness and isolation. Additional evidence in this direction is advanced by those authors who see in the cloak-and-dagger operations of an Israeli spy ring against American buildings in Cairo the confirmation of a possible co-operation between the Israeli and European Secret Services. The fact, however, remains that so far there is too little evidence to sustain this thesis. The official explanation given at the time (and later disproved) was that the number of Egyptian casualties in the Gaza raid was doubled by the accidental setting off of a mine laid many days before by a lorry carrying Egyptian reinforcements. It is also known that the divergence of opinion about the Gaza attack strained the relations between the then Premier Moshe Sharett and Ben Gurion, who was acting as Defence Minister.[2] The fact however remains that

---

[1] See Israel Beer, *Bitaḥon Israel* (Israel's Security), Tel Aviv, 1966.

[2] Bar-Zohar, op. cit., p. 200. Bar-Zohar also shows in *Sefer Hazanchanim* (The Book of the Paratroopers) (Tel Aviv, 1969), p. 99, that contrary to what Ben Gurion had claimed, most of the Egyptian casualties were caused by an ambush laid by the attacking force.

from 1953 to early 1955 we are faced with a dearth of reliable information from almost all sources and with an orgy of conspiracy literature. At the very centre stands the Lavon affair, that 'security mishap' which, according to the consensus of opinion, saw a number of Israeli and Egyptian Jews planting bombs in American buildings in Cairo. Uri Avnery, the Israeli M.P., in a recent book claimed that the aim of this operation was to put an end to the *rapprochement* of the U.S.A. and Egypt, and—a reaction to the American Ambassador and Assistant Secretary for State Byroade's declared intention—to achieve it at the expense of Israel.[1] In opposition to Lavon, but again according to the best principles of the conspiracy theory, other authorities believe that the 1956 Sinai campaign was the result of the Israeli policy of border reprisals. This time, the chief villain is General Dayan, who became Chief of Staff at the end of 1953. Under him the Army was reorganized, and the policy of reprisals against border infiltration seemed a way of restoring the confidence and unity of the Israeli nation—then in great internal trouble. Two particular dates are important historically as proofs of Dayan's determination to take Israel into war. The first is 13 October 1953, when the Israelis caused scores of civilian deaths in the Jordan frontier village of Kibya. The raid shook the Jordan Government and provoked the British Government to open threats of action against Israel. The second is 28 February 1955—the date of the Israeli raid on Gaza, which, according to President Nasser, angered the Egyptian military establishment to such an extent that he was forced to look to Russia for military aid.

The thesis of an Israeli military conspiracy to provoke a war against the Arabs is usually accompanied by different interpretations. One links it with the fight for power inside the Israeli Government, between Lavon, Sharett, and Ben Gurion (who at that time had retired to his Negev kibbutz, Sdeh Boker).[2] Another links it with Western plans to create a Middle Eastern system of alliances against Russia, in which Israel was used as a tool—or a bait—to force Egypt to join the Baghdad Pact. A third interpretation links it with the attempts to stop or slow down the British retreat from Suez, by making London claim it had a 'responsibility' towards Israel for as long as Egypt refused to let Israeli ships use the Suez Canal. The common element in these interpretations of the motivations of Israel's 'conspiracy' policy towards the Arabs, finally leading to the 1956 war, is that the onus of proof, to the effect

---

[1] Uri Avnery, *Israel Without Zionists: A Plea for Peace in the Middle East* (London, 1968), pp. 101 ff.

[2] Bar-Zohar, *The Armed Prophet*, ch. 25, pp. 189–97.

that Israel was not after all the main cause of the Middle Eastern convulsions in the fifties, is left to Israel, and the trouble is that Israel cannot easily offer such proof, at least for the time being.

At a time when the leadership, totally devoted to the survival of the State (whatever the divergence of opinion about what sort of State this might be), fought a daily battle against great political, economic, military odds for the survival of the State; when immigrants who had been pouring into the State in their thousands were losing heart in transit camps which had been turned into permanent settlements; when the Arabs, in a more or less co-ordinated way, and certainly intentionally, transformed the frontiers of Israel into an area of total insecurity, while trying to choke the State with a very effective boycott; when the Great Powers, attempting to organize the Middle East in terms of the Cold War, were divided among themselves about the way to achieve their aim and allowed their agents in the field to use Israel as a bait for anti-Soviet Arab unity; when the economy, the Army, and the population in Israel was in a state of total fluidity (not to say shambles); when the Israeli Government could not avoid the contradictions of a hand-to-mouth and day-to-day policy of survival—in these conditions it is difficult to believe that anyone, least of all a coalition government in a new State, could think clearly about its long-term future and the effects of today's decisions, conditioned by the necessity to survive, on tomorrow's political relations with the Arabs.

One thing is, however, certain. In the midst of this great confusion Israel made several attempts to reach an agreement with the Arabs. Some, such as the negotiations with King Abdullah in 1950, which led to the King's assassination in 1951, are known, others are still secret. The probable reason for their failure and the reason why Israel cannot yet provide a successful answer to the conspiracy theory is that these attempts took place in an Arab Middle East in which considerable political and social ferment was created by the Second World War, by the elation of newly achieved independence in the wake of the end of the Mandate system. The shock caused by the sudden disappearance of British and French power and their replacement in the area by the U.S.A. and U.S.S.R. was still great. A confused situation arose which had nothing, or very little, to do with Israel, but of which Israel was now part. The physical existence of the new State, its determination to live, its impact on Arab society, its new needs—economic, social, military, strategic—acted as a powerful element in the polarization and acceleration of the emotions and changes taking place in the Middle East. A chance of peace was possibly missed in the Lausanne talks in 1950, but probably not after that.[1] Be that as it may, it seems clear that the 1948 war had been not only the war for Israel's independence; it had also been the first war which the Arabs had fought by themselves for themselves. For Israel it was the realization of a dream—for the Arabs the test of it —the dream of independence, sovereignty, national revival, and restoration of past greatness. For Israel, it had been a victory followed by tremendous difficulties. For the Arabs, a defeat which they could not be persuaded to accept as their own (it was all the fault of the corrupt régimes left by the retreating colonial ruler) and was followed by an increasing feeling of power and international importance—due to their strategic situation, to their uncommitted potential and political, strategic, and economic force, to the two warring blocks.

Seen from this point of view, the 1956 confrontation between Israel and the Arabs appears inevitable. It was perhaps tragic for both that it took place so soon and in such politically compromising conditions, linking Israel with France and (less) Britain, and Egypt with Russia. But to think that the tremendous changes and emotions created by the consequences of the Second World War in the Middle East and activated by the creation of a Jewish State in the centre of the Arab world could be settled by an Arab–Israeli political agreement in the atmosphere of world tension which followed the war, is to ignore the realities of life and history.

And so the second Jewish–Arab war came. It did not help to change the basic pattern of conflict—which once more broke out ten years later—but it reinforced both sides in their basic belief.

Israel came out of the Suez affair with the firm conviction that she could no longer be destroyed by the Arabs, but, in fact, that thanks to the results of the Sinai campaign, she had ended the trial period and was entitled to live as a normal State, a still contested but by now ineradicable factor in the area.

Egypt came out of the conflict with the equally firm conviction that whatever her military weakness in the field, her political influence in the world was now an established fact, recognized by all. She had beaten off the attack of two powerful European powers and recovered all the ground lost to Israel with the help—and the competition—of the U.S.A. and U.S.S.R. Egypt was now a leading nation, and Nasser a leading figure in the uncommitted Third World. To transform his tremendous influence into real power, all that was needed now was to canalize the potentialities of Arab nationalism into the proper institutions of an Egyptian-dominated Arab Union. To this end, there was

[1] Eytan, op. cit., ch. 3, 'Lausanne: the Conciliation Effort', pp. 49–64.

little Israel could do in a positive way, but much in a negative way. It was a powerful reminder of the need for Arab unity. All the Arabs had to do now was to become strong and united under Egyptian leadership and wait till the time came for the final settling of scores between the Zionists and the Arabs. The Palestine question, said Nasser to the Palestinian refugees in Gaza in 1962, must wait until the Arabs are united and ready to deal with it.

The main consequence of the 1956 conflict seems thus to be the following: before the Sinai and Suez crises, both Arab and Jewish nationalists struggled to prove their existence—to the colonial powers and to each other; after the 1956 war, both Jewish and Arab nationalism were forced by different, but equally compelling, reasons to search for their own 'post-risorgimento' significance. The problem of defining themselves, in terms of their own rising national, economic, and social aspirations; in terms of an ancient past and a foreign-influenced modernizing future; in terms of traditional national and religious ideologies and of trends in world thought; in terms of political, moral, economic, social, and cultural hopes and shortcomings—became as important as the Jewish–Arab national confrontation.

It became also highly explosive because both sides had a distorted and fearful image of each other (and possibly of themselves) which favoured a Manichaean simplification of the conflict: Israel was 'the enemy' which the Arabs needed in order to provide substance and an external pressure towards coalition for an otherwise loose nationalism. The Arabs fulfilled, on a totally different level, the role of the 'persecutor', which the Jews needed to activate their powerful reflexes of national unity through self-defence.

Chapter 7

The Search for an Identity

One cannot look at the events which followed the Suez war simply as a continuation of the old, well-known pattern of conflict. In any case, for Israel, if not for the Arabs, about whom I do not feel competent to speak in this context, the Sinai campaign represented a watershed in the history of the State, of Zionism, and possibly of the Jews.

Such a far-reaching statement needs to be supported with detailed documentation. I hope to be able to provide it in another book in which I shall attempt to analyse the developments in Israeli politics since the Suez campaign. Thus my present efforts really end here. I have accepted, however, the view of many friends who have urged me to put down, in a tentative way, some of my ideas about the second decade in the life of the Jewish State.

All dates are arbitrary when considered as 'watersheds' in history but some are probably less arbitrary than others. This is particularly true of the Sinai campaign and of the period between November 1956 and March 1957. This seems to me to have been a time of significant change, in spite of an outward appearance of continuity. On the surface little seemed, in fact, to have changed. So much so that in 1966 when the Israeli press was full of recollections of the events which had taken place ten years before, it was difficult to avoid a feeling of *déjà vu*. In 1966, as in 1956, and almost in the same words, Israel was still proposing peace to the Arabs and the Arabs rejecting it. Russia was arming Egypt, Egypt was calling for Arab unity in order to destroy Israel, and the Palestinians were infiltrating, with or without Nasser's blessing, the frontiers of the Jewish State.

That was, however, just the tip of the iceberg of the old 'Palestine question'. At the root of the problem things were changing, possibly on both sides of the frontier, but certainly in Israel where nothing had been quite as before since the Sinai campaign.

First on the list of changes was the question of the physical survival of the State. Before 1956 its existence had been arguable, its ability to integrate immigrants, amounting almost to double the original Jewish population of Palestine, doubtful, to say the least. Before 1956 Israel

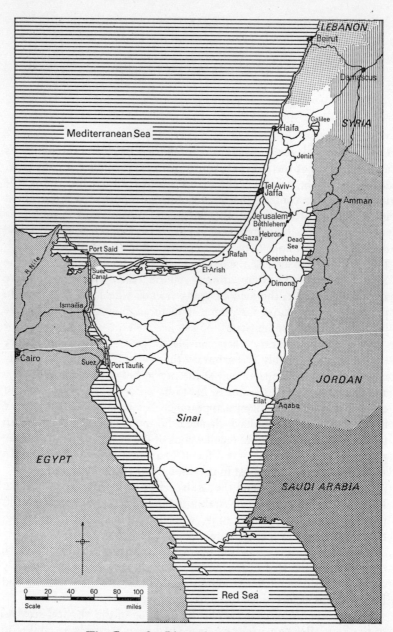

4 The Cease-fire Lines after the June 1967 War

could not really be considered a State, in spite of all the paraphernalia of political independence. It was, rather, a refugee camp under siege desperately trying to strike roots in an underdeveloped colonial country and facing an apparently insoluble combination of economic and social, internal and external challenges. Israel looked more like an articulated provincial municipality, cumbersomely trying to adapt itself to the ill-fitting garments which so many tailors—the United Nations, world Jewry and Zionism, the Arab and Christian nations, were interested in stitching up. It was to a large extent a society based on Jewish colonial structures and institutions which every new wave of immigration was shaking, while demanding from them new energy and ideas for unity, integration, and leadership. From the outside this struggle seemed (to friends) an inspiring or (to enemies) an awful battle of supermen against unbelievable odds. From the inside it appeared as piecemeal improvisation, a miracle of daily ingenuity in the midst of total confusion, unrealistic planning, and bureaucratic inefficiency, where the only clear principle of individual and collective policy was the one expressed by the Hebrew words *ein brera* (no alternative).

It was this lack of choice that helped to mobilize a population unequally participant in the life and struggles of the State. Thus, although in most fields of thought ideology and reality were far apart, in action— war, economic development, foreign policy, and so on—Israel presented a remarkable unity.

After 1956 all this became history. Frontiers were secure, if not entirely peaceful.[1] The Israeli Army, which up to 1953 had suffered from problems of organization and command, had by now established itself as the most efficient military, political, and socially unifying factor in the country. The Sinai campaign had been the crowning achievement of its nation-wide efforts at integration. Reduced immigration, the reclamation of large agricultural areas, the full utilization of abandoned Arab properties, increasing financial aid from America, both from governmental and Jewish sources, the impact of German reparations and, last but not least, the tremendous individual efforts of old and new residents, were beginning to bear fruit. Economically and militarily it was no longer a question of survival, but of choosing between alternative ways of life.

Second on the list of changes came the radical transformation of the demographic structure of Israel. The State, quite paradoxically, had

[1] There were no Israelis killed in border incidents in 1964 and the total number of casualties between 1956 and 1966 was less than a hundred.

become more westernized and more Jewish because it had more oriental-born and fewer Western Zionist inhabitants.

It was less Zionist because Zionist ideals were losing strength as they became a reality. The dream of an independent Jewish State in Palestine having been realized, the ideological climate of the country was, quite naturally, that of the confusion and the indecision of 'the morning after'. It was also less Zionist because the majority of the new immigrants had not been led to immigrate by Zionist ideals as understood by Western Jewish nationalism, but by material and religious factors. For the many thousands of European refugees stranded after the Second World War in the displaced persons' camps in the lands of the Nazi holocaust, Israel was certainly the only place where they could escape the memories of the past and hope for a better future. But when they had finally come, they had been motivated more by hardship than by idealism. In fact, out of some 450,000 European Jews who came to Israel between 1949 and 1965, about 100,000 left again, many thousands even to return to Western Germany. The other half million immigrants originating from Islamic countries also came because of the pressure of the hostility of the non-Jewish (Arab) milieu in their lands of origin. But this pressure was infinitely weaker than in Europe, and what moved them towards Israel was not Jewish nationalism in terms of Zionism (of which they knew nothing) but a genuine national and religious vocation to participate in the Messianic rebirth of the Jewish people. They 'orientalized' Israel and undoubtedly made its social fabric more 'Jewish' than it was before. But there was another factor which contributed to the increase in the 'Jewishness' of the State, while increasing its 'westernization' and that was Arab hostility.

Zionism had never conceived nor worked for a purely ethnic Jewish State. What it had been striving for was a Jewish majority in Palestine (and some, the old Zionist 'Territorialists', were prepared to try to achieve it even outside Palestine). Herzl had envisaged and described —romantically but undoubtedly sincerely—a Zionist State which would be a bridge between West and East, a country and a 'Jewish nation on the march', which would not only remove the Jew from the humiliations of antisemitism but replace him in his old, glorious role of 'translator' of ideas, values, civilization. He thought of the Zionist achievement in Palestine as the first step in the long war of national liberation of oppressed people. Dr. Blayden, one of the founding fathers of Pan-Africanism, who had never met Herzl but who admired his ideas, and had visited Palestine in 1866 and become deeply interested in the Jewish question and later in Zionism, complained that there were not enough 'black Jews' to help to promote the liberation of the African.[1]

The Zionist leaders after Herzl never conceived a Jewish State based solely on Jews. The plans for the partitions of Palestine which they accepted in 1937 and in 1947 were based on a close coexistence of Arabs and Jews in Palestine, although a leading Zionist planner, Dr. Ruppin, was at the time ready to reduce even the small area allotted by the Peel Commission plan in order to achieve a purely Jewish 'Canton'. The 1948 war totally changed such conceptions. It made Israel into a besieged cul-de-sac, technically nearer to Europe—and in fact even to Japan—than to nearby Syria. It put an end to all direct contacts between Arabs and Jews, with the exception of a small Arab minority in Israel, which was socially and politically less important than its numbers (10 per cent of the total population) might imply, since it had lost its leaders. The war transformed the Yishuv of Palestine, which up to that time had been far more Zionist than Jewish, into the State of Israel, which was, out of necessity, ethnically, religiously, ideologically, and politically more European Jewish than Zionist.

The majority of the population was not European-born, but the *élites*, the symbols of national identity, the sources of income and aid, the propagators of education were all deeply influenced by European tradition. Furthermore, the majority of the new immigrants, in fact more than two-thirds of the population, was concentrated in the towns. Some of them, like Jaffa and Askalon, may have had a long and glorious past, but their present was in no way related to the imposing archaeological ruins cared for by the Tourist Department. Their present was, as epitomized by Tel Aviv, built on sand by a population of migrants who spoke mostly Hebrew but who dreamt in the languages of the Diaspora. The French, British, Russian, and Moroccan Israelites, who were so conscious of being Jews abroad, suddenly became Israelis anxious to stress (or, in some cases, to forget nationalities which might be considered socially unacceptable) that they were British, French, or Russian. Twenty-three publications in foreign languages and broadcasts by the local radio in nine different languages were an indication not only of the fragmentation of the cultures but also of the desire of some of them not to give up the past. The Europeans in any case set the standards, because they were better educated, of a higher social class, and politically more influential. They, not the oriental Jews, laid down the pattern of life in Israel which the rest of the population shared. It was

[1] E. W. Blayden, *From West Africa to Palestine* (London, 1873) and *The Jewish Question* (Liverpool, 1898).

the life-style of a petty bourgeoisie, trying to recreate in the new environment of the State some of the atmosphere it had known in the Diaspora, more especially in the Eastern European Diaspora. In the small, standardized two- or three-room apartments (where the European family of four lived fairly affluently and the oriental family of six or eight were crammed in a state of permanent encampment) the refrigerator (usually a gift from a relative in America) dominated the decor, sharing the whitewashed walls with some pathetic, framed picture of a bearded rabbi grandfather and the ugly, functional modern furniture.

It was a provincial life-style in scope and ambition, just as pre-Sinai Israel generally was. Not Judaist in belief but deeply Jewish, and more particularly 'stedtl Jewish',[1] in habits, memories, tastes, and institutions. Not Jewish by solidarity but by a common defensive reaction which Arab hostility continuously provoked. Revolutionary and radical, with socialist and Zionist slogans, but fundamentally traditional in everyday life. It was a puritan society without necessarily living according to puritan morality; Spartan but not militarist; rugged and melodramatic in its own way. Only one Israeli writer, Amos Oz, has so far been able to distil its misery and greatness, its drabness and its petty bourgeois heroism, in that superb novel *My Michael*.[2] It is curious that he should have been an Israeli-born member of the kibbutz aristocracy but it is significant that his novel—whose main theme is the uneventful life of a typical Israeli couple in the years 1950–60—should have become a best-seller in Israel.

Israeli society at that time was in any case fragile and insecure, and not only from the point of view of military security. Like a plant brought by the wind of fate, it had been deposited on rocky ground and had to struggle for breathing space and a patch of soil in which to strike root. The breathing space could be contested by the Arabs, but ground to strike roots in was a purely Jewish affair. In a sense it was the struggle of Zionism, which had robbed Judaism of its universal theistic Messianism, to pierce through Judaism itself in order to reach the common and vital ground of the biblical past from which they might both draw strength. Such an Israel dissatisfied many Jews of the Diaspora who expected the State to provide a solution to their problems of identity but exalted all those who felt that the Israeli military victories —the Sinai campaign included—projected a new image of the self-confident and 'normalized' Jew among the Gentiles. It irritated many

---

[1] A 'stedtl' was a small Jewish town or village in Eastern Europe inhabited by a majority of orthodox Jews.   [2] Amos Oz, *Michael Sheli* (Tel Aviv, 1967).

locally born Israelis who resented being dragged into a way of life too reminiscent of the Diaspora. It terrified the Arabs who had no part in it and little understanding of it. It was perhaps an inevitable but certainly a major disaster that the Sinai campaign confirmed in the eyes of the Arabs the view that the wretched refugee community of Jews left by the Second World War was, in fact, a superhuman, humourless, terribly efficient, aggressive branch of Western imperialism in the Middle East. The alliance with France, at the time still deeply engaged in the Algerian war, did much to strengthen this Manichaean vision.

The Israelis were aware of the situation but not particularly worried by it. Just as the Arabs saw them as a well-oiled machine of foreign aggression, they did not need criticism to tell them how weak and unsettled their society in fact was, how it gnawed away at its own internal harmony. To them, what counted in the Sinai campaign was the practical result paid for with 134 dead and expenses of some 400 million dollars partially offset by the booty captured from the Egyptians. They had achieved almost complete peace around the frontiers for the first time since the establishment of the State. They were enjoying the exhilarating feeling that the country had emerged unscathed from the confrontation with its most powerful Arab neighbour and that the other Arab States, by not joining in the battle, had proved the limited practical value of Pan-Arabism.

They had also won time. How much, nobody could say, but enough, it was hoped, to integrate the thousands of newcomers still living in temporary accommodation; time to reap the fruits of economic investments; time for a new generation of indigenous Israelis to grow up; time, above all, to think and plan the future of a State whose real nature and vocation nobody could as yet tell.

Finally there were many new hopes. The hope of finding a way of coexisting with the Arabs; of joining the European Common Market; of having a role to play in the development of the new countries of Asia and Africa; of transforming Israel into a sort of Middle Eastern Switzerland, capable of deterring and helping with a strength derived more from political and social stability and from economic and scientific development than from military force. Looking back at the time between the Sinai campaign in 1956 and the Six-Day War in 1967, one understands why so many writers and journalists have fallen into the habit of dividing this period into two different, almost diametrically opposed phases, the first one (from 1958 to 1964) full of hope, and the second one (from 1964 to 1967) full of disillusion and crisis. Although the two periods overlapped in many ways, there is no doubt that the general mood of affluent Israel in 1964–5 was far gloomier than the mood of the still very poor Israel of 1958.

Early hopes and later disillusionment did not, of course face one another as opposing poles, but were rather co-ordinated in a chapter of Israel's history which was marked by swift changes and their consequences. The switch from hope to frustration, from illusion to disillusion, from success to crisis, must also be related to the particular character of the Jewish State at the time: a land of universal appeal in the framework of a 'mini-State', where rapid switches from provincialism to universalism—and vice versa—seem to have been a conditioned reflex of its population.

To understand the great acceleration of events which took place in a short space of time and in spite of an outward appearance of stagnation, one should perhaps go back to the late fifties and re-read some of the statements made in Israel when the State was celebrating its tenth anniversary—and compare them with what was said six years later.

The *Israel Government Yearbook*, for example, is a publication traditionally used by Israeli Premiers to expound their views on the State and its future. In 1956 Ben Gurion's article published just before the Suez operation, as I have mentioned, was significantly called 'Southward'. In 1957 Ben Gurion's programmatic paper was entitled 'Israel and the Diaspora', an indication, perhaps, of the preoccupation the Premier already felt with a possible break or misunderstanding between Israel and the other Jews in the world, some of whom remained critical of the participation of the State in the Suez operation—although happy about its outcome—and increasingly disinterested in the stereotyped clichés of Zionist appeals. In 1958 Ben Gurion did not write an article in the *Yearbook* but one of his closest collaborators, Shimon Peres (later to become Israel's Deputy Defence Minister and then Secretary General of Ben Gurion's splinter party, Rafi), summarized, in a conversation with the author, the outlook for the next ten years in the formula: 'We fought to survive, we shall have to fight to prosper.' Peres also believed that one of the main changes which had taken place in the Middle East was that, whereas in the past the great powers had been interested in 'what was happening inside the Middle East', from now on they would try to get the Middle East 'interested in what was happening outside it'. He also believed that Israel's future, with the help of France and possibly Germany, was to be found in Europe and that the main thing required from Israel—whose population he expected to grow to 4 or 5 million by 1968—was ability to act. 'Writers and ideologists will come later,' he said.

For Naḥum Goldmann, the most outstanding and one of the most outspoken Zionist personalities of the Diaspora, the main problems which Israel would have to face between 1948 and 1968 were those linked with the integration of immigrants, economic independence, relations with the Diaspora and with the Arabs. In all four cases he was particularly preoccupied by the necessity of finding appropriate new diplomatic and institutional formulas which might safely transfer the old Zionist wine into new bottles. On the whole, the impression gathered from the forecasts made in 1958 for the next ten years was one of continuity through expansion; an impression which was not to be confirmed by subsequent events.

In 1964, for instance, Professor Eisenstadt, the leading Israeli sociologist, was convinced that the impact of industrialization on the State in the seventies would be as great if not greater than the military and political impact of the Arabs. He felt that the main problem Israel would have to face would be the social one created by the adoption of higher technology. In a nation in which, he claimed, the number of professionals was rapidly increasing and in which they were supposed by some of the leaders 'to uphold the ideals which the leaders themselves cannot or do not want to uphold', the real challenge to the State would be whether or not a new system of principles could be devised, whether or not people could identify themselves with their jobs and feel that their work was part of their responsibility to the nation, and whether the parties would become a federation of different ethnic and other groups, distributing benefits to each, or be able to develop a new ideology.[1]

Moshe Shamir, the writer, was blunter. He wrote that 'behind the fence of material prosperity we face spiritual catastrophe'. He believed that if nothing was done 'to arouse the real spirit of the people' of Israel 'nihilism and cynicism' would become prevalent among the younger generation.[2]

Thus, in six years of continuous economic growth, of relative security, of spectacular development, a 'credibility gap' had opened between what the people had achieved and what they wanted to achieve. It was not just a question of choice between leaders and parties, although these were by no means unimportant. A strange *malaise* diffused itself throughout the Israeli nation, raising the question of how and why the 'land of milk and honey' was turning into a land of frustration and discontent just when honey and milk were, in fact, beginning to flow for everyone, at the rate of an average income of $750 *per capita* per annum, one of the highest along the Mediterranean coast.

[1] *Jerusalem Post*, 17 April 1964.   [2] ibid.

It was clear to most people that the Jewish State which had emerged from the Sinai war was quite different from the State that had gone into the war, or at least it had suddenly become conscious of being different. The change was not due to an altered balance of forces, internal and external. It was rather a result of the feeling that the nation was growing out of the straitjacket of the slogans, values, institutions, habits of the formerly colonial Zionist society, without having anything to put in its place. 'We look like monkeys to the tourist,' wrote Moshe Shamir,[1] and the desire to find a new image combined with the difficulty of making it fit contradictory realities and aspirations became a major source of frustration and discontent. The 'Establishment', the parties, and the bureaucracy naturally tried to appease this feeling by showing the considerable material achievements and by throwing the responsibility for the crisis onto the younger generation—the 'espresso generation'— which seemed to have lost the taste for old-fashioned pioneering patriotism. There was an outcry when one Tel Aviv University sociologist showed that the teaching of the Book of Judges, in the nationalistic atmosphere of the Israeli secondary schools, could promote chauvinism;[2] there were protests when a newspaper interviewed students in the best high school in Jerusalem and heard teenagers laugh at old-fashioned worlds like 'Zionism', 'fatherland', and 'pioneerism'. These same youngsters were soon to prove to their elders that they could fight for their country probably much better, even if with much less enthusiasm for war and uniforms, than the previous generations. Still the mood was such that the gloomiest forecasts were made. A recurrent one was that the country was on the verge of civil strife and many intellectuals believed that Ben Gurion's desire to change the electoral system was in fact a disguised attempt to introduce a régime of authoritarian premiership in Israel. This pessimistic mood was due in large part to the material achievements of the country, to the fact that people were for the first time able to think seriously about their own internal problems rather than external ones.

In the military sphere, border security and the friendship with France made it possible for the first time to purchase arms in quantity and of a quality limited only by the financial resources of the State. It also allowed the military to rethink the whole defence structure of the country, preparing themselves for a highly technological future conflict, for which Israel—with its reserves of skilled personnel and scientific

[1] ibid.
[2] George Tamarin, 'Three Studies of Prejudice in Israel', Dept. of Psychology, Tel Aviv University.

resources drawn from both the State and the Diaspora—was much better equipped than the Arabs.

Israel was certainly not happy about the return of the Egyptians to Gaza in spite of the assurances given to the contrary by the United States. Nor was it satisfied with the arrangement which briefly allowed Israeli goods to go through the Suez Canal on non-Israeli ships. But if Israel had lost Gaza, the Egyptians had acquired the onus of controlling the vast mass of Palestinian refugees in that area; if the Canal stayed closed, the Straits of Aqaba were now opened, with the result that Israel not only had free access to the Indian Ocean but also that its southern port of Eilat and its desert hinterland could now be better developed under the commercial impetus of a rapidly developing maritime trade than from the doubtful sparks of a costly pioneering agricultural effort in the Negev.

No less important to security was the new position achieved by Israel in Europe with the help of France and by her growing economic collaboration with Western Germany. In this way the State acquired new markets and new possibilities of quick modernization. This *rapprochement* also offered for the first time space for diplomatic manoeuvring in the Western world, one of the two 'anchorage' points to which the ship of the Jewish State could be tied in the disturbed waters of the Middle East (the other 'anchorage' being the non-Arab countries of Africa and Asia).

For any Frenchman or Frenchwoman of some social standing a trip to Israel became a 'must', after Henri, the Count of Paris, pretender to the throne of France, decided to come to Tel Aviv and recall the adventures of his crusader ancestor, St. Louis (King Louis IX), in the Middle East, in front of the bosses of Israel's trade unions, gathered for the occasion on the fifth floor of the Histradut building, which the Israelis call the 'Kremlin'. From 1956 onwards a countless number of official and unofficial French missions visited Israel, and a countless number of declarations stressed the 'eternal friendship' between the two countries. On the occasion of Israel's tenth anniversary, even the President of the French Jewish 'Consistoire' publicly disavowed his previous, almost traditional anti-Zionist stand and proclaimed that 'after the creation of the State of Israel all Jews are united in total support of Israel'.[1]

Whatever the feeling of Jewish and non-Jewish French intellectuals over the Suez operation, no guests were absent from the gala opera performance given on the occasion of the tenth anniversary of the

[1] *La Terre Retrouvée*, April 1958, special 10th anniversary issue.

creation of the State. Israel even came into French internal politics. When Pierre Hervé, an anti-Stalinist communist candidate who had written antisemitic articles, had to fight the pro-Jewish, left-wing resistance fighter Claude Bourdet in a Paris by-election, he did not hesitate to accuse him of being anti-Israeli because of his criticism of the Suez affair. In fact Israel's co-operation with France was more criticized in Israel than in France (communists excluded). Already in January 1957 Ben Gurion had to refute strong Mapam accusations of sharing an aggressive military alliance policy with France by stating very clearly that it was his duty to work with France.[1] With or without a formal treaty (which in fact was never signed because of French reluctance to enter into a formal alliance with Israel) the Government in Jerusalem saw in the co-operation with France the new corner-stone of its foreign policy and it hoped that it would not crumble with the end of the Algerian war, which had been the basic element in the Israeli–French *rapprochement*.

Quite apart from the supply of costly but practically unlimited military supplies, France was now standing by Israel at the United Nations and offering credits to make good the American aid which had been stopped during the Sinai crisis. The French Government and French capitalists made possible the construction of the first large pipeline carrying oil from Eilat to the Mediterranean and promised to supply Israel with oil from French sources in case of emergency. The State-owned car factory, Renault, established a car assembly plant in Haifa. Air France became the only airline to fly from Israel to the Far East. The fact that the same two firms were also first to cool down their relations with Israel (Renault broke their agreement with Israel in October 1959 to resume sales in the Arab States, and Air France refused to give Paris–New York landing rights to the Israeli national airline, El Al, in January 1960 on the advice of the French Government) were ominous signs which, however, did not seem to modify the essence of the strong French–Israeli collaboration. As early as March 1958 the first of many partnerships between French electronic and other highly sophisticated industries and an Israeli Histadrut firm was established. In May 1958 the Institute of Nuclear Physics was opened in Rehovot. It marked not only an Israeli military break-through into the company of the most advanced nuclear countries of the world, but also the beginning of closer nuclear collaboration with France, which led to the construction of the nuclear centre at Dimona. Increased trade between the two countries was accompanied by big French investments in Israel

[1] Michael Bar-Zohar, *Suez Ultra-Secret* (Paris, 1964), ch, ix, pp. 248 ff.

and by an extraordinary expansion of French cultural influence in a formerly anglicized part of the world. French and Hebrew school and university certificates were equalized; reciprocal military service admitted; French embassies in Arab and communist countries issued tens of thousands of entry visas to France for Jews directed to Israel, and on one occasion French trade unionists interrupted a general strike to let a train of Jewish immigrants pass through France. This trend, apparently, did not change with the advent of de Gaulle to power. The General certainly took his distance from Israel, putting a brake on the military side of the scientific collaboration which he believed to be an exclusively French domain. But it was more a matter of style than of content, and the Israelis preferred a cooler but stronger man at the helm of French policy to a more friendly but weaker politician like Guy Mollet. In June 1960, when Ben Gurion met de Gaulle in Paris, the whole conception of the two countries' *entente* was revised and strengthened. The common hostility to the Arabs ceased to be the main point of contact. De Gaulle gave unconditional approval to Israel's activities in Africa, reiterated France's support against any attempt to destroy Israel, gave his blessing to a new supply of military and airforce equipment, and seemed very pleased with the definition given by Ben Gurion of the future Israel as a State more interested in the development and numerical increase of its population than in the extension of frontiers. The later visit to Paris of Ben Gurion in 1961 and of his successor, Levi Eshkol, in 1964 seemed to confirm de Gaulle's determination to continue to co-operate with Israel while establishing equally good relations with the Arabs.

Israel's second important, but far more controversial link with Europe was with Germany. The Israeli Government had to be careful in its relations with Bonn because of the passionate reaction of at least a part of its population and the traditional anti-German stand of some of the parties—Herut in the opposition, Aḥdut Haavoda and Mapam in the coalition. In January 1958 Aḥdut Haavoda had brought the Government to a crisis over the alleged leakage of information concerning Israeli supplies of light arms to the German Army. Another crisis was brought on in 1959 by Mapam, for roughly the same reasons. In March 1960, however, an important step forward in the relations between the two countries was taken. Ben Gurion and Adenauer met in New York, not only breaking the psychological ice of direct contact between the German and Israeli Government leaders but also laying the foundations for some important military and economic agreements. These agreements were later to be at the epicentre of a violent debate in the Israeli administration itself. The frequent and discreet trips of Israeli military personnel to Germany, the visit paid by the German Defence Minister, Franz-Josef Strauss, to Israel and his interest in its military industries contributed to wider co-operation in the field of skilled technology. Meanwhile commercial exchanges between the two countries grew at a fast rate.

In 1960 again one aspect of the German–Jewish question became tragically focused in world opinion: the arrest of Adolf Eichmann in Argentina and his trial in Jerusalem played an ambivalent role—both cathartic and embittering—in the development of contacts between the two nations.

But a fact also considered important in Jerusalem was that through France and Germany the Jewish State could acquire a larger margin for political and economic manoeuvring in relation to the, up till then, all-powerful Anglo-Saxon influence. France—and to a lesser degree Germany—also contributed to Israel's penetration in Africa. Africa, with Europe, was a political and diplomatic 'anchor' to which the Israelis hoped to tie their ship of state.

It was a French-speaking African President, Maurice Yaméogo from Upper Volta, who in 1961 opened the long list of Heads of State who, after years of diplomatic quarantine, agreed to set foot officially on Israeli territory. But even that first and—for the Israelis—historic visit had been preceded by many attempts to by-pass the Arab siege by establishing contact with the African and Asian world.

After the 1955 Bandung Conference, which marked the lowest point of international isolation ever touched by Israel, Israeli diplomacy had steadily worked to reverse the situation. By the end of the same year an Israeli goodwill mission had attended President Tubman's re-election ceremonies; another had gone to Ethiopia, a third to Burma, while increased immigration from Iran had not only brought additional citizens to the State but also closer political and economic links with Persia, which had not yet recognized Israel *de jure*. In 1957 a consulate was opened in Ghana (there was another in Addis Ababa) and an important Israeli mission attended the independence ceremonies at Accra. This was to be the real beginning of Israel's penetration in sub-Saharan Africa and one of her brightest diplomats, Ehud Avriel, was chosen to carry it out: the same man who had organized the military and diplomatic co-operation with Czechoslovakia in 1948. But, at the time, Asia, not Africa, was still the Israelis' most coveted diplomatic goal, and some hopes were still pinned on India, which had recognized Israel *de jure*, however only allowing a consulate to be opened in Bombay. The former

Premier, Moshe Sharett, went to Asia on a fruitful goodwill tour in 1956, soon followed by Dayan and Peres, who, in their respective roles as Chief of Staff and Director-General of the Ministry of Defence, visited Burma in January 1958. They established then the basis for Israel's first large-scale military and technical co-operation with a developing country. In April 1958 Mrs. Golda Meir made the first of many tours of African capitals, while Pinchas Sapir, the then Minister for Commerce, toured Asia. The fruits of their on-the-spot diplomacy were quick to appear: Israeli exports to Afro-Asian countries rose from almost nil to 20 million dollars and represented 5 per cent of the total of Israeli exports by 1968. At the same time, the meeting of African Heads of State at Accra in April 1958 failed to condemn Israel, in spite of strong Egyptian pressure. It was the first clear sign that the new States of the black continent were reluctant to be mixed up in the Palestine question, which they considered a non-African quarrel. The presidential visit of Izhak Ben Zvi to Burma in 1959 was the first ever made by an Israeli Head of State beyond his country's borders. It took place in return for the visit of Burma's Prime Minister U Nu to Israel, which had driven the by now siege-obsessed Israelis to a degree of almost hysterical patriotic enthusiasm. But it was the year 1960 which consecrated the new policy. In the wake of the creation of the independent African States Israel saw her diplomatic mission, as well as her experience acquired through many years of 'parliamentary, socialist nation-building' in Palestine, welcomed by all the new States, with the exception of Mauretania and Somaliland. A special department was created by the Ministry of Defence and, on a smaller scale, by the Ministry of Agriculture. The internal political competition of the ministers (Golda Meir, Moshe Dayan, and Shimon Peres[1]) often acted as an additional spur for new initiatives overseas.

The story of Israel's co-operation with developing countries is an oft-told tale. It is best epitomized by the fact that the Israelis referred to the first successful international conference for the application of science to the development of new countries, at Rehovot in 1960, as their 'answer to Bandung'. This attitude, supported by slogans such as 'Israel only helps others to help themselves', 'Better to be wrong on a decision taken by oneself than to be right on a foreigner's advice', 'Learn from Israel, cemetery of foreign advisers' plans', was not only the recognition of Israel's limited means, but also offered the Africans a welcome change from cumbersome and often ineffective international aid. It was an expensive challenge for the Arabs to take up. It provided

[1] Foreign Minister, Agricultural Minister, and Vice-Minister of Defence respectively.

irritating competition for the communist countries, who disliked being told by the Africans that Zionism was the 'Israeli version of practical Marxism'. Even a country like Great Britain did not like her military advisers, from Sierra Leone to Uganda, being replaced by Israeli officers, but for Israel it was a policy which paid handsome dividends. It established the Jewish State on the diplomatic map of the Third World; it gave Israel new weight, new diplomatic dimensions, and new prestige; it diverted the attention of the Israeli public from the narrow confines of the local frontiers, opening new horizons of interest, action, and adventure for the young; it absorbed many, still young, retiring army officers; it helped to increase exports and to diversify sources of imports, loosening Israeli dependence on Western sources in some vital fields such as diamonds, timber, and meat. From the political point of view it reinforced the theory and the vision—so dear to Ben Gurion—of the existence of a Moslem area in Africa and in Asia, where a large majority of the population could in time be detached from Arab influence, and possibly serve as an indirect means of overcoming Arab hostility. Israel's close relations with Turkey and her even closer collaboration with Iran were followed, in spite of Egyptian efforts to the contrary, by the establishment of diplomatic and economic links with independent Cyprus. The Kurdish revolt in Iraq, the Yemeni war, the enthusiasm showed by Moslem rulers, such as President Ahidjo of Cameroon, Tombalbaye of Chad, for Israel's role in the developing world, had reinforced the Israelis' belief in the possibility of collaborating with a secular, moderate, pro-Western Moslem group, which could be opposed to the radical, communist-oriented Arab group. This idea, which mainly concerned the non-Arab Middle East, was put forward by Ben Gurion himself to de Gaulle in their talks in Paris in 1960 and 1961 and does not seem to have elicited much interest. But, on the other hand, the French President was full of appreciation for and fully supported Israel's 'special role' in Africa. It was also in and with the African countries that Israel conceived the diplomatic project of obtaining from the United Nations a resolution calling for direct talks between the Arabs and Israel. For two subsequent years, in 1962 and 1963, this resolution was the main diplomatic target of Israeli diplomacy in New York, but it was always defeated by the combination of Arab and communist votes. It was, for Israel, a depressing exercise in brinkmanship but also a display of its new influence in the United Nations through the vast network of relations with African, Asian, and Latin-American countries. In some cases, new African friends, such as Madagascar, Ivory Coast, Ethiopia, Niger, and Dahomey, were to prove far more faithful to Israel in the trying days before the 1967 war, than old 'allies' such as France or even the U.S.A.

More important from the Israeli point of view was the exotic escape which the collaboration with the Third World provided from the dilemma between ideology and practice in the Zionist State. International co-operation with the Afro-Asian and—later—Latin-American countries provided, in the words of the late Premier Levi Eshkol, 'the first opportunity for the Israelis to give instead of receive'.[1] For a society of refugees, voluntary or involuntary, in search of an identity, the feeling of being sought after was psychological bliss.

As time passed and relations with the Afro-Asian countries switched from slogans and colourful 'diplomatic tourism' to serious economic, social, and military involvement in more than thirty countries, the Israelis were faced with some unexpected problems. The first was how to fulfil the expectations of the developing countries with the limited means at their disposal. This called for the development of techniques and for ingenuity in the application of technical aid which transformed the State into a major source of 'micro-co-operation', while the Western and communist powers were getting into trouble with their cumbersome and often inefficient schemes of 'macro-co-operation'.

Another problem was the Israelis' need to explain themselves to people who knew nothing of Jews and antisemitism and who on the whole took little notice of the Palestinian quarrel. The Israeli was a 'white' who refused to be equated with the Europeans; a Westerner who claimed to be Asian; tribal next-of-kin to Jesus who had nothing to do with Christianity—at least with the version exported by Europe to the colonies; a Marxist who believed in parliamentary democracy and individual freedom. The demand for a clearer image of Israel was as powerful among the returning Israelis from Afro-Asian countries as the demand for African masks and Asian ivories among those who stayed at home.

It would be quite wrong to think that this mood was based on a transient, exotic fashion, although such a fashion existed and contributed to the inevitable appearance abroad of the Israeli parvenu, or as the then Minister of Agriculture Moshe Dayan named it after a tour of Africa, 'the boastful Israeli' (*haisraeli hamashwitz*). Co-operation with the Third World was important because it opened, especially to the young Israelis, new horizons and new challenges. It gave Israel the feeling of being called upon to play a positive international role, that of

[1] In a speech to French businessmen in Paris in 1957, when he was Minister of Commerce and Finance.

modernizer and innovator, and of contributing ideas and experience which reminded the Jew of the best historical moments in his traditional role as mediator of cultures.

Obviously the basic condition for Israel's extending technical aid to underdeveloped countries was to achieve at home a high level of development and economic affluence. This she had been able to do thanks to the efficient utilization of large foreign capital investment. The pundits, of course, worried about the growing dangers of inflation; the industrialists and the businessmen accused the Histadrut of following a policy of socialist economic monopoly, which was as unimaginative as it was out of date. Everybody was conscious of the fact that production and productivity were not increasing as fast as demand; that the country tended to live above its means; that it was feeding on its own imported capital; that it was too dependent on private Jewish and governmental (mainly American) foreign aid and grants. But even after all this and much other bitter criticism had been taken into consideration economic improvements were still impressive. While the Government continued to fight, with limited success, against both inflation and foreign expenditure, because of military imports, development of the country's infrastructure, and absorption of immigrants, a feeling of increased personal well-being developed—unevenly, but conspicuously—throughout the country. Rationing had gone by 1958 and immigrants were no longer forced to stay for long periods in depressing transit camps. Abandoned Arab property, buildings in the cities and large tracts of land in the countryside, had been put into full use, providing an important element of financial support for many immigrants, especially for those who had arrived from the Arab countries. The Government had invested massively in the development of the country's infrastructure, helped in this by the Histadrut, which had taken the initiative of starting or participating in many development projects whose chances of profitability were considered too dubious for private capital. These investments, financed by capital provided by American grants and Jewish donations, by American, and later French, loans and credits, and by the successful floating (from 1952) of Development Bonds in most Western countries, had begun to bear fruit. No less important were the reparations from Western Germany. They probably saved Israel from bankruptcy during the crucial financial difficulties of 1953, and they provided afterwards a steady source of government income on which the authorities could base long-range policies in some important fields, such as naval and railway communications, telephone and electricity services, and regular supplies of essential raw materials. Because the Government wanted to avoid as far as possible the Israeli public coming into direct contact with German products, it directed the purchases of German goods towards raw materials or semi-finished products, rather than towards consumer goods. The German reparations to Israel, amounting to almost 800 million dollars over a period of twelve years, were accompanied by personal restitutions from Germany to individuals who had suffered under Nazism. These unilateral payments brought into Israel 1 billion dollars between 1955 and 1968, and they still remain an important source of foreign capital for the State. They were also to become, as we have seen, a cause of social tension in the country.

Leaving aside the first eight months of Israel's life, during which the country used up most of its wartime savings in Britain, total capital transfers between 1949 and 1966 amounted to 7 billion dollars, almost double the amount offered by the Marshall Plan to Europe. Over $4·5 billion came from unilateral transfers from Jewish institutions, from German reparations to the State ($775 m.), American grants ($315 m.), German restitutions to individuals ($1·1 billion), and private transfers ($835 m.). The remaining $2·5 billion came from loans ($1,650 m.) and private investments ($850 m.).

These impressive figures do not convey the full extent of the economic development of the State. The population of Israel had grown four times in size between 1948 and 1967—to 2,700,000 inhabitants—an average increase of 6 per cent per year, most of which, however, was concentrated in the first years of existence of the State. Diminishing immigration over the years, accompanied by a growing rate of production and foreign help, explains the Israelis' feeling of relief as they emerged from the almost intolerable security and economic difficulties of the fifties into the growing affluence of the sixties. To this affluence local Israeli production contributed an increasing share of capital and labour. As the country became almost independent of food imports, purchasing abroad concentrated more and more on machinery and raw materials for a diversified industry which was slowly exporting its product to foreign markets. In 1948 Israel imported iron nails; in 1966 it exported industrial goods valued at $400 million, among them aeroplanes and electronic appliances. Altogether, exports (services, tourism, and agricultural exports included) had risen from $48 million in 1949 to almost a billion dollars in 1967. This meant a total revolution in the economic structure of a country which, ten years before, still considered itself to be mainly agricultural, and whose social values and many of whose political personnel still belonged to an ideological world based on the almost religious veneration of agricultural work.

Imports had also grown, enlarging the $120 million trade deficit of 1949 to a deficit of $570 million in 1964. This was a staggering figure for a country of 2·5 million people, but it never really impressed either the Government or the public, who knew that in 1949 Israel exports covered one-third of the imports, while in 1966 they covered three-quarters of them, of which a large part was made up of military supplies, whose cost had grown sixteen times between 1952 and 1966 in foreign currency alone. They also knew that the number of actual taxpayers in the Jewish State did not match the number of Israeli taxpayers. At least 1 million Jews throughout the world were making regular economic contributions to the development of the State. On the whole, and in spite of much criticism, the population tended to think that a Government which had helped to multiply the number of children at school by five, those at university by seventeen, the tonnage of the merchant marine by 200, which had won two wars against the Arabs and obtained the recognition of the State by three-quarters of the independent nations of the world was, after all, a government which could be trusted with the responsibility of more delicate problems of social, cultural, and institutional nation-building. But it was unfortunately in these vital fields that technocracy, opulence, and organization alone showed their inadequacy in providing solutions to old and new tensions, which the post-Sinai feeling of security and subsequent developments had in fact exacerbated.

The most important of these problems, which for many years occupied the front pages of the newspapers, was the integration of the oriental immigrants and—to a lesser extent—the integration of the Arab minority in the westernized Jewish society of the Zionist State.

The oriental Jews and the Israeli Arabs presented three main challenges to Jewish society in Israel: economic, cultural, and ideological. The economic challenge was the least complicated. Practically all the oriental immigrants belonged to the lowest income group of the population. Not only did they earn less than the European-born Israelis, but their control of the distribution of income was limited both by their place in society and by the fact that some sources of income, such as the German reparations, were not available to them. At the same time they contributed an indispensable labour force, which was a condition of the development of the Israeli economy. The development and the industrialization of society left them lagging behind the rest of the population because of their limited supplies of skill and capital. While general economic progress improved their lot, it also widened the gap between them and the European-born Israelis and thus their feeling of being discriminated against, especially once they had begun to understand the implications of official slogans still proclaiming equality as a supreme national aim. In this respect, although their conditions were quite different, the position of the Arab minority was not very different from that of the orientals. Both groups felt that their weight in numbers, votes, and labour was not reflected in their share of the national income and even less in their social status. Social status was obviously linked to income, but not exclusively. Men's needs are not equal, certainly not where communities brought up in different cultures and with different values are concerned. What was, for instance, the advantage of influence if the accepted values of the *élite* in Israel called for a measure of puritanism which belittled the outward show so dear to the Mediterranean mind?

But there were more serious cultural snags. The skills of the oriental Jews—traders, artisans, or ordinary workers—were not of a kind liable to be fully exploited in an industrialized economy like the Israeli one. They lacked technical education, although their culture was, in many ways more refined than that of many European-born Israelis. Their children were handicapped in the competition for higher education. In the large families of oriental immigrants crowded into small flats the facilities for studying were certainly inferior to those in the houses of the small European Jewish families. The children also received less help from their parents, quite apart from the economic strain imposed on them by keeping their children at school. The situation was no different with the Arab minority, which also lacked proper teachers, modern textbooks, and which was cut off from its natural cultural environment. In spite of conspicuous government efforts to promote higher education among oriental Jews and—from 1962 onwards—among Israeli Arabs, the percentage of those from both communities in further education lagged far behind the percentage of European Jews. The oriental Jews, who accounted for 50 per cent of the elementary school population, had only about 10 per cent of the pupils in the higher classes, and less than that in the universities. But education is not, in most cases, an end in itself: it is a means of obtaining better jobs. Here again, the Israeli Arabs and the oriental immigrants were handicapped by different but equally important obstacles. Their share of influence on the Government being inversely proportional to their number, they could not enjoy the benefits of a co-optation which was open to the European-born part of the population by reason of their seniority of residence in the country, of vested interests, party affiliations, and relations. For the Israeli Arabs there was the additional obstacle of security which kept them out of many government jobs in the diplomatic service, the Army, and so on.

There was, however, a distinct difference between the two groups from the ideological point of view. The oriental immigrants shared the Judaism of the State. They might not have been Zionists, in the sense the veterans of the second *aliah* were, they might be indifferent to the call of socialism, pioneerism, or collectivism, but they were Jews who had not even needed the appeal of modern nationalism in order to come to Israel and participate in the nation-building process of the State. What of the 230,000 Arabs? How could they share in a Jewish or Zionist enterprise from which they were sentimentally, ideologically, religiously, and even ethnically cut off because of their belonging to the Asian–Arab world? In the first year of the State they fought to preserve their lands from what they thought was a determined effort by the Israeli authorities to deprive them of them. But in time, the impact of urbanization and industry was stronger than the allegiance to traditional village life. Thousands of young Arabs took up residence in Jewish quarters, worked in Jewish factories, Hebraizing their names (just as some oriental immigrants had Germanized theirs) in the hope of being accepted by the westernized *élite* of the country, and often marrying Jewish girls after the religious conversion of one party. Both groups, in a different way, underwent the same process of change. They saw their traditional way of life disrupted by the impact of westernization and modernization and yet they remained marginal to the main structures of power, influence, and thought in Israeli society. This combination of economic, cultural, and ideological frustration bred resentment in both groups and manifested itself in limited violence and much argument after the Sinai operation. On the whole, the tension between the two Jewish Israels and between the Jewish and Arab Israelis proved to be much less serious than the gloomy forecast of the late fifties had indicated. Looking back to those years it is significant that it was in Nazareth, not in a Jewish town, that the first shots of the battle against discrimination were fired, and more specifically on 1 May 1958. On that day eighteen people were wounded and a hundred arrested in Nazareth. The troubles had been without doubt exploited by political agitators. But there was something deeper and more local at stake which had nothing to do with Nasser or the communists. A leading member of the Mapai Party, and one of the most distinguished Israeli poets, Nathan Alterman, saw the implications of the Nazareth riots more clearly than the political pundits. In a moving poem, which he published in the Histadrut paper *Davar*, he proclaimed: 'The agitators raised them [the

Nazareth Arabs], it is true. But from the moment they rose, their anger was real. And let us add, to our consternation, that it was our fault. The right was with them and the right will be with them until the great change.'[1]

The same could have been said of the troubles which, a year later and for a long period hence, followed in the development towns inhabited by oriental immigrants. There were disorders in the Wadi Salib quarter of Haifa, in Migdal Emek and Beersheba, and in many other places. Such disturbances spurred the Government into embarking on a crash programme of education, welfare, and technical training which undoubtedly eased the lot of many of the poorer Israelis, but it did not really tackle the problem of the 'fundamental change' with which Alterman was so rightly concerned.

The change was in fact not so much a righting of wrongs as the creation of new rights. It was not so much a matter of redistribution of income and influence—important as this might be—as of the creation of a new common identity for the whole nation. In no field more than that of religion was the need for new common denominators more evident and deeply felt.

It has become common in Israel to call the strife between the groups, organized and non-organized, which favoured a religious, theocratic régime for Israel and those who defended the right of a Jewish state to be secular, by the German word *Kulturkampf*. Nothing could be more misleading. In Israel there is no real fight between secularism and religion, no serious demand for separation between 'Church and State'—at least in the European sense—in spite of some demands made by small but vocal groups. The religious hierarchy of Judaism is too loose, too decentralized, too articulated, to present the type of religious-political challenge which the Roman hierarchy presented to the European States. Whatever the irritating impingement of religion on the politics and day-to-day life of individuals, the fact remains that the religious struggle in Israel is not a battle between the lay and the Orthodox but rather a battle of competing orthodoxies.

There is the old, unresolved battle between Judaist-Judaism and Zionist-Judaism. There was the battle between official Israeli rabbinical authority and the rabbinical authority of immigrant groups—such as the Beni Israel from India—which refused to submit to the rules of the Jerusalem rabbinate and called for the intervention of the State and of parliament in a matter in which the Government and the parliament had obviously no legitimate status or authority. There was the battle between Judaist-Jews and Christian-Jews, namely the converts of the Christian missions in Israel who wanted the Israeli Government—because of its official agnosticism—to accept the existence of Christian Jews in a Jewish State which for the first time in the history of Judaism had claimed not to be confessional. In a way, there was also a battle between Jewish nationalism and Islamic nationalism, inasmuch as the Arab minority of Israel could not play a full part in Israeli society because it was not Jewish and because the Arabs, even those who accepted the Jewish State, were kept tied to a different basic national identity by their adherence to the faith of the Prophet (the absence of any form of civil marriage meant intermarriage must be accompanied by one party's religious conversion). Islam, like Judaism for the Jews, was the root of national Arab consciousness. The struggle was a many-sided one and we should perhaps pause for a moment to recapitulate the situation.

After the Sinai war there emerged an Israeli State whose survival was no longer threatened, even if its existence was not yet recognized, by its Arab neighbours. It was the scene of rapid economic and industrial expansion and was moving away very quickly from the colonial, agricultural, and egalitarian socialist basis of two decades before. Some political and military problems—relations with the Arabs, for instance—were not solved but put in cold storage as it were by a combination of circumstances, linked with the military power of Israel and the deep divisions in the Arab world.

There were other problems which were purely Israeli: for instance, the social and cultural problem created by the unexpected arrival of a majority of oriental Jewish immigrants in a State essentially conceived for the European Jews who stayed out of it; the problem of the very nature and meaning of the State, born out of the matrix of a Zionist, non-Judaist, nationalist European movement, now obliged by the force of internal and external circumstances to establish itself as the centre of Jewish national identity; the problem of the integration into the new nation of communities which by culture, faith, origin, and loyalties were distinct from the main cultural or religious body of Israeli society; the problem of modernization and westernization which provided some solution to the enormous tensions in Israeli society, some common ground for co-operation in productivity but at the same time intensified the problem of personal alienation.

It was only natural that all these pressing problems should reflect themselves in the delicate mechanism of the State's institutions and more particularly the political institutions.

It is in this connection that the 'Lavon affair',[1] should be recalled, a sequence of events connected with Pinchas Lavon, the former Defence Minister, and which represents in my view the ten-year-long Israeli version of what in other countries have been the struggles for religious, class, and party power. The 'Lavon affair', as a problem of succession of power from the generation of the 'founding fathers' to that of the 'administrators' is also a reflection of the Israelis' special brand of colonial revolution. It represented, in many senses, the same crisis of authority which occurred in almost every new state of the Third World after a period of colonial rule. The transfer of power from one generation of politicians to another is invariably linked with the destruction of the charismatic image of the 'founding father', of the official 'liberator'. In so far as the 'Lavon affair' destroyed the political popularity of the most charismatic figure of heroic Zionism, the process was not very different from that which toppled Ghana's Nkrumah or Indonesia's Sukarno. The outstanding difference is, however, to be found in the fact that in only two countries of the 'emerging world', India and Israel, has the transfer of power from the 'founding fathers' to another, wider group of leaders (in Israel this change is often referred to as the switch from the lions to the foxes) strengthened and not weakened the democratic institutions. I cannot speak for India, but I believe it safe to claim that in Israel democracy has come out of the Lavon affair stronger, not because Ben Gurion was pushed out of politics, but because the electorate, having been obliged to choose between Lavon's political Messianism and Ben Gurion's political pragmatism, refused to allow one trend to prevail over the other. It watched with sorrow and increasing boredom as these two powerful personalities murdered each other, and finally backed a non-charismatic leader, Levi Eshkol, who was committed both to Ben Gurion's pragmatism and to Lavon's Messianism and who knew that both conceptions were essential—if taken in small doses—to the civic health of Israeli society.[2]

Before I give a brief account of the Lavon affair, it must be recalled that in Israel political power is essentially vested in four centres: the Histadrut, the Party bureaucracy, which means the bureaucracy of the Mapai (now Labour) Party, the Defence Ministry, and the Treasury, both of which control the distribution of the country's income. The Army has no political role, for the simple reason that—the nation as a

---

[1] For a concise description of the 'Lavon affair' see Bar-Zohar, *The Armed Prophet*, pp. 249–58, 365–8, 373 ff.; see also Uri Avnery, *Israel without Zionists* (New York and London, 1968), ch. 7; S. N. Eisenstadt, *Israeli Society* (New York and London, 1967), pp. 329–32.

[2] V. D. Segre, 'Israel : A Society in Transition', *World Politics*, vol. XXI, no. 3, April 1969, pp. 345–65.

whole being permanently in a state of mobilization and the senior officers being pensioned at a very low age—the High Command has never been able to develop a separate political consciousness; instead it reflects the opinions and trends of all sections of the population. The Defence Ministry was conceived as a civilian organization with strong anti-militaristic tendencies and is in fact often in open disagreement with the General Staff. Up to now only one officer has been allowed to retain his place at G.H.Q. while holding an important position in the Ministry, and this with much soul-searching on both sides. No less paradoxcially, the power of the Treasury—and to a certain extent of the other economic ministries—has grown thanks to the co-operation with non-socialist sources of foreign capital, Jewish and non-Jewish, mobilized by socialist Ministers often in open opposition to, or at least in competition with, Histadrut interests. The Defence Ministry and the Treasury are real forces inside Israeli society because of their control of the source and distribution of a large part of the country's resources. They have developed, out of necessity, more than any other ministry, an efficient, specialized bureaucracy with a highly developed sense of civic responsibility, a tradition of initiative and a devotion to duty equalled only by their attachment to efficiency and technology.

Compared with them, the other ministries—such as the Foreign Ministry or the Ministry of the Interior—have far less power and importance. Perhaps less important than any other is the Premier's Office, which—supreme in authority when associated with another portfolio—holds very little real or constitutional power by itself.

In the fifties, Pinchas Lavon, then Minister of Agriculture, was considered by some to be Ben Gurion's successor, for reasons which would be too long to relate here but which were, to a great extent, linked with his extraordinary analytical intelligence and his skills as a political debater. When Ben Gurion retired to the Negev, he was prevented by his party colleagues from appointing Eshkol in his place, with Lavon as Defence Minister. The Premiership went to Moshe Sharett and for the first time the Premiership and the Defence portfolios (which under Ben Gurion were held together) were split, with Lavon getting the lion's share, the Defence Ministry.

For reasons which still need much research in order to be properly assessed Lavon switched from total loyalty towards Ben Gurion to wavering loyalty towards Sharett, mainly on the matter of policy towards Egypt. He became the centre of a cloak-and-dagger controversy (still the object of a total security black-out in Israel) usually referred to as a 'security mishap'. It has been said, by several authorities and by the

Arabs themselves, that this mishap was occasioned by the activities of an Israeli-sponsored espionage net in Cairo, which was caught (and some of its members later hanged) while attempting to sabotage American and British installations in that city. The 'affair' took place in July 1954, when Egypt was firing the last rounds against Britain over the evacuation of the Suez Canal, when Nasser was fighting his battle for power both against Neguib and against the Muslim Brotherhood (who attempted to assassinate him) and when the Cairo régime was stubbornly refusing to be dragged into the British-sponsored Baghdad Pact. Was the secret Israeli operation aimed at involving Egypt in a fight with U.S.A. and Britain? Was it a plot, used if not mounted in Israel by Ben Gurion's partisans against Lavon and Sharett, to force Ben Gurion to return to power? Was it connected with a fundamental divergence of opinion in the Israeli Government and in the Army's High Command regarding the foreign and military policy to be followed? I am not in a position to answer this question here. The fact is that Lavon was forced to resign, that Ben Gurion took his place at the Defence Ministry and in November 1955 became Prime Minister again: first with Sharett as Foreign Minister, then without him. The exclusion of Sharett from the Government created a political crisis inside the leadership of Mapai and the second *aliah* establishment which has not yet entirely blown over. But, in spite of all this, the whole affair could have been forgotten at this point; in any case it did not damage Lavon's political reputation. In 1959 he was back as a powerful and militant Secretary General of the Histadrut, a role which he could have hardly obtained without the consent of Ben Gurion. Because of his position, his abilities, and his personal resentment against a number of Ben Gurion's followers who had tricked him, in his opinion, into the 'security mishap', Lavon became the political meeting point of all those interests which, after the Sinai campaign, opposed Ben Gurion's intention to hand over his power to some of the younger elements in the party (General Dayan who left active service in 1958, the Director General of the Defence Ministry, Shimon Peres, and so on) who had emerged as men of action and responsibility in the Sinai crisis. Such possible succession was linked, in the mind of many Israeli politicians and intellectuals, with the fear that Ben Gurion—who demanded at the time changes in the electoral system—might transfer to his young partisans not only power but also a régime in which power would in fact be removed from the party caucus's control. True or not, the 'Lavon affair' reopened in 1960 over the question of the 'rehabilitation' of Lavon over the alleged responsibility for the security mishap (on new evidence brought forward by a criminal trial). Lavonists and Ben Gurionists were polarized now into two blocs inside Mapai with almost equal strength but with a growing support for Lavon from non-Mapai members in student circles and intellectuals. For the first time Israel saw street demonstrations in favour of a political leader. Ben Gurion forced the issue by demanding that his party choose between him and his opponent. His victory over Lavon was a Pyrrhic one, and as a result he was forced to hand over control of the Party to Levi Eshkol and Pinchas Sapir, the two figures in Mapai most representative of the second *aliah* establishment. This led to the political death of Lavon and two years later to the retreat of Ben Gurion from power, but it salvaged some of the influence of Ben Gurion's followers inside the Party, a thing which would have been impossible had Lavon had his way.

The third phase of the Lavon affair, which led to the secession of Ben Gurion from his party in 1965 and to the formation of a Ben Gurionist splinter party—Rafi, is far less important because it did not change the results of the 1960-2 battle. The 1967 war brought Dayan back into the Government in the all-powerful position of Minister of Defence, and Rafi—without Ben Gurion—soon returned to the fold of Mapai (with Ahdut Haavoda in the Labour Party but not Mapam, which remained an electoral ally of the Labour Party but had not yet merged with it).

What was really important in the second phase of the Lavon affair was—apart from the debatable question whether Ben Gurion and the young guard wanted or not to change the present political régime in Israel—the polarization of two political philosophies, two opposing camps. In this there was a reflection not only of personal animosity but of the struggle for the development and the adaptation of the political institutions of the Israeli State to the new realities of Israeli society. More important, it was an attempt to impose solutions on some of the State's basic problems: it was, in fact, a battle between Zionist Messianism and practical Zionism.

The first rounds in this battle were fired in 1958 in the Party's election of the Councils of local parties when Lavon called Dayan and his friends 'pseudo-intellectuals', and were followed up in April 1959 at the Mapai convention. Here Lavon fought very forcefully against 'Young Mapai' in front of the 1,900 delegates. He defended the 'primacy of the Histadrut'; he denied the existence of ethnic problems in the country which, according to him, and not without some truth, arose 'more from geographical conditions than from community of origin'. Dayan was equally forceful in the criticism of the party and of the Histadrut. He scored a certain success when a resolution was passed to the effect that 'those who do not go into agriculture are not necessarily to be considered careerists'. But he did not win much support for himself or his friends inside the party organization.

The charge of 'careerism' and of 'activism' returned frequently in Lavon's attacks. In a, by now, famous ideological article published in 1962, and significantly entitled 'A Chosen People and a Normal Society', he claimed that the traditional Socialist Zionist *élite*, formed by the pioneers, the labourers, and the disinterested civil service, had to maintain its hold on the top of the Israeli social pyramid if Israel were to remain a 'chosen society'.[1] They should also oppose the attempt of the 'parvenus' to dislodge them, namely the attempts of the 'careerists', of the 'successful men' who had made their way up 'without effort' through the opportunities offered by the military victories or by the development funds, and of the State 'apparatus'—in other words, the technocrats and the bureaucrats who thought that Israel was a 'society like other societies'.

> I believe [wrote Lavon] that the state of Israel requires additional dimensions, not in technology and not in numbers . . . It is clear [this dimension] cannot be expressed in the economic field . . . What would have been the reaction of Degania 'A' or 'B', of Ein Harod or Afikim, if a member of Mapai would have been elected president of the golf club twenty years ago? . . . If there is no serious about-turn . . . we shall be a completely normal society without any special attraction. We shall then be, in the last analysis a *Levantine country* [my italics].[2]

Nothing could be more revealing than such a statement both in connection with the battle between the old and new *élites* and the contempt with which Lavon (but also Ben Gurion) regarded Middle Eastern—'Levantine'—culture. Lavon's statement was certainly not that of a 'proletarian Marxist' but rather that of a conscious member of the Israeli collective agrarian aristocracy, who was speaking with the authority of a former 'High Priest' of the Labour 'Church', the Histadrut. But there was more to it than that. There was something very Jewish—in spite of his secularism—about Lavon's ideas. There was the feeling that Israel could not escape her vocation as the country of the chosen people, her Messianism, and that this vocation could only be expressed through the élitist, egalitarian, pioneering, rural, and labouring side of Israeli society.

[1] Translated and reprinted in *New Outlook*, v, February 1968, pp. 3–8.
[2] ibid.

Just as Lavon was a fundamentalist, so the main theoretician of the 'Young Mapai' group, Shimon Peres, was a pragmatist. Long before he became the Secretary General of Ben Gurion's Rafi splinter party, he had tried to formulate the basis for a new type of leadership of Israel, one which could modernize and remould the institutions of the State and acquire the authority to run the Government in virtue of the new forces created by the social transformation of the State. In a perhaps more confused way than Lavon, but certainly more rationally than Dayan, Peres formulated the belief that technocracy and meritocracy, not seniority and ideology, should be the leading principles of a modern administration. Not only did he reject Messianism in all its forms, but back in August 1959 he had chosen as an introduction to one of his programmatic articles a quotation by Berl Katzenelson, the revered Socialist Zionist, which had said

Our movement was born in confusion, the confusion of Uganda [where the Zionist territorialists wanted to settle at the turn of the century] of a Russian Revolution that aborted not only through repression by Nicolai's army but through failure and discouragement from within. It is largely from this confusion that the Labour movement in Palestine sprang, and that it fed, finding in it the power to tread unbeaten paths.[1]

Action on the basis of naturally confused realities, not clarity in irrelevant and impracticable ideology, was thus to be the guiding principle of the new technocratic generation of Israel. There could be no division of the nation, said Peres, into 'wicked and righteous'. Israel should strive to become 'a third force for a world torn between two opposing ways of life'. The State should offer its contribution not by discussing 'what to achieve' but 'how to achieve'. For the Young Mapai's enemies this was 'dangerous activism'. For Peres and his friends 'action should come first, theories later'.[2] When the break with the Party was finally consummated in 1965, the Rafi platform and Peres, its Secretary General, put forward the idea of political pragmatism, of social engineering, of technocracy to be used to achieve a higher standard of living, of science to increase productivity and military strength, of a fully-fledged electoral programme: an antidote to emigration, frustration, and recession. The new Ben Gurionist party suffered a bitter defeat (but remained a political factor) because the electorate felt that the choice between plantocracy and technocracy, between outdated Socialist Zionist ideology and new technological pragmatism, was not the answer to the nation's pressing and basic problems—how to com-

[1] Quoted by Shimon Peres in the *Jerusalem Post*, 13 August 1959.
[2] *Jerusalem Post*, 12 February 1965

bine old and new in a more harmonious institutional and ideological form.

But perhaps, deep in the national consciousness, there was more to it than that. Although Ben Gurion had been a bitter enemy of Jabotinsky and of his Revisionist movement, he had, in fact, realized most of Jabotinsky's aims. Ben Gurion proclaimed the supreme importance of statehood, *mamalachtiut*, over all other Zionist trends. He not only created the national army which Jabotinsky had envisaged as the most powerful tool for the achievement of the Zionist ideals, but realized Jabotinsky's dream of transforming the army into a national school of civic virtue. Ben Gurion again acted very much in the spirit of Revisionism when he fought for and achieved the suppression of the parties' separate system of elementary education and installed a single national programme of basic studies for Israeli children. The policy of border reprisals, the theory that the Jews could best defend themselves by attacking the enemy—which are today standard military policy in Israel —had already been proclaimed in the thirties by Jabotinsky as the only possible national policies in times of emergency. They were the very opposite of the policy of *havlaga* (self-restraint) then preached by the Zionist Organization. On this divergence of opinion Jabotinsky and the Irgun broke away from Ben Gurion and the Hagana. So, as I have shown, in many ways Ben Gurion realized Jabotinsky's policy. It is quite possible that the battle between him and Lavon will one day appear as simply another chapter in the generation-long conflict over the meaning of a Jewish State. This, after all, has been and still is the fundamental problem facing Zionism and Israel. I shall not dwell here on this problem, which I have discussed elsewhere.[1] However, I think it important to record the opinion of the Israeli writer, Amos Oz, who was, as a friend of Lavon's and as one of the founders of Lavon's splinter group, 'Min Hayesod', involved in the last stages of the Lavon affair. In an article published in 1962, Oz puts forward forcible arguments to support the thesis that Ben Gurion's (and Jabotinsky's) State of Israel is in fact a kind of revenge by secular Jewish nationalism on traditional Judaism. Certain Israeli efforts to exalt new Jewish strength as opposed to past Jewish weakness, to prize action above study, clear, abrupt language above the cautious, traditional religious style: all this seems to Amos Oz to be the result of a deep hatred for the (Jewish) past.[2]

[1] In *The New Middle East*, December 1969.
[2] Amos Oz, 'Hamedinah Kifeulat Tagmul' (The State as an Action of Reprisal), *Min Hayesod*, 21 June 1962.

Be that as it may, the fact remains that the Israeli electorate in 1965 refused to choose between Ben Gurion and Lavon, between the self-styled technocrats and the self-styled Zionist puritans. They pushed both contenders out of active politics and chose in their place a moderate man, Levi Eshkol, known for his talent for compromise, a man of the old Zionist plantocratic establishment (he belonged to the second *aliah* and was a member of the kibbutz Degania) and of great administrative and bureaucratic experience. He was no sooner in office than he had to tackle another critical aspect of Israeli life in the mid-sixties, the economic recession currently known as *mitun* (slow down). This economic crisis was predictable and had in fact been expected.

After the great expansion created by the government policy of devaluation of the Israeli pound in 1962 and the unification of the many existing rates of exchange, consumption and prices had again begun to rise more quickly than production. By 1964 some pockets of unemployment were already apparent in development towns and in the building sector, both private and public, as a consequence of the end of German reparations and of reduced immigration.

The main trouble was inflation. In 1965 the G.N.P. grew by 7 per cent in real terms, the total amount of available resources went up only by 5 per cent, while the means of payment increased by 9 per cent, or 15 per cent more than in 1964. Contrary to official statements, much of this increase was due to direct or indirect government expenditure, which in aggregate terms came near to IL (Israeli pounds) 1 billion of overspending. This was due to the adjustment of civil servants' salaries, which, agreed to in principle by the Government, let loose an avalanche of public expenditure once the authorities got caught in the pressure of many competing groups in a situation of over-employment. The rising demands for salary increases and the lack of manpower in all sectors generated an almost uninterrupted chain of strikes, led by the best-paid groups of the country's salaried personnel, often in open defiance of the trade unions' orders. Foreign investment dropped by almost 50 per cent between 1963 and 1965, but under the stress of the general elections of 1965, the Government did not take any steps to check inflation, reverting to increased foreign borrowing—$216 million in 1965 as compared with $84 million in 1964—to meet increased spending. Employment decreased by 1 per cent in agriculture, modestly increased in industry (by 1·3 per cent), while rising dangerously in services (3·5 per cent in transport, 3·9 per cent in commerce and finance, 4·1 per cent in electricity and water supply, 4·4 per cent in other services).

The policy of 'moderation' finally adopted by the Government had some harsh effects soon after its application simply by reducing public expenditure. Although the exact number of unemployed could never be correctly assessed owing to the large number of non-registered Arab workers who had simply left the Jewish areas (mainly the building sector) to return to their farms, it was commonly believed that some 100,000 Israelis were out of work by the beginning of 1967. It was a hard situation which drove many young people, especially those in the professions, to seek work abroad. In 1966 more Israelis left the country than immigrants came in, a phenomenon which added to the general feeling of frustration. But in spite of inevitable hardship, the economic crisis had many positive results. It made a redistribution of the working force possible; it freed many productive industries from the burden of over-employment; it forced government and subsidized private industries to replan their production and cut politically valuable, but economically useless activities; it gave the country a salutary shock, which was prolonged by the feeling of austerity and national unity which followed the oubreak of the June War. It is thus not in the economic recession of the mid-sixties that one must look for the causes of the 'great disillusionment' which followed the euphoria of the late fifties. It is on the moral and institutional plane that the real causes should be sought.

The moral disillusionment came from the old conflict between Zionism and Judaism, in the broadest sense. No one in Israel doubted the supreme necessity of protecting Jewish bodies from physical destruction in order to protect Jewish values from extinction—more through assimilation than through persecution. But a Jewish refuge having now been effectively created, how much idealism could be traded for security, how much Jewish universalism for Jewish nationalism? Nobody could really answer this question, but to many it was clear that the responsibility for evading the answer could not be left to Arab hostility alone, and when people came to think over the problem in the abstract, the situation did not look very cheerful. Here was a State which had been established to revolutionize Jewish life—by a process of a 'national' normalization of the Diaspora Jews—and which instead of attracting Jews was loosing them at a considerable rate. Here was a Hebrew society, speaking the language of the Bible, living in the land of the Bible, and socializing its children in the name of the Bible, and at the same time believing that Jewish survival in Israel was now based on a very un-Biblical principle: that of numerical superiority. If the Jewishness of the State depended on the concentration of Jewish bodies— whether they were conscious of being Jewish or not—per square mile, how could the feeling of national claustrophobia, of a 'national ghetto' be avoided? And if quality, not quantity, was the source of life for Judaism, what kind of quality could be acceptable to a besieged country which, after all, owed its survival to the efficiency but also to the number of its battalions? The dilemma was a real and difficult one. It reflected on the institutions, which were in trouble, not because they were inefficient or outdated, but because they were supposed to perform, surrounded by inertia and technicalities, a nation-building role for which they were no longer receiving inspiration and guidance from the nation's leaders and *élites*. It was said at the time that the Zionist State was to Judaism what the barbarian kingdoms of Italy were to Imperial Rome; a continuity of symbols and language which in fact concealed a total break in tradition. True or not, this was not the cause of the disillusionment. Nostalgic as the Israelis might have been for the glory of Judaism—the Nobel prizewinner S. Y. Agnon was the recognized bard of this nostalgia—they were aware that Zionism had grown out of the ruins of nineteenth-century Judaism, not created them. The crisis was deep because the Zionist 'barbarians' who had set out to renovate Judaism suddenly felt that their sense of purpose and direction had abandoned them, that the winds of confidence were no longer blowing into the sails of a national ship which, paradoxically, now looked very secure, and that the institutions of the State were, like oars, beating the air instead of cutting into the water. More depressing was the fact that no one seemed now to really know the way, in spite, or because, of the many hands holding the tiller.

Then the June War came, unexpected by the Israelis who believed that Nasser was too busy in the Yemen and at home to face the challenge of war. Unexpected too by the Great Powers, and certainly by Russia which did its utmost to stir up a little crisis and, when it had lost control, in vain tried to avoid the conflict. Then the Arabs became involved in a disastrous war, more as a result of their own quarrels than as a result of a decision to put an end to Israel's existence, at least at that particular time. The war came and changed the map of the Middle East and the balance of power between Arabs and Jews in the area and outside it. It was openly and officially fought for less than a week; it then continued in a more subdued form after a cease-fire was accepted by all the contenders. What it meant to the Arabs I am unable to say. To the Jews and to Israel, it was as much a revolution as a war.

The 1948 war had been first and foremost a war of independence for the colonial community of Jews in Palestine. The overwhelming majority of the Diaspora Jews took an interest in this struggle more as a duty of solidarity and honour towards the persecuted than for their own sake.

The 1956 war, against Egypt, had neither been specifically Jewish nor specifically Zionist, but a strictly Israeli affair. It was carried out according to local political logic, disapproved of by many Jews in the Diaspora (who felt at the same time relieved that Israel escaped with minor bruises), and in collaboration with non-Jewish and non-Zionist partners. It helped to open a new maritime frontier towards the Indian Ocean, a part of the world which was as new to Zionism (in spite of Herzl's romantic dreams and Ben Gurion's early desert camel rides to Eilat) as it was historically un-Jewish.

The 1967 war was different and, to some extent, revolutionary, because it was the first war fought by a Jewish independent State for the survival of the Jews in Palestine since the time of the Romans. Whether the Israeli fears of extermination were justified or not is a matter of controversy. The Arabs certainly did their best—and bitterly regretted it afterwards—to produce this impression with their wild declarations. But for the Jews (and many non-Jewish sympathizers) the survival reflex was a genuine and lasting one. It brought forth a community of feeling and effort which for the first time saw anti-Zionist religious zealots joining hands with anti-Zionist Jewish communists for the purpose of preserving the Zionist State. The June War was, unlike the two previous wars, deeply Jewish also in its symbolism. It was not the destruction of the Egyptian army in the Sinai but the recovery of the Wailing Wall and of Jerusalem which fired the Jewish imagination all over the world. Indirectly, it produced more social integration inside Israel and more unity between Israel and the Diaspora than twenty years of Zionist propaganda.

The war also marked the triumph of technocracy and industrialization over improvisation and agriculture. It was virtually won in three and a half hours by an Air Force supported by highly organized technical ground services. It left no room for 'pioneers' initiative' or 'marching farmers'. It was a coolly planned and coolly executed operation, in which victory was brought about by superior skill, organization, and mass media, with no place for ideology of any sort, except the ideology of efficiency. But it was not the achievement of one party. The country and the leadership suddenly discovered the irrelevance of the dichotomy between historicism and pragmatism, between ideology and activisim. It was the contradictory, visceral, fearful, and hopeful common Jewish survival reflex—the consciousness of identity with a fate, not with an idea—combined with modern science and technique which mobilized the Jewish nation. All the rest suddenly became superficial, irrelevant, meaningless. The leaders and the parties which joined together in a spontaneous reaction of common patriotism—and fear—stuck together after the war, less because of continued external danger than because of unwillingness to show, by supporting new policies independently, the poverty of their ideas. No better example of such a feeling could be found than in the pathetic efforts of the most radical, ideological, and plantocratic party of the Socialist Left—Mapam—to find an honourable way of associating with the newly formed, moderate, Jewish, and bourgeois-minded, anti-communist Israeli Labour Party.

The necessity of mixing old and new was equally evident in Israel's relations with the Diaspora. It was soon realized that a still warring Israel, subject to economic restrictions but with a strong case for the defence of Jewish national rights, religious honour, and traditional symbols—such as the right to Jerusalem and of access to the Wailing Wall—was more attractive to the Jews of the Diaspora than the old Zionist theories. The trend of emigration was reversed with the war, with thousands of Israelis returning home, not only because they had undergone a change of heart but because of the new attitude of the Israeli Government towards them. Treated with contempt before the war, they were now officially considered as new immigrants and granted the same economic facilities as the newcomers. As for the Jews of the Diaspora, they also came in increased numbers: 20,000 in 1967, 30,000 in 1968, more than 40,000 in 1969. Some were refugees from Arab and communist countries. Many were young people from France, America, and England to whom the new dimensions and the new dangers of Israel represented a challenge and an appeal. More important, the need for technicians and qualified professionals in the expanding, war-geared economy opened many opportunities to Diaspora Jews to pursue, in Israel, the same activities they had been performing abroad. Significant of the change was the fact, that for the first time, the presidency of the Weizmann Institute of Science—which Einstein had declined—was accepted by another world-famous Jewish Nobel prizewinner, Professor Sabin, the discoverer of the anti-polio vaccine. And with the change in heart and approach came a change in the relations between the State and the Diaspora. The traditional financial contributions from the Diaspora took less and less the form of charity and more and more that of gainful investment. In 1968 a formal conference of Israeli and Diaspora economic representatives established the permanent framework of an organization of Jewish–Israeli co-operation which amounted to the creation of a Jewish–Israeli common market. Its effect was immediately felt by the economy with exports increasing by 20 per cent in just over a year.

It would, however, be wrong to believe that the consensus of the Diaspora was total. The 1967 victory also drew violent reactions from those Jews, and they were numerous, who militated in the 'New Left'. For them, a victorious Jewish State polarizing Jewish enthusiasm and the loyalty of the Diaspora was an anathema similar to that which Zionism had been for religious Orthodoxy fifty years before. It is not difficult to find the reason for this attitude. For a Jew of the 'New Left', incapable of being and unwilling to be a Jew according to the Jewish or Zionist rules, but still conscious of the indifference or the hostility which the 'progressive' camp felt for his separate identity—the American Negro looking on the liberal Jew as a white oppressor, the communist despising the Jew for his cosmopolitanism, and so on—the victory of Israel was a deprivation of his (perhaps masochistic) pleasure derived from the role of victim and witness. The regret experienced by many Diaspora Jews, and probably by the majority of Israelis, on seeing the State of Israel an occupying power, remains genuine. Less genuine, perhaps, is the fervour with which the anti-Zionists (Jewish and non-Jewish) set the Jewish State up as a prototype of reactionary nationalism, racial discrimination, and colonialist aggression. To many Jews, Jewish anti-Zionism seems to be much more than a matter of politics. It is one manifestation of a permanent trend of Jewish revolt against a separate Jewish identity (now emotionally centred on Jewish nationalism as it once was on Jewish religion) that we find expressed throughout the centuries by contradictory currents, such as Hellenization, early Christianity, assimilation, and also by secular Zionism.

For many non-Jewish anti-Zionists, antagonism towards Israel tends often to become a contemporary version of antisemitism which draws strength and justification, but not original inspiration (as in the case of Russian anti-Zionism), from the Middle East crisis. This antisemitism has elicited a reaction from the Israelis, expressed in the stubbornness of Israel's demand for a security which is not solely based on political guarantees.

Israel's reluctance, on the basis of past experience, to go back to the unsettled situation of 1967 without firm commitments from the Arab States to peace is understandable. But under closer scrutiny, these commitments are not on the whole territorial. They must include the psychological acceptance of the Jewish State by the peoples of the Middle East and more particularly by the Palestinians who are, after all, the main justification for the Arab Governments' struggle against

Israel. No Arab State is at present able or willing to make this acceptance, if for no other reason, for the fact that the Arab Governments have lost all right and power of control over the Palestinians.

As for the dialogue between Israelis and Palestinians: this is certainly taking place, in spite of military occupation, terrorism, and reprisals, and at a more intense rate than in the past fifty years, through an unprecedented integration of Jewish–Arab economies, daily human intercourse, and reciprocal cultural influence. But it has not yet turned into a political dialogue because both sides are still seeking to define their respective national personalities and the aims which they are set on achieving. And to this effect, on both sides, border tension and a situation of patriotic unity are certainly more advantageous than a phoney peace. For the moment neither side has yet revealed its true intentions, in spite of many official declarations to the contrary.

The representatives of the Palestinian organizations say that they want 'to liberate the Israelis from Zionism' and create 'a true, democratic, bi-national State in Palestine' where people should count for what they are, not for what they are affiliated to. While the sincerity of these views is questionable in view of the demand contained in the Covenant of the Palestinian Organizations[1] (approved in Cairo in July 1968) that all Jews who emigrated to Palestine after 1917 should re-emigrate in the case of an Arab victory, this new line of policy is interesting for two reasons. First, because it shows that the Palestinians—like the rest of the Arabs—are prepared to accept the Jews as individuals but not yet as an organized political community. Second, because the Palestinians seem to admit—unlike the rest of the Arabs—the idea of an equally balanced bi-national Arab–Jewish State in Palestine. If realized, this would obviously be the most powerful State in the whole region. Implicitly, it amounts to an admission that, while all Arabs are still fearful of the role which a Jewish political community would play inside the, so far, disunited Arab and Islamic community, the Palestinians can conceive already of the possibility of joining the Jews in their position on the margins of both Eastern and Western society: an idea which, I believe, is the direct consequence of the creation of an articulate Palestinian Diaspora and a Palestinian nation of Arab refugees, politically hostile to, but socially and psychologically not so distant from, the Jewish Diaspora and the Israeli nation of Jewish refugees.

The Israeli position since the June War has evolved considerably in spite of the crystallization of political positions. The Arabs, who want to liberate the Israelis from Zionism, seem to be misinformed about the

[1] For full text see *The New Middle East*, March 1970.

number of Zionist 'sacred cows' which have been slaughtered in Israel in the last two years. One of them is the Zionist contention that the survival of a Jewish State is a function of the seclusion of a large Jewish majority from the non-Jewish world. Whatever the final régime to be established in reunited Palestine, be it a wartime Jewish military administration or a peacetime partition of the country between Israelis and Palestinians, the Jews of Israel will be faced with the challenge of intimate coexistence with a non-Jewish people which—as a religious, social, and cultural group—is infinitely more numerous than and potentially equally as powerful as the Jewish one. Thus, once more, the Israelis are faced with the Jews' old challenge of having to safeguard their identity and assure their national survival by quality rather than quantity. For the time being they are as afraid as the Arabs are afraid of a Jewish State in their midst. While they do not mind the creation of a powerful political Palestinian entity linked with the rest of the Arab countries and controlling both sides of the Jordan, and possibly more than that, entitled to extra-territorial rights of passage to Jerusalem and to the Mediterranean, they are still fearful of the role of individual Arabs inside their own society.

Historically this is a total and curious reverse of positions. The Jews, who never based their survival on numbers, have now become very conscious of their importance. The Arabs, as heirs of the Empire of the East and as modern representatives of the Islamic nation, should not be fearful of independent territorial enclaves. The political society of the Middle East has always consisted of such enclaves and the oriental political genius was to make them coexist for its own benefit. It was the challenge of Western individualism to the traditional Eastern way of life that from the time of Alexander made the oriental mind—the Jewish mind included—feel uneasy and that originated suicidal heresies.

The clue to this reversal of historical positions is probably to be sought in the substitution of secular nationalism for religion in both Judaism and Islam. The fact that Arabs and Jews are killing each other on the basis of foreign national ideals, imported from their Western Christian oppressors, has turned the present political tragedy of Palestine into a colossal historical farce.

When two old civilizations like Judaism and Islam meet in a struggle as violent as the one over Palestine, it is difficult to believe that their fight is just one more outdated tribal territorial confrontation. Deep down behind the current emotions, interests, and fears there must exist on both sides the unconscious feeling that something more important is at stake.

However, it seems clear that now already both sides are no longer fighting for territory but for time—time to grow new, genuinely collective personalities from the traumatic experiences of persecution and colonialism; time to take stock of strength and convictions, after centuries of partial or (for the Jews) almost total political, social, and economic stagnation; time to overcome alienation and inferiority complexes; time to trade faith for fatalism, future for past, action for inertia.

Appendix

Table 1.   Population, by Population Groups, 1949–1960
(Estimates, Thousands)

Year (end)	Total population	Jews	Moslems	Christians	Druze
1949	1,173·9	1,013·9	111·5	34·0	14·5
1950	1,370·1	1,203·0	116·1	36·0	15·0
1951	1,577·8	1,404·4	118·9	39·0	15·5
1952	1,629·5	1,450·2	122·8	40·4	16·1
1953	1,669·4	1,483·6	127·6	41·4	16·8
1954	1,717·8	1,526·0	131·8	42·0	18·0
1955	1,789·1	1,590·5	136·3	43·3	19·0
1956	1,872·4	1,667·5	141·4	43·7	19·8
1957	1,976·0	1,762·7	146·8	45·8	20·5
1958	2,031·7	1,810·1	152·8	47·3	21·4
1959	2,088·7	1,858·8	159·2	48·3	22·3
1960	2,150·4	1,911·2	166·3	49·6	23·3

Source: *Statistical Abstract of Israel* (Jerusalem, 1961), p. 27.

Table 2. Jewish Population by Continent of Birth, 1948–1960
(Absolute Numbers and Percentage)

Mo. Day Yr.			Total		Israeli-born		Asia		Africa		Europe and America	
			Number	%	Number	%	Number	%	Number	%	Number	%
11	8	1948	716,678	100·0	253,661	35·4	57,768	8·1	12,236	1·7	393,013	54·8
12	31	1949	1,013,871	100·0	279,173	27·5	132,493	13·1	56,159	5·5	564,046	53·9
12	31	1950	1,202,993	100·0	311,100	25·8	188,578	15·7	80,542	6·7	622,773	51·8
12	31	1951	1,404,392	100·0	353,220	25·2	289,565	20·6	98,576	7·0	663,031	47·2
12	31	1952	1,450,217	100·0	393,873	27·1	292,603	20·2	106,965	7·4	656,776	45·3
12	31	1953	1,483,641	100·0	433,298	29·2	292,017	19·7	109,725	7·4	648,601	43·7
12	31	1954	1,526,000	100·0	470,811	30·9	292,860	19·2	121,033	7·9	641,305	42·0
12	31	1955	1,590,519	100·0	509,979	32·1	292,349	18·4	152,859	9·6	635,332	39·9
12	31	1956	1,667,455	100·0	548,273	32·9	293,474	17·6	196,207	11·8	629,501	37·7
12	31	1957	1,762,741	100·0	588,191	33·4	296,923	16·8	218,920	12·4	658,707	37·4
12	31	1958	1,819,148	100·0	625,969	34·6	302,372	16·7	220,980	12·2	660,827	36·5
12	31	1959	1,858,841	100·0	666,466	35·9	303,736	16·3	224,058	12·1	664,581	35·7
12	31	1960	1,911,189	100·0	708,140	37·1	303,480	15·9	228,141	11·9	671,428	35·1

Source: *Statistical Abstract of Israel* (Jerusalem, 1961), p. 43.

Table 3. Jewish Immigrants by Continent of Birth, 1919–1960
(Absolute Numbers and Percentage)

Period	Absolute Numbers					Percentage				
	All Continents	Asia	Africa	Europe	America and Oceania	All Continents	Asia	Africa	Europe	America and Oceania
1919–5/14/1948	452,158	40,776	4,033	377,487	7,579	100·0	9·5	9·0	87·8	1·8
5/15/1948–12/31/1960	968,748	507,074		442,248		100·0	53·4		46·6	
5/15/1948–12/31/1948	101,819	4,739	8,192	76,554	478	100·0	5·3	9·1	85·1	0·5
1949	239,076	71,624	39,156	121,753	1,344	100·0	30·6	16·7	52·1	0·6
1950	169,405	57,771	25,525	83,632	1,006	100·0	34·4	15·2	49·8	0·6
1951	173,901	103,326	20,123	49,533	671	100·0	59·5	11·6	28·5	0·4
1952	23,375	6,701	10,024	6,131	516	100·0	28·7	42·9	26·2	2·2
1953	10,347	2,871	4,889	2,025	549	100·0	27·8	47·3	19·6	5·3
1954	17,471	3,305	12,188	1,325	641	100·0	18·9	69·8	7·6	3·7
1955	36,303	1,323	32,143	1,942	620	100·0	3·6	89·3	5·4	1·7
1956	54,925	2,739	44,878	6,674	631	100·0	5·0	81·7	12·2	1·1
1957	69,733	5,249	24,112	38,889	874	100·0	7·6	34·9	56·2	1·3
1958	25,919	7,597	3,893	13,626	802	100·0	29·3	15·0	52·6	3·1
1959	22,987	7,635		15,348		100·0	33·2		66·8	
1960	23,487	6,801		16,684		100·0	29·0		71·0	

Source: *Statistical Abstract of Israel* (Jerusalem, 1961), p. 86.

Index